POUND / JOYCE

POUND / JOYCE

The Letters of Ezra Pound to James Joyce,
with Pound's Essays on Joyce

Edited and with Commentary by Forrest Read

x

A NEW DIRECTIONS BOOK

CONTENTS

Introduction

During the winter of 1913 Ezra Pound was in Sussex with William Butler Yeats, acting as the elder poet's secretary. Temporarily free of the rush of London, each was assessing the other's work and both were laying out new directions. When Pound had almost completed an anthology of new poets, the Imagists, he asked Yeats if there was anyone he had forgotten to include. Yeats recalled a young Irish writer named James Joyce who had written some polished lyric poems. One of them had stuck in Yeats's mind. Joyce was living in Trieste. Why not write to him?

Pound wrote at once. He explained his literary connections and offered help in getting Joyce published. A few days later Yeats found "I Hear an Army Charging upon the Land" and Pound wrote again to ask if he could use it. Joyce, who had been on the continent for nearly ten years, cut off from his nation and his language and so far all but unpublished, was surprised and encouraged. He gave Pound permission to use the poem and a few days later sent a typescript of his book of short stories *Dubliners* and a chapter of a new novel called *A Portrait of the Artist as a Young Man*, along with news that he would soon have a play ready. A prolonged correspondence began, which grew into a long-standing friendship. Because of World War I the two inventors of modern fiction and poetry did not meet until June 1920, when Pound persuaded Joyce to come to Sirmione, Catullus's resort on Lago di Garda. But between 1914 and 1920 a constant stream of letters flowed between London and Trieste, London and Zurich. Pound transmitted his spontaneous reactions as typescripts of *Dubliners*, *A Portrait*, *Exiles*, and *Ulysses* arrived, then sent the chapters on to the magazines of which he was a correspondent or editor. As the books appeared he crystallized his insights in a series of reviews and essays, the first sustained criticism of Joyce's work. Pound's efforts and essays slowly created an audience and put Joyce across.

Pound's struggle to get into print "the men of 1914," as Wyndham Lewis called Pound, Joyce, Eliot, and himself, is well known. He is the colorful figure who enlivened literary London and Paris, then

1

championed *les jeunes* from Rapallo. "The Pound question" presents him as the tireless advocate of economic doctrine, Confucianism, and fascist political ideas, an American pariah who spent thirteen years confined in Washington under indictment for treason. But relatively little attention has been given to the extent of his relations with Joyce, especially during and just after the First World War when modern literature took its shape. For one thing, the letters did not come to light until the Cornell University Library bought Stanislaus Joyce's papers in 1957. Pound wrote nearly eighty letters to Joyce between 1914 and 1920, sixty-two of which have survived (most of Joyce's letters to Pound—he wrote some sixty during that period—have apparently been lost). He wrote numerous essays and articles on Joyce's work, some of which have never been reprinted and others of which are out of print. Since the two writers were together in Paris off and on from 1921 to 1924 they did not correspond, and after Pound moved to Rapallo late in 1924 both correspondence and meetings became infrequent, partly because of Pound's indifference to the extravagances of *Finnegans Wake*. Nevertheless their friendship continued and each remained aware of the other and his work. Joyce memorialized their association fulsomely in *Finnegans Wake*. Pound continued his consideration of Joyce in his critical writings and his poetry; his best memories were spoken over Rome Radio in 1941, after Joyce had died and a second war had begun, and in *The Pisan Cantos*. The present volume gathers together all of Pound's surviving letters to Joyce, most of which are published for the first time, all of his essays and articles on Joyce's work, his radio broadcast, various anecdotes of the time, and a number of miscellaneous pieces and extracts.

When Pound discovered him Joyce was at the end of his tether. Before he left Ireland for good in 1904 he had published in Dublin and London only some essays and book reviews and a few poems and stories. Since then he had lived in Pola, Rome, and Trieste, working as a language teacher and a bank clerk. In 1907 *Chamber Music*, brought out by Elkin Mathews, who was soon to become Pound's publisher, received some slight notice. Since 1905 he had been trying to get *Dubliners* published, but an exasperating series of efforts had resulted only in unfulfilled contracts, broken plates, and a burned edition. He had also been turning his false start, *Stephen Hero*, begun in 1904, into a new kind of novel. But the frustration of trying to publish his book of stories unexpurgated continued to rankle; he was writing desultorily, his time eaten into by English

2

language lessons, by the added responsibility of two children, and by periods of discouragement. Sometimes his plight cast him into despair, sometimes it amused him. He wrote to Nora's uncle Michael Healy on November 2, 1915:

> Today is the feast of S. Justin Martyr, patron of Trieste, and I shall perhaps eat a cheap small pudding somewhere in his honour for the many years I lived in his city. As for the future it is useless to speculate. If I could find out in the meantime who is the patron of men of letters I should try to remind him that I exist: but I understand that the last saint who held that position resigned in despair and no other will take the portfolio.[1]

Joyce did not know the hands he was already in. Already Pound was what Horace Gregory later called "the minister without portfolio of the arts."

Pound had arrived in London in 1908 as a modern troubadour with his first volume of poems, printed in Venice, in his pocket. Within five years he had met most of the important artists in London, young and old, and had published five books of verse and numerous translations. At first he had seemed to be trying, as Yeats said, to provide a portable substitute for the British Museum. In 1909 and 1910 he lectured on medieval literature and expanded his lectures into *The Spirit of Romance*, "An Attempt to Define Somewhat the Charm of the Pre-Renaissance Literature of Latin Europe." But *The Spirit of Romance* was part of the "background" or "history" of a modern epic poem he was already preparing to write. By 1909 he was calling his poetry "my history of the woild" and "a more or less proportional presentation of life." He had determined to conflate the Europeanism of Dante and the native American strain of Whitman, had outlined the requirements for an "Epic of the West," and had begun to conceive his life as a modern Odyssean adventure and a subject for epic poetry.

Certainty about his purpose and his direction grew out of his return to America for a prolonged visit during 1910 and 1911. Excited by the possibilities of a new Renaissance that would grow from a merging of American and European cultures, he returned to London in 1911 and launched himself on his main work—to promote such a Renaissance. He was drawing on his American vitality and on his studies of medieval and Renaissance literature, his aim sharpened by Ford Madox Ford's impressionism, especially his urging

[1] *Letters of James Joyce*, I, page 86.

3

about Flaubert's *mot juste* and about live contemporary speech, and by ideas current in the group around T. E. Hulme, the "School of Images" of 1909. In 1911 and 1912, in the double manifesto "I Gather the Limbs of Osiris" and "Patria Mia" (the result of his trip to America), written for A. R. Orage's Guild Socialist weekly *The New Age*, he propounded the motives and methods of *The Cantos* and probably began drafting the first versions. In 1912 too he formulated the Imagist Manifesto, became foreign editor of Harriet Monroe's new magazine, *Poetry* of Chicago, and embarked on his evangelical struggle to reform English poetry. At the same time he suddenly began to modernize his own verse with the poems of *Ripostes* and *Lustra*, extending Imagism to an urban impressionism modeled on the forms and methods of the Roman poets of the Augustan Age. Stirred by these new impulses and encouraged by his successes in America, he was moving toward the center of the London scene as a leader of the *avant garde*. When he wrote to Joyce in 1913 he had recently gained a place in *The New Freewoman*, soon to become the better-known *Egoist*, and had just published his important "The Serious Artist." He was about to help prepare *Blast*, the famous outburst against sedate Georgian London. Pound was becoming what Wyndham Lewis called a "Demon pantechnicon driver, busy with moving of old world into new quarters," a kind of moving van or storage warehouse who carried other people's furniture in his editing and in his writing. He was also becoming (in the literal sense of pantechnicon) an "expert," major or minor, in a bewildering number of technics. As if poetry, literary criticism, journalism, editing, impresarioship, scholarship, and polemics were not enough, he was discovering new music, new painting, and new sculpture, and establishing a reputation for cooking, carpentry, and tennis.

"In the midst of many contrivings," already as many-faceted and inventive as the "factive personality" of his *Cantos*, Pound the Odyssean-impresario would have earned the admiration and envy of Leopold Bloom himself. He gave Joyce practical help and encouragement when he most needed it. He got Joyce printed. When he had to he made sure that Joyce got read: what Pound called "the party of intelligence" began to coalesce by passing around *A Portrait* in "a much-handled file of Egoists or . . . a slippery bundle of typescript." Pound and Harriet Shaw Weaver conducted a high-powered publicity campaign that antedated the days of slick advertising, and Pound tirelessly negotiated with publishers and wrote reviews. It was largely through Pound that Joyce maintained his contact with his own literature and language during the isolation of

4

the war years. Furthermore, at critical moments Pound was able to drum up financial support from such varied sources as the Royal Literary Fund, the Society of Authors, the British Parliament, and the New York lawyer John Quinn. To help Joyce through one of his eye operations, he even went so far as to try to sell authentic autographs of King Ferdinand and Queen Isabella (date: 1492).

Pound illustrated his mixture of practicality, resourcefulness, and extravagant generosity during the frustrating efforts in 1916 to find a publisher for *A Portrait*. John Marshall of New York had agreed to publish a book entitled *This Generation,* in which Pound intended to discuss "contemporary events in the woild-uv-letters, with a passing reference of about 3600 words on vorticism." But then Marshall expressed interest in *A Portrait*. Pound, seizing the opportunity, acted immediately. First he wrote Marshall, then informed Miss Weaver:

> I have just written him direct a very strong letter re Joyce, advising him to print the Joyce in preference to my book, if his capital is limited. I can't go further than that.
>
> I advise you to send *him* (i.e., mail to him not to Kreymborg) at once the leaves of *The Egoist* containing the novel *and also* the bits the printer cut out. He may as well have it all, and at once while my letter is hot in his craw.
>
> My other letter was to Kreymborg for Marshall, I think the two letters ought to penetrate some one skull.

On the more quixotic side are Pound's attempts to prescribe from London for Joyce's eyes (Odysseus too was an eye expert, *vide* the Cyclops, though in another sense!) and the efforts to get expert advice from a Philadelphia (Pa.) specialist. The atmosphere was one of urbane good humor and gusto; it had room for affections, confidences, enthusiasms, and rages, and it produced puns, limericks, and parodies.

Pound's and Joyce's financial plights resulted in amusing ironies. Pound lived in "high-hearted penury" in London. His "gate receipts" from November 1, 1914, to October 31, 1915, the first year of his marriage, were £42/10. He was forced into a bewildering variety of journalistic work and into making his own furniture. He accompanied Yeats to Sussex as his secretary during three winters, 1913–1916. When he wrote lauding the end of *A Portrait* he remarked that Joyce probably couldn't have completed the book " 'in the lap of luxury' or in the whirl of a metropolis with the attrition of endless small amusements and endless calls on one's time, and endless trivialities of enjoyment." Pound himself knew what the whirl of the metropolis was like; his gusto as impresario of the serious literary movement was often accompanied by misgivings that he was allowing his serious poetic impulse to waste from lack of use. But he was almost wholly in the dark about Joyce's course of life. Joyce lived a quite unspartan life in Trieste and Zurich. His penury was largely self-inflicted; he was always willing, even eager, to be dependent, and despite his success at finding windfalls he always considered his plight deplorable. During one financial crisis Pound actually suggested that the great metropolitan might construct his own furniture or move to a village in the country, reminding him "Various young writers here have done so." Pound might have been aghast or even indignant had he known the luxuries Joyce allowed himself.

But although he may not have known the causes of Joyce's pleas and discouragements and indecisivenesses, Pound's energetic action was just what Joyce needed to sustain him, not only materially but emotionally. Pound's tireless efforts produced only a trickle of money—nothing like Miss Weaver's series of benefactions or Edith Rockefeller McCormick's subsidy. But the symbolic value must have far outweighed the actual cash. Recognition from the Royal Literary Fund, *Who's Who*, the Society of Authors, and the custodians of the Privy Purse was a kind of official recognition; if Joyce did not relish the thought of being supported by the British government, which he would soon have more reason for resenting than merely the fact that he was an Irishman, he could nevertheless feel that the foremost writers in English acknowledged him and that he had a place among them. When John Quinn began to buy his proofsheets and manuscripts, he could even feel that he had a place in posterity. Joyce had to have his books published, accepted, and respected; indeed, as he himself frequently said, he often had to rely on others to convince him that he was a writer. Once he lost faith sufficiently to stick the "original original" manuscript of *A Portrait* into a stove.

Encouragement from such a variety of sources helped keep Joyce working at a pitch of intensity and rapidity. Nor can the editorial deadlines that Pound represented be discounted. Further, Pound repeatedly acquiesced, and often insisted, that Joyce should *not* do the kind of journalistic work he himself was forced to do, but should devote himself persistently to *Ulysses*. Pound's determination that *Ulysses* should be finished, and that Joyce should leave Trieste for a place that would enable him to finish it unharried, brought about their meeting in 1920. That moment was clearly a crucial one.

Afflicted with indecisiveness, as the exchanges surrounding the event show, the wavering Joyce finally submitted to Pound's "fixed idea" that he should come to Sirmione. Although Pound confessed, "The curse of me and my nation is that we always think things can be bettered by immediate action of some sort, *any* sort rather than no sort," this time the "curse" was the one thing needful and persistence worked. In July Joyce moved to Paris.

Pound's comments to Joyce about Joyce's work were usually enthusiastic. Of course he was struck immediately by the scrupulous prose of *Dubliners* and *A Portrait*, and told Joyce so on receiving the first typescripts, but that did not prevent him from writing spontaneously to "let off steam" in praise of a new chapter of *A Portrait* after it had come out in *The Egoist*. Even when he had reservations he was frank and liberal. He thought *Exiles* not up to Joyce's other work but still gave Joyce the full benefit of his critical judgment; he wrestled with the play much of one night, wrote Joyce a long letter, and, though he was never to alter his initial objections, composed next morning a long essay on *Exiles* and modern realism. When he boggled at the jakes episode in "Calypso" he was downright in both his practical and literary judgments. As an editor he feared censorship; the November 1917 issue of *The Little Review* had just been suppressed because of a story by Wyndham Lewis. But that was not his only reason. He was not merely afraid of having editresses jailed, he wrote, but was reluctant to have them jailed over a passage he thought overdone, "not written with utter maestria" (in this instance Pound penciled out a number of the more "realistic" passages; Joyce at once demanded that they be restored for book publication). When he received "Sirens" in 1919 he objected to the apparently chaotic opening and to Joyce's once more "going down where the asparagus grows." But after a series of objections that reveals throughout his own lack of dogmatic certainty, he could close the letter with a self-reversing, back-page postscript: "*And* you may be right—Anyhow send along this record of uncertainty."

Pound maintained this critical deference throughout the years of *A Portrait* and *Ulysses*. Only when he had done his best with the early parts of *Finnegans Wake* and decided that he could not make enough of it did he finally draw his line against Joyce's "experiment." It is doubtful that Joyce ever accepted Pound's specific criticisms; later he said that once he had made up his mind he was right, nothing could affect his texts. Whether and to what extent Joyce was interested in Pound's work, or whether Pound's experiments in poetry may have offered him suggestions for his own work, is still an open question. At any rate, Joyce's gratitude for Pound's help was considerable. He never stopped citing Pound as a "wonder worker." It is hard to guess what might have happened if Pound had not persistently rushed Joyce's chapters into print hot from the writer's pen. Joyce himself wondered whether without Pound's efforts his books would ever have been finished or put before the public.

The letters and essays printed here are the best single record of Pound's open-minded liberality. In his relations with Joyce he reveals an aspect of himself not so easily discernible elsewhere. He usually seems to speak as "the high and final Ezthority," totally sure of himself and totally right. In his published letters he justifies himself to William Carlos Williams and Professor Felix Schelling, badgers editresses Harriet Monroe and Margaret Anderson, instructs young poets, critics, and researchers. His most familiar voice ("Naow lemme tell yuh!") is the exasperating facsimile of American frontier dialect that led Gertrude Stein to call him "a village explainer, excellent if you were a village, but if you were not, not." Pound has become almost a figure of mythology: the flamboyant *enfant terrible*, the *avant-garde* bohemian who wanted to stay ahead of both the status quo and his walking companions, the flailing iconoclast whom Wyndham Lewis called a "revolutionary simpleton." In his letters to Joyce, however, Pound speaks as a writer to a respected equal. Like other men he lives in uncertainties and doubts, frequently confiding discouragement about his own work and revealing the difficulties of his artistic struggle. Most striking, however, is his unusual respect for Joyce as "the stylist," even "Cher maître."

Joyce appeared to Pound as the great new urban writer, a great synthetic expresser of the modern consciousness. In many ways 1914–1924 was for Pound, indeed for modern writing itself, the Joyce decade. Sometime about 1912, when Pound had become aware of the modern city and was going about London "hunting for the real" in order to modernize himself and his poetry, he had playfully evoked a hypothetical Joyce:

> Sweet Christ from hell spew up some Rabelais,
> To belch and . . . . . and to define today
> In fitting fashion, and her monument
> Heap up to her in fadeless excrement.[2]

In numerous other statements he uncannily prognosticated Joyce's work. When the books began to arrive Pound saw at once that Joyce

[2] Ezra Pound, *Guide to Kulchur*, London: Faber and Faber Limited, 1938. New Directions edition, Norfolk, Conn., 1952, page 96.

was what he had been looking for and trying to become, the "donative" author. Such an author

> seems to draw down into the art something which was not in the art of his predecessors. If he also draw from the air about him, he draws latent forces, or things present but unnoticed, or things perhaps taken for granted and never examined. . . . Non è mai tarde per tentar l'ignoto. His forebears may have led up to him; he is never a disconnected phenomenon, but he does take some step further.[3]

Joyce was both perfecting nineteenth-century realism and realizing in literature the motives of Pound's *avant-garde* experiments. He had the sharp eye for seeing life as it is and presenting the urban surface intensely, yet he also presented "a sense of abundant beauty," combining the objective fact and the sensitive response. *Dubliners* made the city a formal principle for the first time in modern English literature; the lives of the Dubliners were not subdued to the conventional form of the story, but were presented according to the pressures of the city and the form of an emotion. In *A Portrait* Joyce transformed his own personal experience to explore the artist's expanding inner life, contrasting it to Dublin's urban surfaces and its stultifying moral and intellectual milieu. He was achieving a full stylistic and formal expression in the settings, events, rhythms, consciousnesses, emotions, and historical perspectives of *Ulysses*. Later, recalling his 1912 quatrain and the arrival of Joyce's works, Pound confirmed " 'Ulysses' I take as my answer."

Joyce was the most consistently absorbing cause of Pound's London years, not only a focus for his versatile activities but also a touchstone of literary innovation. Pound's account of the emergence of modern literature from the war years emphasizes Joyce:

> Emerging from cenacles; from scattered appearances in unknown periodicals, the following dates can function in place of more extensive reprint: *Catholic Anthology*, 1915, for the sake of printing sixteen pages of Eliot (poems later printed in *Prufrock*). Criticism of Joyce's *Dubliners*, in *Egoist*, 1916 [*sic:* 1914], and the series of notes on Joyce's work, from then on. Instrumentality in causing Joyce to be published serially and in volume form, *Egoist*, *Little Review*, culminating with the criticism of *Ulysses* in the Mercure de France, June 1922.[4]

[3] "I Gather the Limbs of Osiris," Installment IV, *The New Age*, X, 8 (December 21, 1911), page 179.

[4] "Date Line," *Make It New. Essays by Ezra Pound*, London: Faber and Faber

9

The war years were the years not only of the gradual growth and appearance of Joyce's mock-epic in prose but also of Pound's counterpart in poetry, *The Cantos*. Nor is it a coincidence that their work continued to run parallel as Joyce embarked on *Finnegans Wake* and Pound unfolded his "big long endless poem." Of all modern writers, Pound and Joyce are the two who decided at an early age to follow the classic vocation of preparing themselves to write epic: as moderns, to use their personal lives "to forge in the smithy of my soul the uncreated conscience of my race"; as classicists, to adapt the motives, methods, and forms of the epic tradition to modern use. Both developed a single idea toward an ever larger, more inclusive, synthetic form. The similarity of their motives and methods is reflected in Pound's essays. As a group, these essays show how Joyce's work served as a kind of goad or catalyst while Pound was absorbed in his own public and artistic struggle. While Pound's life and contacts in London and his excursions into the past through books were supplying him with the kind of material he needed for his poetry, his association with Joyce enriched and expanded his thinking about literary methods and form along lines that Joyce was exploring.

But if the essays are a record of Pound's exploratory artistic thought, his letters to Joyce reveal his problems—probably because he was able to see how Joyce was solving similar ones. Late in 1915, in the midst of a period of intensive work on the first drafts of *The Cantos*, Pound took fire while reading Joyce's work and embarked on theoretical speculations about literary form. In his 1917 letters he begins to inform Joyce about his efforts with the first published versions and to confide his misgivings. While his essay of 1918 pushes his insights into Joyce deeper, his letters reveal an uncertainty about his own poetry. This period of self-assessment coincides with a crisis in his public and artistic career, partly uncertainty and partly growing pains. He did not overcome it until he finally settled in Paris in 1921. The year 1922 was an *annus mirabilis* not only for modern literature but himself. *Ulysses* and *The Waste Land*, which Pound blue-penciled during the winter of 1921–1922, were published. In his 1922 essays on *Ulysses*, which he had been able to read complete in book form, he summarized ten years of thought about Joyce and about literary method and form. These climactic essays suggest one of the most interesting aspects of the association be-

Limited, 1934; *Literary Essays of Ezra Pound*, edited with an introduction by T. S. Eliot, Norfolk, Conn.: New Directions, 1954, page 80.

tween the two writers. For by the summer of 1922, in a burst of creative energy after two fallow years, Pound had roughed out the cantos for the first installment to appear in book form, *A Draft of XVI Cantos* (1925). Even more important, sometime between 1922 and the summer of 1923 he had completely altered the form of his poem, and perhaps the conception, by making the first section begin with Odysseus. He went a step further than Joyce, for instead of beginning with Stephen-Telemachus and instead of concluding in the bed of the desirable female, *The Cantos* opens with Odysseus leaving Circe's bed for an even more arduous adventure.

In *Guide to Kulchur* (1938), Pound designated "the nineteen teens, Gaudier, Wyndham L. and I as we were in *Blast*," "the sorting out"; the 1920's were "the *rappel à l'ordre*" and the 1930's "the new synthesis, the totalitarian." [5] He immediately qualified his designation by inserting a brief chapter on Joyce, but the polemical and ideological "prospect" of "the new synthesis" made him define Joyce as "retrospect" and *Ulysses* as "the monumental," a satiric memorial to the cultural morass of the prewar era. In 1922, however, he hailed *Ulysses* as an "epoch-making report on the state of the human mind in the twentieth century (the first of the new era)." The letters and essays of 1918–1922 reveal how he responded first to its vitality and to its achievement in literary method and form, as well as to its summary of the European consciousness. The opening of one of his 1922 essays confirms Joyce's achievement as an essential literary breakthrough:

> All men should "Unite to give praise to Ulysses"; those who will not, may content themselves with a place in the lower intellectual orders; I do not mean that they should all praise it from the same viewpoint; but all serious men of letters, whether they write out a critique or not, will certainly have to make one for their own use.

As Pound recalled later, the completion of Joyce's "super-novel" which "poached on the epic" left him "free to get on with my own preferred job." [6] This is not the place to analyze how Pound's critical study of the motive, method, and form of Joyce's work may have influenced his own poetic development, but the letters and essays collected here indicate that the effect was considerable.

[5] *Guide to Kulchur,* page 95.
[6] "Augment of the Novel," *New Directions in Prose & Poetry, 6,* Norfolk, Conn.: New Directions, 1941, page 707.

THE TEXT

In this volume I have tried to present all the material directly relevant to the association between Pound and Joyce. To make it as intelligible as possible it is presented chronologically, with enough information about both writers so that a reader can maintain a focus on those parts of their respective careers that touched each other. The chronological divisions reflect here merely residences and main periods in the writers' lives. The war years, 1914–1918, were Pound's most active in London and his heyday with *Poetry* and *The Little Review;* Joyce remained relatively undisturbed in Trieste and Zurich, similarly in exile. Between the end of the war in 1918 and the meeting in 1920, while the Versailles peace conference was trying to turn the world back to the nineteenth century, both writers were uprooted; Joyce was seeking new conditions and Pound both new conditions and a new direction. They were together in Paris from 1921 to 1924; after 1924 Joyce remained in Paris almost until his death in 1941, while Pound moved to Italy, where he lived until he was brought back to the United States in 1945 to face charges of treason. For the period 1914–1920 I have relied mainly on Pound's letters and essays; thereafter I have based my commentary on the scattered materials available. I have not cited extensively from memoirs of the period, preferring to let this material speak for itself. If I have presented too much background or too much interpretation, it has been in the service of intelligibility and liveliness. I have tried as much as possible to make the book read as a narrative, striving to maintain an accurate proportion throughout.

I have also included the enclosures that were part of Pound's literary chronicling service. These not only explain the contents of some of Pound's letters but also demonstrate the exigencies of trying to promote new writing under transalpine and even transatlantic conditions while a war was in progress. The most extensive, the amusing correspondence between John Quinn and a New Haven book dealer concerning some corrected proofsheets of the 1917 American edition of *A Portrait* (Appendix B), lightens up a corner of literary history and enriches the tone of the Pound-Joyce correspondence. Appendix A presents selections from Pound's letters to Elkin Mathews, his publisher, about the subject matter and language of *Lustra*. This controversy was the simultaneous counterpart of Pound's battle for *A Portrait* and elicited from him his most forcible statements against publishers' and printers' censorship.

Finally, Appendix C gives the passages Pound deleted from the "Calypso" episode of *Ulysses* before sending it on to *The Little Review* in 1918.

NOTES ON EDITING

Pound was one of the early users of the typewriter for composing both poems and letters; most of the unpublished letters to Joyce are typescripts. In writing to "the stylist" he was much more conscious of *le mot juste* than he was in his letters of the 1930's, when he became one of the century's most prolific correspondents. He first typed the letter directly, frequently crossing out words or phrases with the typewriter. Then he picked up his pen and went through his typescript, altering and adding words, phrases, sentences, or occasionally a paragraph, and concluding this process of composition and correction with his signature.

I have tried to preserve as much of this combined spontaneity and care as possible. The letters published here for the first time, December 1913 through June 1920, are typescripts unless the designation *longhand* appears at the head of the text below the date and address. When Pound typed additions to a typescript letter or wrote longhand additions to a longhand letter, I have indicated them *insert*. When he added to a typescript letter in longhand I have indicated it *longhand*. In both cases Pound's addition follows the designation; the designation and the whole phrase or paragraph are included in the running text, within square brackets, whether the phrase was added between the lines, or in the margin, or separately. Thus, in the sentence "The contrast between Blooms [*insert:* interior] poetry and his outward surroundings is excellent," the word "interior" was added between the lines. I have preserved crossouts when they seem to have been more than mere typing errors, e.g., "God knows where you have been and what you have gazed upon with your [*crossout:* myopic] microscopic [*crossout:* eye] remarkable eye."

It is interesting to observe that in his typescripts Pound used the symbol £, rather than the x, for his crossouts. Throughout his career he used this mark as a monogram for "Pound." He also used it to represent groups of poems. For instance, he wrote what he called a "series of Exultations" in which "Each poem is to some extent the analysis of some element of life £." [7] The series is a group

---

[7] From a letter to Viola Baxter, ?–1910, at Yale.

of personae; "王," the life behind them, gives them a kind of proportional unity. When writing to Joyce he referred to *Lustra* as "£." Such monograms are an elementary indication of Pound's belief that personality could give a certain sort of unity to apparently different poems, or that a collection of different elements could be held together by the force of the creative mind, one formal principle of *The Cantos*. The Chinese ideograph Ching (正 = precise, upright, orthodox) appealed to him in the same way (e.g., *Canto* LI). Later came "Money Pamphlets by £" and the "Square $ Series."

I have corrected obvious misspellings but have preserved grammatical idiosyncrasies and personal habits of punctuation and paragraphing. Since Pound liberally sprinkles his letters with dashes and other informal punctuation, I have used five asterisks (*****) in the few instances where it seemed advisable to delete a name or a word. Conjectures and a few omitted words have been placed in square brackets. Dating of letters is regularized, in both form and position; variations in addresses are preserved but position and form have been modified.

Unless otherwise noted, all the letters reproduced, including enclosures by other correspondents, are in the Joyce Collection at Cornell. The locations of other quoted, unpublished materials are indicated in the commentary, either directly or in parentheses, e.g., "(at Yale)."

Twelve letters from Pound to Joyce (July 1920 to December 1937) were previously published in *The Letters of Ezra Pound 1907–1941*, edited by D. D. Paige, New York: Harcourt, Brace and Company, 1950 (abbreviated *Letters*). All quotations in the commentary from Pound's letters to other correspondents are from this volume, indicated by date, unless otherwise noted. I have included three published letters from Joyce to Pound—one from *Letters of James Joyce*, edited by Stuart Gilbert, New York: The Viking Press, 1957, and two from *Letters of James Joyce*, Vols. II and III, edited by Richard Ellmann, New York: The Viking Press, 1966—as well as extracts from Joyce's letters to other correspondents. All quotations in the commentary from Joyce's letters are referred to those volumes.

Most proper names are identified, where possible in the running commentary, otherwise in footnotes. For the few cases where such names are not immediately identified, the Index may be consulted. Names are not identified when they are self-evident or irrelevant to the relations between Pound and Joyce. Matter from this volume is quoted in the commentary without cross reference.

For Pound's essays I have used the text as first printed but indicated reprints. For references to books and periodical articles, I have given full bibliographical information only where texts are quoted or pages cited. For fuller information on Pound's books and articles the reader may consult Donald Gallup's invaluable *A Bibliography of Ezra Pound*, London: Rupert Hart-Davis, 1963. When citing from Pound's early periodical publications I indicate both the original publication and, when an early work has been reprinted, the title of the last and therefore most easily available collection. First citations of periodicals give place of publication.

ACKNOWLEDGMENTS

For permission to publish most of the previously unpublished material in this volume, and to reprint Pound's essays and selections from his other volumes, I am indebted to Mr. and Mrs. Ezra Pound. I am grateful also to Mary A. Conroy for permission to draw extensively from John Quinn's letters to Pound and Joyce, and from his letters to E. Byrne Hackett relating to the proofsheets of *A Portrait*. For permission to publish a letter or part of a letter I should like to thank David Fleischman, heir of Leon Fleischman; the Estate of Edmund Gosse; Mrs. Ben W. Huebsch; Jane Liverdale for the Estate of Harriet Shaw Weaver; George Philip and Francis Richard Wells for the Estate of H. G. Wells; and Miss Anne Yeats and Michael Butler Yeats for the Estate of William Butler Yeats. I have been unable to locate the heirs of Augustine Birrell and E. Byrne Hackett.

I am grateful to Mrs. Pound and James Laughlin for advice and for help in gathering materials. Professor George H. Healey of the Department of Rare Books at Cornell University gave helpful advice and the Cornell University Library acquired essential microfilms. Also helpful was Donald Gallup, Curator of the Collection of American Literature at The Beinecke Rare Book and Manuscript Library, Yale University. Robert W. Hill, Keeper of Manuscripts at the New York Public Library, aided in contacting the heirs of John Quinn. The following also made available material from their collections: the Rare Books Department, University of California, Berkeley; the State University of New York at Buffalo; Hamilton College; and Harvard University. The libraries at Cornell, Yale, California, and Buffalo gave permission for publication. The English Department of Cornell University generously made grants for travel and for preparation of typescripts. Professors Richard

Ellmann, Gordon N. Ray, and Thomas Connolly provided unpublished letters from Pound which were in their possession. Professor Arthur Mizener helped with an early draft of my commentary. Dr. Edward Hart of Ithaca, N.Y., explained some of Pound's optical terminology.

For previously published materials, acknowledgment is made to Harcourt, Brace and Company for extracts from *The Letters of Ezra Pound;* to The Viking Press for extracts from *Letters of James Joyce*, Vols. I, II, and III, from *Finnegans Wake*, and from *Exiles;* to Random House for extracts from *Ulysses;* and to Holt, Rinehart and Winston for Joyce's dream, from *James Joyce*, by Herbert Gorman. Also, to the Society of Authors, acting for the Estate of James Joyce, for several items, and to David Garnett for his father Edward Garnett's opinion about *A Portrait*.

I should like also to thank the editors of *The Drama* and *The English Journal*, in which two of Pound's essays originally appeared, and those editors of now defunct periodicals who helped in the making of modern literature. Olga Rudge deserves thanks for collecting several of Pound's radio broadcasts, and Richard Ellmann and the Oxford University Press for their indispensable *James Joyce*. I reiterate my gratitude for Donald Gallup's bibliography, which makes serious study of Pound possible. Last but not least, I feel a special debt to James Laughlin and New Directions, the pioneers who printed and have kept in print so much of Pound's work.

1913-1918

When Ezra Pound first wrote to James Joyce in December 1913 he was enjoying an interlude from his busy affairs in London and America. He had come to Stone Cottage, Coleman's Hatch, Sussex, as Yeats's secretary, partly to ease the drain on his meager finances and partly out of "duty to posterity." He was working with Ernest Fenollosa's notes on the Chinese language, Chinese poetry, and the Japanese Noh drama, which he had recently received from Fenollosa's widow, and putting the final touches on *Des Imagistes,* his summary of Imagism; he wrote about twenty new poems. He had also recently met Henri Gaudier-Brzeska; excited about his sculpture, he was probably preparing to launch vorticism and to aid Wyndham Lewis and Brzeska with *Blast.* Pound presented himself to Joyce as an agent for *The Egoist* and *The Cerebralist* in London (only one issue of *The Cerebralist* ever appeared), the *Mercure de France* in Paris, *The Smart Set* in New York, and *Poetry* in Chicago. He had recently rejoined *Poetry,* after having resigned in disgust, "pending a general improvement of the magazine." At the moment his editorial connections were extensive and expanding.

As for Joyce, he had just received an unexpected windfall: in November Grant Richards, the London publisher who had once contracted to print *Dubliners* but had decided against it, agreed to reconsider it. Almost simultaneously Joyce received Pound's unsolicited offer of help. By chance, Pound struck at exactly the right moment. Sometime around New Year's Day 1914 Joyce's answer to his letter arrived and the Joyce decade had begun.

15 December 1913   *10, Church Walk, Kensington. W.*
James Joyce ESq.

Dear Sir: Mr Yeats has been speaking to me of your writing. I am informally connected with a couple of new and impecunious papers ("The Egoist" which has coursed under the unsuitable name of "The New Freewoman" 'guere que d' hommes y collaborent' as the

17

Mercure remarked of it—and the "Cerebrilist" which means God knows what—anyhow they are about the only organs in England that stand and stand for free speech and want [*longhand:* (I don't say get)] literature. The latter can pay a little, the former practically can not pay at all, we do it for larks and to have a place for markedly modern stuff.

I also collect for two American magazines which pay top rates, I can not however promise publication in them as I have no absolute powers for accepting mss.

This is the first time I have written to any one outside of my own circle of acquaintance (save in the case of French authors). These matters can be better dealt with in conversation, but as that is impossible, I write.

"The Smart Set" wants top notch stories. "Poetry" wants top notch poetry, I do not answer for the editorial conception of "top notch" but they pay 2 bob a line and get most of the best people (and one hell of a lot of muck). As I dont in the least know what your present stuff is like, I can only offer to read what you send, Essays etc. could only go into the "C" or "E." [*longhand:* either is a very good place, if you want to speak your mind on something The Spectator objects to.] Appearance in the Egoist may have a slight advertising value if you want to keep your name familiar.

Anyhow there are the facts for what they are worth. Please, if you send anything, mark quite clearly what you want done with it, minimum price as well as price desired. [*longhand:* etc.

I am bonae voluntatis,—don't in the least know that I can be of any use to you—or you to me. From what W. B. Y. says I imagine we have a hate or two in common—but thats a very problematical bond on introduction.]

Yours sincerely
Ezra Pound

26 December 1913   *Stone Cottage, Coleman's Hatch, Sussex*
James Joyce Esq.

Dear Mr Joyce: Yeats has just found your 'I hear an Army' and we are both much impressed by it.

This is a business note from me and compliments from him.

I want permission to use the poem in my anthology of Imagists. I can give you a guinea fee down, if that's good enough, and whatever more your share in profits of the anthology come to (if they come to

18

anything—this is not the usual graft anthology, the contributors are to share proportionately, if the book earns anything)

yours sincerely
Ezra Pound

4 January 1914   *Stone Cottage, Coleman's Hatch, Sussex*
                     (*mail address, 10, Church Walk, London. W.*)

Dear Mr Joyce:

[*longhand:* Thanks for the use of the poem] I sent on your fee from London yesterday (for poem to go in Anthology). I will send copies of papers in a day or so if I can find some.

About the stuff you have on hand, of course I can't tell until I see it, but I will forward it as follows: I will send the stories to the Smart Set (saying nothing about their suppression [*longhand:* I take it they have*n't* appeared at all]) I dare say you know the magazine, BUT it has a new editor.[1] He likes D. H. Lawrence's work but wrote recently about one story "Glorious stuff, wish to God we could print it, but we should find the magazine suppressed and I should be languishing in a cell as I believe the phrase is" [*longhand:* He says he wants and does want realism.]

However we can try him first as he pays more or less decently. Yeats says the tales shocked the modesty of Maunsell or something of that sort. "The Egoist" wont mind that (The Egoist is the present name of what will be marked FREEWOMAN in the copies I send you) only the Egoist cant pay, and one keeps it, as I said, for [*crossout:* personal utterance, or] propaganda, or for stuff that is too personal to sell to the usual magazines, or too outspoken.

We want it to be a place where a man can speak out. It is not a device for getting a man who ought to be paid, to work for nothing, which is more than I can say for some arty magazines. . I think they would probably be glad to have some of the essays, or possibly the novel if you cared to give it them. The Smart Set wouldnt print anything serially, and I've no influence with any magazine that might.

I found with the "Horses of Diomedes"[2] that it was rather easy to find a publisher *after* the Freewoman had printed about half of it. I don't know how much advantage it would be to you. The actual

[1] H. L. Mencken had joined the staff. Willard Huntington Wright was editor through the January 1914 issue; Mencken and George Jean Nathan became co-editors with the January 1915 issue.

[2] Remy De Gourmont, *Les Chevaux de Diomede* (1897), translated by C. Sartoris, *The New Freewoman,* August–December 1913, *The Egoist,* January–March 1914.

size of the book would also have to be considered before I could tell what they would do with it.

As for the play, there's the Abbey [3] for performance (? ? ? ?) and for publishing, The Glebe [4] (which is doing the anthology) might print it, or they might do the novel.

Publication in the Egoist would help toward that

"Poetry" as you will see, prints only verse and a few notes by the staff. They pay 2 s. per line but are slow about getting things in and very wobbly about their judgement. They get some good stuff and a lot of bad.

The Glebe pays a royalty, as book publication would.

The whole question re/ the Egoist, is how much the publicity and the 'keeping in touch' is worth. The Mercure de France (Dec 15) quotes a page and a half from my article on Tagore in said paper, that for what it is worth, shows how much such appearance gets the matter about. And then there is the mere convenience of getting a number of copies of a thing one wants for friends.

That is about the 'lay of the land' or lie of the land or whatever, at present.

yours sincerely

Ezra Pound

In addition to giving Pound permission to print "I Hear an Army," asking about "the literary situation," and inquiring about placing his work, Joyce sent a copy of a letter he had circulated to Irish newspapers in 1911, now brought up to date for use as a preface. Pound printed it without comment in his *Egoist* column as "A Curious History." Meanwhile Joyce finished the first chapter of *A Portrait* and sent it to Pound with *Dubliners*.

A CURIOUS HISTORY.[5]

The following statement having been received by me from an author of known and notable talents, and the state of the case being now, so far as I know, precisely what it was at the date of his last letter (November 30th), I have thought it more appropriate to print his communication entire than to indulge in my usual biweekly comment upon books published during the fortnight.

Mr. Joyce's statement is as follows :—

[3] The Abbey Theatre, Dublin, a center of the Irish revival where Yeats's plays were produced.

[4] Alfred Kreymborg and Man Ray founded *The Glebe* to publish volumes of new writing. *Des Imagistes* was published as *Glebe*, I, 5 (February 1914).

[5] *The Egoist*, I, 2 (January 15, 1914), pages 26–27.

The following letter, which gives the history of a book of stories, was sent by me to the Press of the United Kingdom two years ago. It was published by two newspapers so far as I know: "Sinn Fein" (Dublin) and the "Northern Whig" (Belfast).

Via della Barriera Vecchia 3²ᴵᴵᴵ
Trieste, Austria.

Sir, May I ask you to publish this letter, which throws some light on the present conditions of authorship in England and Ireland?

Nearly six years ago Mr. Grant Richards, publisher, of London, signed a contract with me for the publication of a book of stories written by me, entitled "Dubliners." Some ten months later he wrote asking me to omit one of the stories and passages in others which, as he said, his printer refused to set up. I declined to do either, and a correspondence began between Mr. Grant Richards and myself which lasted more than three months. I went to an international jurist in Rome (where I lived then) and was advised to omit. I declined to do so, and the MS. was returned to me, the publisher refusing to publish, notwithstanding his pledged printed word, the contract remaining in my possession.

Six months afterwards a Mr. Hone wrote to me from Marseilles to ask me to submit the MS. to Messrs. Maunsel, publishers, of Dublin. I did so; and after about a year, in July, 1909, Messrs. Maunsel signed a contract with me for the publication of the book on or before 1st September, 1910. In December, 1909, Messrs. Maunsel's manager begged me to alter a passage in one of the stories, "Ivy Day in the Committee Room," wherein some reference was made to Edward VII. I agreed to do so, much against my will, and altered one or two phrases. Messrs. Maunsel continually postponed the date of publication and in the end wrote, asking me to omit the passage or to change it radically. I declined to do either, pointing out that Mr. Grant Richards, of London, had raised no objection to the passage when Edward VII. was alive, and that I could not see why an Irish publisher should raise an objection to it when Edward VII. had passed into history. I suggested arbitration or a deletion of the passage with a prefatory note of explanation by me, but Messrs. Maunsel would agree to neither. As Mr. Hone (who had written to me in the first instance) disclaimed all responsibility in the matter and any connection with the firm I took the opinion of a solicitor in Dublin, who advised me to omit the passage, informing me that as I had no domicile in the United Kingdom I could not sue

21

Messrs. Maunsel for breach of contract unless I paid £100 into court, and that even if I paid £100 into court and sued them, I should have no chance of getting a verdict in my favour from a Dublin jury if the passage in dispute could be taken as offensive in any way to the late King. I wrote then to the present King, George V., enclosing a printed proof of the story, with the passage therein marked, and begging him to inform me whether in his view the passage (certain allusions made by a person of the story in the idiom of his social class) should be withheld from publication as offensive to the memory of his father. His Majesty's private secretary sent me this reply:—

Buckingham Palace.

The private secretary is commanded to acknowledge the receipt of Mr. James Joyce's letter of the 1st instant, and to inform him that it is inconsistent with rule for his Majesty to express his opinion in such cases. The enclosures are returned herewith.

11th August, 1911.

(The passage in dispute is on pp. 193 and 194 of this [the Maunsel] edition from the words *But look* to the words *play fair.*[6]

I wrote this book seven years ago and hold two contracts for its publication. I am not even allowed to explain my case in a prefatory note: wherefore, as I cannot see in any quarter a chance that my rights will be protected, I hereby give Messrs. Maunsel publicly permission to publish this story with what changes or deletions they may please to make, and shall hope that what they may publish may resemble that to the writing of which I gave thought and time. Their attitude as an Irish publishing firm may be judged by Irish public opinion. I, as a writer, protest against the systems (legal, social, and ceremonious) which have brought me to this pass.

Thanking you for your courtesy,

I am, Sir,

Your obedient servant,

JAMES JOYCE.

18th August, 1911.

I waited nine months after the publication of this letter. Then I went to Ireland and entered into negotiations with Messrs. Maunsel.

[6] "Ivy Day in the Committee Room," *Dubliners,* New York: The Viking Press, Compass Books edition, 1958, page 132.

They asked me to omit from the collection the story, "An Encounter," passages in "Two Gallants," the "Boarding House," "A Painful Case," and to change everywhere through the book the names of restaurants, cake-shops, railway stations, public-houses, laundries, bars, and other places of business. After having argued against their point of view day after day for six weeks and after having laid the matter before two solicitors (who, while they informed me that the publishing firm had made a breach of contract, refused to take up my case or to allow their names to be associated with it in any way), I consented in despair to all these changes on condition that the book were brought out without delay and the original text were restored in future editions, if such were called for. Then Messrs. Maunsel asked me to pay into their bank as security £1,000 or to find two sureties of £500 each. I declined to do either; and they then wrote to me, informing me that they would not publish the book, altered or unaltered, and that if I did not make them an offer to cover their losses on printing it they would sue me to recover same. I offered to pay sixty per cent. of the cost of printing the first edition of one thousand copies if the edition were made over to my order. This offer was accepted, and I arranged with my brother in Dublin to publish and sell the book for me. On the morning when the draft and agreement were to be signed the publishers informed me that the matter was at an end because the printer refused to hand over the copies. I took legal advice upon this, and was informed that the printer could not claim the money due to him by the publisher until he had handed over the copies. I then went to the printer. His foreman told me that the printer had decided to forego all claim to the money due to him. I asked whether the printer would hand over the complete edition to a London or Continental firm or to my brother or to me if he were fully indemnified. He said that the copies would never leave his printing-house, and added that the type had been broken up, and that the entire edition of one thousand copies would be burnt the next day. I left Ireland the next day, bringing with me a printed copy of the book which I had obtained from the publisher.

JAMES JOYCE.

30th November, 1913.   *Via Donato Bramante 4,*[II.,] *Trieste*

The other events in the world of publication have been the appearance of a new volume of poems by Arthur Symons. The pub-

lisher neglects to send it to us for review. A similar complaint
against him appeared recently in "The Outlook," over a popular
novel.

"The English Review" for the month contains the outpourings of
Messrs. Crowley, Edmund Gosse, and George Moore. Mr. Moore has
succeeded in falling below even his usual level of mendacious pusil-
lanimity.

EZRA POUND.

17 and 19 January 1914   *10, Church Walk, Kensington, London. W.*
Saturday

Dear Joyce: I'm not supposed to know much about prose but I
think your novel is damn fine stuff—I dare say you know it quite as
well as I do—clear and direct like Merimee.

I am sending it off at once to THE EGOIST, it seems a crime not
to get you paid for it but you recognize the difficulties and the rows
any publisher would make.

I hope to god THE EGOIST dont jibe at one or two of your
phrases, but I shall try to keep the burden of argument from your
shoulders.

Confound it, I can't usually read prose at all not anybody's in
English except James and Hudson and a little Conrad.

I am writing this at once. have just finished the reading.

Monday.
Have been deeved with interruptions.

I think the stories good—possibly too thorough, too psychological
or subjective in treatment to suit that brute in New York. I suppose
AN ENCOUNTER is impossible (for a magazine) still I shall send
the three of them with my recommendation, for what that's worth.
Wright thinks me a bit cracked, and regards himself as the sane
normal and practical male. He has exactly twice as much sense as
the common american editor, a sort of double zero leaning toward
the infinitesimal. Anyhow we'll have a go at him and see what can be
done.

How about verses. Have you anything more that stands up objective as your "I hear an Army". That potty little magazine in Chi-

24

cago pays well, and as I have resigned in a rage they are now for a little space docile and desirous of pleasing me by taking my advice.

I hope to have proofs of the "Artist" in a week, , but you know what a hell printers and papers are, one NEVER knows till the stuff is out of the office.

Pardon lack of ceremony in this note, but I'm just getting resettled in London and everything has to be done all at once.

yours sincerely
Ezra Pound

Pound sent *The Smart Set* "An Encounter," "The Boarding House," and "A Little Cloud." The enclosure in the following letter was probably a rejection of Joyce's stories. Frank Harris, whose help Pound considered seeking, was in Brixton jail during February for contempt of court in connection with a libel suit brought against him and his magazine, *Modern Society*, because of an article on a divorce case.

14 February 1914   *10, Church Walk, Kensington, London. W.*

Dear Joyce: I enclose a prize sample of bull shit. Wright has left the S. S. for a job on the Tribune and the magazine will fall back into its earlier courses.

Please send back the letter. Frank Harris will be out of quod in another week and I will try to set him on the war path in your behalf.

Also, as you see, the S. S. is disposed in your favour IF you have any sugar tits for 'em.

yours in some hurry
Ezra Pound

NEW ADDRESS

[c. 1 April] 1914   *5, Holland Place Chambers, Kensington. W.*

Dear Joyce: Your second chapter has arrived O.K., you know how good I think your work is so I needn't go into that.

The "Portrait" is at least getting you a "Gloire de cenacle". Lewis, Hueffer (Ford) and every one with whom I have spoken of the novel have all called it good stuff.

25

The "Araby" has gone to America and I haven't heard from it.

I have written to ask about the type being kept set up. I am afraid it hasn't been kept, and dont suppose there would be much use in starting plates now, but we'll see.

The proofs aren't sent to me. I guess the editorial secretary must do them. I asked that they be sent you. However they seem to be all right. The second chapter seems clear enough.

Lewis is starting a new Futurist, Cubist, Imagiste Quarterly,[7] I think he might take some of your essays, I cant tell, it is mostly a painters magazine with me to do the poems. He likes the novel but isn't very keen on the stories. AND he cant pay. Still there'll be a certain amount of attention focused on the paper for a few numbers anyhow and it might be a good place to have your name. I wish I could find some more remunerative openings but I dont do much in that way for myself and . . . . la' la' . . .

Lets hope for a heaven with no Gosses.

yours ever
Ezra Pound

Grant Richards finally brought out *Dubliners* on June 15, 1914. Pound's first review of Joyce reflects his current interest in realistic prose and in impressionistic rendering of local ambiance, especially the urban milieu and its effects on mind, manners, and emotion; hence his comparison of *Dubliners* to the work of the Scandinavian impressionists August Strindberg and Herman Joachim Bang, and to the regional novels *Madame Bovary* by Flaubert and *La Doña Perfecta* by Benito Pérez Galdós. His efforts to modernize his own poetry to catch up with the achievements of nineteenth-century prose led him to compare *Dubliners* also to the work of poets who seemed to be moving in a similar direction. He had favorably reviewed Frost's *A Boy's Will* and D. H. Lawrence's *Love Poems and Others* in *Poetry* in the spring of 1913. In the fall he had written an important series in *The New Age*, "The Approach to Paris" (the basis of his later "A Study in French Poets").[8] There he had discussed among other things the poetic realism of Charles Vildrac and

---

[7] *Blast,* I, appeared June 1914; *Blast,* II, the second and last issue, July 1915.

[8] "The Approach to Paris," seven installments, *The New Age,* XIII, 19–25 (4 September through 16 October 1913). Revised and expanded, "A Study in French Poets," *The Little Review,* IV, 10 (February 1918). Further revised, *Instigations of Ezra Pound,* New York: Boni and Liveright, 1920, and *Make It New,* 1934.

Francis Jammes; he had been particularly interested in efforts by the unanimist Jules Romains and by Henri-Martin Barzun to devise a neo-Whitmanian epic style for encompassing the modern city and the modern mind. When Joyce's work began to arrive Pound was fully open to receive it.

"DUBLINERS" AND MR JAMES JOYCE [9]

Freedom from sloppiness is so rare in contemporary English prose that one might well say simply, "Mr Joyce's book of short stories is prose free from sloppiness," and leave the intelligent reader ready to run from his study immediately to spend three and sixpence on the volume.

Unfortunately one's credit as a critic is insufficient to produce this result.

The readers of THE EGOIST, having had Mr Joyce under their eyes for some months, will scarcely need to have his qualities pointed out to them. Both they and the paper have been very fortunate in his collaboration.

Mr Joyce writes a clear hard prose. He deals with subjective things, but he presents them with such clarity of outline that he might be dealing with locomotives or with builders' specifications. For that reason one can read Mr Joyce without feeling that one is conferring a favour. I must put this thing my own way. I know about 168 authors. About once a year I read something contemporary without feeling that I am softening the path for poor Jones or poor Fulano de Tal.

I can lay down a good piece of French writing and pick up a piece of writing by Mr Joyce without feeling as if my head were being stuffed through a cushion. There are still impressionists about and I dare say they claim Mr Joyce. I admire impressionist writers. English prose writers who haven't got as far as impressionism (that is to say, 95 per cent. of English writers of prose and verse) are a bore.

Impressionism has, however, two meanings, or perhaps I had better say, the word "impressionism" gives two different "impressions."

There is a school of prose writers, and of verse writers for that matter, whose forerunner was Stendhal and whose founder was Flaubert. The followers of Flaubert deal in exact presentation.

[9] *The Egoist*, I, 14 (July 15, 1914), page 267; *Literary Essays*, pages 399–402.

They are often so intent on exact presentation that they neglect intensity, selection, and concentration. They are perhaps the most clarifying and they have been perhaps the most beneficial force in modern writing.

There is another set, mostly of verse writers, who founded themselves not upon anybody's writing but upon the pictures of Monet. Every movement in painting picks up a few writers who try to imitate in words what someone has done in paint. Thus one writer saw a picture by Monet and talked of "pink pigs blossoming on a hillside," and a later writer talked of "slate-blue" hair and "raspberry-coloured flanks."

These "impressionists" who write in imitation of Monet's softness instead of writing in imitation of Flaubert's definiteness, are a bore, a grimy, or perhaps I should say, a rosy, floribund bore.

The spirit of a decade strikes properly upon all of the arts. There are "parallel movements." Their causes and their effects may not seem, superficially, similar.

This mimicking of painting ten or twenty years late, is not in the least the same as the "literary movement" parallel to the painting movement imitated.

The force that leads a poet to leave out a moral reflection may lead a painter to leave out representation. The resultant poem may not suggest the resultant painting.

Mr Joyce's merit, I will not say his chief merit but his most engaging merit, is that he carefully avoids telling you a lot that you don't want to know. He presents his people swiftly and vividly, he does not sentimentalise over them, he does not weave convolutions. He is a realist. He does not believe "life" would be all right if we stopped vivisection or if we instituted a new sort of "economics." He gives the thing as it is. He is not bound by the tiresome convention that any part of life, to be interesting, must be shaped into the conventional form of a "story." Since De Maupassant we have had so many people trying to write "stories" and so few people presenting life. Life for the most part does not happen in neat little diagrams and nothing is more tiresome than the continual pretence that it does.

Mr Joyce's "*Araby*," for instance, is much better than a "story," it is a vivid waiting.

It is surprising that Mr Joyce is Irish. One is so tired of the Irish or "Celtic" imagination (or "phantasy" as I think they now call it) flopping about. Mr Joyce does not flop about. He defines. He is not an institution for the promotion of Irish peasant industries. He accepts an international standard of prose writing and lives up to it.

He gives us Dublin as it presumably is. He does not descend to farce. He does not rely upon Dickensian caricature. He gives us things as they are, not only for Dublin, but for every city. Erase the local names and a few specifically local allusions, and a few historic events of the past, and substitute a few different local names, allusions, and events, and these stories could be retold of any town.

That is to say, the author is quite capable of dealing with things about him, and dealing directly, yet these details do not engross him, he is capable of getting at the universal element beneath them.

The main situations of *"Madame Bovary"* or of *"Doña Perfecta"* do not depend on local colour or upon local detail, that is their strength. Good writing, good presentation can be specifically local, but it must not depend on locality. Mr Joyce does not present "types" but individuals. I mean he deals with common emotions which run through all races. He does not bank on "Irish character." Roughly speaking, Irish literature has gone through three phases in our time, the shamrock period, the dove-grey period, and the Kiltartan period. I think there is a new phase in the works of Mr Joyce. He writes as a contemporary of continental writers. I do not mean that he writes as a faddist, mad for the last note, he does not imitate Strindberg, for instance, or Bang. He is not ploughing the underworld for horror. He is not presenting a macabre subjectivity. He is classic in that he deals with normal things and with normal people. A committee room, Little Chandler, a nonentity, a boarding house full of clerks—these are his subjects and he treats them all in such a manner that they are worthy subjects of art.

Francis Jammes, Charles Vildrac and D. H. Lawrence have written short narratives in verse, trying, it would seem, to present situations as clearly as prose writers have done, yet more briefly. Mr Joyce is engaged in a similar condensation. He has kept to prose, not needing the privilege supposedly accorded to verse to justify his method.

I think that he excels most of the impressionist writers because of his more rigorous selection, because of his exclusion of all unnecessary detail.

There is a very clear demarcation between unnecessary detail and irrelevant detail. An impressionist friend of mine talks to me a good deal about "preparing effects," and on that score he justifies much unnecessary detail, which is not "irrelevant," but which ends by being wearisome and by putting one out of conceit with his narrative.

Mr Joyce's more rigorous selection of the presented detail marks him, I think, as belonging to my own generation, that is, to the "nineteen-tens," not to the decade between "the 'nineties" and today.

At any rate these stories and the novel now appearing in serial form are such as to win for Mr Joyce a very definite place among English contemporary prose writers, not merely a place in the "Novels of the Week" column, and our writers of good clear prose are so few that we cannot afford to confuse or to overlook them.

16 July 1914   *5, Holland Place Chambers, Kensington, London. W.*
Thursday

Dear Joyce: Thanks for your letter and for Chapter III. I am trying to make the Egoist print it in longer installments. I think you have bundled up the hell fire preaching very finely. The intonation of cant etc.

I have done a little punctuating, I hope correctly, in one or two places that seemed difficult.

My article on you is very bad, but I simply can't afford to rewrite articles for the Egoist. One can do only a certain amount of work unpaid. I wish it were better.

Thanks for the very amusing cutting from Trieste. [*longhand:* re Blast] [1] I should like to have seen the Corriere. England, the press, is mostly sullen resentment. [*longhand:* one man even singled out the obituary notice of Gore for his criticism.] [2]

INTERRUPTIONS

Tuesday, July 21

Your letter just come.
I believe in your prose all right enough.

[1] "I Vorticisti Sorpassano in Audacia I Futuristi. Versi da Una a Trecento Sillabe!," *Il Piccolo della Sera,* Trieste. Pound printed the account in his *Gaudier-Brzeska: A Memoir,* 1916 (republished, New York: New Directions, 1960, pages 51–52).

[2] The painter Frederick Spencer Gore, 1899–1914, *Blast,* I, page 51.

I am afraid "my" review is all in the air. An american dangling before me enough money just not to run it.

However I can send the two poems to that Chicago rag if you can stand it. They pay, dammm 'em. That's their recommendation. Also they mean well but . . . . . .

On the whole they are remarkably good considering that they just have to print some American stuff.

About the novel. By all means send the whole of it to a publisher. The book can perfectly well appear simultaneously with the last installment in the Egoist. No publisher will get it out before that time even if he begins now. You've waited long enough for your recognition.

I haven't a decent photograph at the moment but Arbuthnot has asked me for a sitting and you are welcome to the result when it comes . , tho it won't much adorn the landscape.

With this letter being interrupted I cant remember what I [*cross-out:* wrote you] have written to you. However I dont think I have left out any news worth telling. We have been having Vorticist and Imagiste dinners, haciendo politicas etc. God save all poor sailors from la vie litteraire.

yours ever
Ezra Pound

The outbreak of World War I temporarily interrupted postal service between Austria and England. Joyce was unable to continue sending *A Portrait* until he arranged a Venetian forwarding address, that of Italo Svevo's father-in-law; no installment appeared in the November *Egoist*. Pound meanwhile was disturbed by the outbreak of the war and occupied with the repercussions of *Blast;* consequently a hiatus of eight months appears in the correspondence, during which no letters seem to have been written—at least none have survived.

In September 1914 Pound discovered T. S. Eliot, who was studying philosophy at Oxford, as he had discovered Robert Frost in 1913, and began similarly to promote Eliot's work. During the winter of 1914–1915 he tried unsuccessfully to promote the idea of a College of Arts as a means of finding employment for the vorticists and of sustaining civilization. In Trieste Joyce continued his work on *Exiles* and *Ulysses*. Pound had put him in touch with H. L. Mencken, now co-editor of *The Smart Set*, who in May 1915 printed "The Boarding House" and "A Little Cloud." Meanwhile, in February, in the last article of "Affirmations," a survey of the music, painting, sculpture, and poetry of the decade as seen by a vorticist, Pound delivered his most outspoken early praise of Joyce. Except for his mention here of D. H. Lawrence, an earlier admiration whom Joyce supplanted as the best of his generation, Joyce was the only prose writer Pound singled out.

from "THE NON-EXISTENCE OF IRELAND" [3]

. . . Coming down to the present, I can find only one man calling himself Irish who is in any sense part of the decade. I refer to the exile James Joyce. Synge fled to Paris, driven out presumably by the local stupidity. Joyce has fled to Trieste and into the modern world. And in the calm of that foreign city he has written books about Ireland. There are many books about Ireland. But Joyce's books are in prose. I mean they are written in what we call "prose" par excellence.

If there is anything wearying in this life it is "arty" unmetrical writing; the spilling out of ornaments and sentimental melancholy that came in the wake of the neo-symbolist writers and which has had more than its day in Ireland, as it has had elsewhere. It is a joy then to find in Mr. Joyce a hardness and gauntness, "like the side of an engine"; efficient; clear statement, no shadow of comment, and behind it a sense of beauty that never relapses into ornament. So far as I know there are only two writers of prose fiction of my decade whom anyone takes in earnest. I mean Mr. Joyce and Mr. D. H. Lawrence. Of these two the latter is undoubtedly a writer of some power. I have never envied Mr. Lawrence, though I have often enjoyed him. I do not want to write, even good stories, in a loaded ornate style, heavy with sex, fruity with a certain sort of emotion. Mr. Lawrence has written some short narrative poems in dialects which are worthy of admiration.

Mr. Joyce writes the sort of prose I should like to write were I a prose writer. He writes, and one perhaps only heaps up repetitions and epithets in trying to describe any good writing; he writes with a clear hardness, accepting all things, defining all things in clean outline. He is never in haste. He writes as a European, not as a provin-

[3] *The New Age*, XVI, 17 (February 25, 1915), page 452.

cial. He is not "a follower in Mr. Wells' school" or in any school whatsoever. Life is there. Mr. Joyce looks without bewilderment. He finds no need to disguise things to himself. He writes with no trace of morbidity. The sordid is there, but he does not seek for the sordid. He has the sense of abundant beauty. Often we find a writer who can get a certain delusive sense of "power" out of "strong" situations, or by describing rough life. Mr. Joyce is not forced into this. He presents his people regardless of "bareness," regardless of their not being considered "romantic" or "realistic" material. And when he has written they stand so that the reader says to himself, "this thing happened"; "this is not a magazine story made to please some editor, or some current taste, or to 'ring a bell in the last paragraph.' " His work is not a mode, not a literary endeavour. ·

Let us presume that Ireland is ignorant of Mr. Joyce's existence, and that if any copy of his work ever reaches that country it will be reviled and put on the index. For ourselves, we can be thankful for clear, hard surfaces, for an escape from the softness and mushiness of the neo-symbolist movement, and from the fruitier school of the neo-realists, and in no less a degree from the phantasists who are the most trivial and most wearying of the lot. All of which attests the existence of Mr. Joyce, but by no means the continued existence of Ireland.

Joyce was trying to arrange book publication of *A Portrait* with Grant Richards. In March 1915 the literary agent James Brand Pinker, at the suggestion of H. G. Wells, wrote Joyce offering to handle his novels. Joyce asked Pound, who was helping him with Richards, to interview Pinker. As a result Pinker became Joyce's agent, a post he held until his death in 1922. A few days after the next letter Pound sent Joyce an inscribed copy of *Cathay*, his renderings of Chinese poetry from Fenollosa's notes, which was published on April 6. Joyce's copy is at Yale.

[c. 29 March] 1915   *5, Holland Place Chambers, Kensington. W.*

Dear James Joyce: I took the final chapter of your novel to Grant Richards this a.m.

Also I saw Pinker. I enclose his draft of agreement. It is straight and fair enough. He is agent for Conrad and Henry James etc. etc. and I think he will probably do better for you then any one else could. I should fill in the agreement and send him your play.

33

If you have an agreement with Richards for the novel I suppose that is done for, but if any dispute arises I dare say Pinker will advise you. I liked the man on meeting him, he says he is interested in literature etc. etc. wants men who take their work seriously and so on. My impression is that his interest should be an asset and possibly a very considerable one.

I am now up and about and feeling quite fit. I shall send you a little book of poems from the Chinese in a few days.
Pinker, by the way, seemed to think Grant Richards not quite good enough, but I think a bird in the hand has a certain value. If Richards doesnt give you good terms then you have [*crossout:* the] Pinker to fall back upon. Best Wishes, yours ever.

Ezra Pound

In May Italy entered the war and communications were cut off once more. In June the Joyce family moved from Trieste to Zurich, having been allowed by the Austrian government to seek asylum in neutral Switzerland. In his June letter, held up until Joyce announced his arrival in Zurich, Pound answered Joyce's persistent request for a photograph of himself. He declined to send a photograph taken by Alvin Langdon Coburn, whose cubist experiments with the vortoscope allied him with the vorticists (the photograph was used as the frontispiece to *Lustra*, 1916). One of the photographs that he did enclose was of the well-known bust by Gaudier-Brzeska, one of the attractions of the London years. Pound later had the bust brought to Rapallo; the stone eyes gazed seaward from a roof terrace during the thirteen years he was confined in Washington. When he returned to Italy in 1959 it was moved to a garden terrace at Brunnenburg, the castle of Pound's son-in-law and daughter, Prince and Princess de Rachewiltz, where it now looks out over the valley of the Passirio and the South Tyrol city of Merano.

[c. June] 1915   *London (no address)*

Dear Joyce: I presume it is entirely vain and useless to write to you, at least until we know that the Italians have rescued Trieste.

Nevertheless I will do this and keep the note until I hear.

Dont worry about your book, for a first book of short stories it has not done badly. Short stories collected into volumes are notoriously unsaleable. My wife is just reading the book for a second time and saying "They are excellently good, aren't they."

Yeats was saying, when I told him your disappointment, "Not so bad. It is the second book always, that sells the first."

Of course Grant Richards have given you abominable terms, but even that will wear off. If you're not wrecked in the bombardment of your domicile.

I will see that your play is read by the agent of one very practical American dramatic company, which does a big business. (For whatever good that will do.)

Also I solemnly swear that I will someday send you a photograph, at present I am torn between conflicting claims. I have an excessively youthful and deceptive photograph (very rare edition). I have several copies of a photo of a portrait of me, painted by an amiable jew who substituted a good deal of his own face for the gentile parts of my own. I have the seductive and sinister photograph by Coburn which I expect to have photograved in order to sell my next book of bad poems. It is like a cinque, or quattrocento painting. My father-in-law says "A sinister but very brilliant italian." My old landlady said "It is the only photograph that has ever done you justice," and then as she was sidling out of the door, with increasing embarrassment. "Ah, ah. I . I hope you wont be offended, sir, but it is [*crossout:* a good] rather like the good man of Nazareth, isn't it sir?"

Dante, you remember at the beginning of the epistle to Can Grande (at least I think it is there) mentions a similar predicament about presenting one's self at a distance. It is my face, no I can not be represented in your mind by that semitic image [*insert:* alone (which I enclose)], it is my face as it may have been years ago, or my face greatly beautified, or as I enclose, my face as immortalized by vorticist sculpture, which I enclose, this bust is monumental, but it will be no use to the police, it is hieratic, phallic, even, if you will consider the profiles not shown in the photograph.

No, I will either, get a new photo, or send you the photogravure in good time.

3 July 1915   *London (no address)*

Dear Joyce: Rejoiced to hear you are in a safe place. I enclose a note written some days since.

I have got the promise of an efficient American agent for a large theatre co. to read your play as soon as Pinker forwards it. I hope you did not leave it behind in Trieste.

If you are hard up, there is as you may know a Royal Literary fund, or some such thing for authors in temporary distress. De la Mare has just been given a pension. And if you arent worth ten De la Mares I'll eat my shirt.

Anyhow I will write to Wells and see if he can stir up the literary fund. You wont get a pension yet a while as you haven't been sitting in the pockets of *Sir* Henry Newbolt and co. for the past six years.

Gaudier Brzeska has been killed at Neuville St Vaast, which is pretty sickening seeing that he was the best of the younger sculptors and one of the best sculptors in all europe. I am very sick about it.

Enough for to night. I'll get this into the mail at once.

ever yours
Ezra Pound

Characteristically, Pound at once began to "stir up" the Royal Literary Fund.[4] The Fund was clearly more conservative than Pound's vorticist group (*Blast* II had just appeared) ; it included writers like Sir Henry Newbolt, poet, man of letters, and like Pound an anthologist of new verse, who had just been knighted, and Edmund Gosse, the influential biographer, critic, and poet. Pound therefore got Yeats to approach Gosse, while he wrote to H. G. Wells. Pound sent Joyce a note from Yeats (at Yale) and Gosse's and Wells's replies (at Cornell), along with his own covering note. (Wells's *Boon, The Mind of the Race, etc.*, 1915 was an encyclopedic parody of the mental state of the contemporary literary world.)

[c. 10] July 1915   *5, Holland Place Chambers, Kensington. W.*

Dear Joyce: Here is the result of the last 48 hours of agitation.

Will you send on "the facts"?

Do you want a job in the censors office?

yours ever
E. P.

[4] For all the letters relating to the application, *Letters of James Joyce*, II, pages 349–363, passim, and *The Letters of W. B. Yeats,* edited by Allan Wade, London: Rupert Hart-Davis, 1954, pages 596–600.

8 July 1915 *18, Woburn Buildings, W.C.*

My dear Ezra: Can you get into communication with Joyce and get the facts. I am writing to Gosse about Joyce's literary gift.

Yrs
W B Yeats

July 1915 *52, St. James's Court, Buckingham Gate. S.W.*

Dear Pound: I'm no good with the R. L. F. because (1) I have hurt Gosse's feelings re *Boon* & (2) I have stopped my subscription on account of the[? Cressland] grant.

Hueffer says he can get Joyce a job at the War Office (Censorship). Also I will telephone Pinker.

Yours ever
H. G. Wells

7 July 1915 *17, Hanover Terrace, Regent's Park, N.W.*

My dear Yeats: I am confined to my room by an acute attack of lumbago. But I am very much interested in what you tell me of Mr. Joyce. I shall be delighted to do all I can. The great thing is for you to make perfectly sure of the *facts*. It does no good to start on mere gossip. Where are the wife and children? Are they with him at Zurich? Who is his representative in this country? Can you send me some account of his works, for I am ashamed to say I know nothing of them?

In a few days I hope to get about again, but I have been now in my bedroom for a week, and I cannot report myself better.

Yours very sincerely
Edmund Gosse

Joyce sent Pound "the facts," Pound relayed them to Yeats, and Yeats sent them on to Gosse, with whom he proceeded to conduct a persuasive series of exchanges. Gosse directed A. Llewelyn Roberts, secretary of the Fund, to take up Joyce's case. (Gosse supported Joyce's applications for government aid during the war but regretted his support after he had read *Ulysses*.) Joyce sent the Fund information about his circumstances, his writing, his income, and his

37

health, adding that he was asking Yeats and Pound to support his application. Yeats had already written to the Fund about Joyce's "beautiful gift," calling "I Hear an Army" "a technical and emotional masterpiece," and *Dubliners* and *A Portrait* signs of "the promise of a great novelist and a novelist of a new kind." Pound corroborated Joyce's "facts" and added his own special arguments in Joyce's favor.

3 August 1915 [5]   *10 Church Walk, Kensington, W.*

A. Llewelyn Roberts, Esq.
Secretary, Royal Literary Fund,
40 Denison House, 296 Vauxhall Bridge Rd. S.W.

Dear Sir: Re/ your request for information regarding James Joyce.

He is a refugee from Trieste. He kept on teaching in that city until the last possible moment. He is now searching for work in Switzerland. He has a wife and children. He has, also, some eye trouble that is likely to incapacitate him for several weeks at a time.

He has degrees from Dublin and, I think, Padua, and various certificates from commercial training schools so he feels he may find work later. The schools are now shut for the summer, I believe.

I understand that he arrived in Zurich with clothing suitable for Trieste but not for the Swiss temperature. A relative of his wife's has advanced him a little money, now nearly or wholly gone. This relative is not a man of means and can scarcely be expected to advance or give more money. My own gross takings for the month of July were £2/17 so I am not in a position to help Mr Joyce directly, though I should be glad to do so. (I do not think he would accept assistance unless he were on the edge of necessity.)

I do not imagine that my opinion of Mr Joyce's writing can have any weight with your committee, still it gives me a certain satisfaction to state that I consider Joyce a good poet, and *without exception* the best of the younger prose writers. (This is not an opinion influenced by personal friendship, for I was [*longhand:* became acquainted] drawn to the man through his work.)

The book "Dubliners" is uneven. It has been well received but I think he has received nothing yet from his publishers.

[5] *Letters of James Joyce*, II, pages 358–360. I have dropped two longhand notes which are not Pound's: ("B.A.R. Univ. Dublin)." at the end of paragraph one, and "Two—boy & girl, 10 & 8 in 1915," inserted after "children" in paragraph two.

His novel "The Portrait of the Artist as a Young Man" has not yet appeared in book form. It is a work of indubitable value, and permanence. It is appearing serially in a paper called "The Egoist." This paper is conducted by enthusiasts who can not afford to pay their contributors.

Your older magazines are so sunk in sloth and stupidity that it [is] impossible for anyone under ninety and unrelated to your detestable victorian rhetoricians to get published in them. Joyce was in Trieste and without friends of influence and I therefore induced him to print this novel in such an out of the way place rather than to leave it longer hidden awaiting the caprice of commerce. This move has been justified, since it has interested several well known authors in Mr Joyce's work.

I would point out that Mr Joyce's work has been absolutely uncorrupted. He has lived for ten years in obscurity and poverty, that he might perfect his writing and be uninfluenced by commercial demands and standards. "Ho sofferto fame tre anni a Lipsia, come magister, io non m'arrendi [sic]. [6]

His style has the hard clarity of a Stendhal or a Flaubert. (I am not using these comparisons in a fit of emotional excitement. I have said as much in print already and the opinion is one which has stayed with me for over a year without diminution.) He has also the richness of erudition which differentiates him from certain able and vigorous but rather overloaded impressionist writers. He is able, in the course of a novel, to introduce a serious conversation, or even a stray conversation on style or philosophy without being ridiculous. With the rest, or with most of your novelists, save Henry James and Thomas Hardy, any author who lets a flash of his own personality leak out through the chinks of his story is lost, utterly and hopelessly lost, and we know we can not possibly care a hang what such an author says, or invents for his characters.

If it might be permitted me, to exceed slightly the request you have made to me for information, and if as a foreigner, viewing as a spectator the glories and shames of your country, I might say that it seems to me ridiculous that your government pensions should go for the most part to saving wrecks rather than in the fostering of letters. Thus you give a pension to De la Mare (God knows I am thankful for any good fortune that may befall Walter de la Mare, [crossout: but here] he is a man who has written a few charming poems, who has been worried to death, who is practically at the end

[6] "I starved for three years at Leipzig, as a teacher, I would not give up."

of his tether and who is unlikely to write anything more of any value. Pensioned and put to rest.

On the other hand you have a really great writer like Joyce, capable of producing lasting work if he had any chance of leisure, such chance of leisure as a small pension might give him.

I know it is not my place to make suggestions to your august committee, but I do very strongly make this suggestion. I assure you that [*longhand:* England's] thoughtfulness, in the midst of war, in stopping to pension De la Mare, has had a good effect on my country. America will have given England more credit for that [*longhand:* small] act than she will have given to Germany for a propaganda of Kultur. The effect on a foreign nation is perhaps irrelevant but it may be considered.

I do not know how these things are arranged, and I am, I believe, persona non grata to most of my elders but that fact might be overlooked for the moment in a matter so intimately concerning the welfare of English letters as I believe Mr. Joyce's welfare to be.

I trust I have given the information that you desire. I shall be glad to supply any more data that I can. Joyce has two children aged 5 and 8. The eye trouble is the after effect of malarial fever. The school term b [*longhand:* begins in October, but there is of course no absolute certainty that he will be able to find a position.]

respectfully yours,
Ezra Pound

The Royal Literary Fund granted Joyce £75, which Richard Ellmann says eased him while he was writing the early Bloom episodes of *Ulysses*. When Joyce wrote in September to thank Yeats, Yeats replied: "I am very glad indeed that "The Royal Literary Fund" has been so wise and serviceable. You need not thank me, for it was really Ezra Pound who thought of your need. I acted at his suggestion, because it was easier for me to approach the Fund for purely personal reasons. We thought Gosse (who has great influence with the Fund people, but is rather prejudiced) would take it better from me. What trouble there was fell on Ezra" (at Cornell).

In May Pound had agreed to help find a producer for *Exiles*, a task he was to continue off and on for more than two years. He carried on an exchange of notes with Joyce's agent, J. B. Pinker (these are in the possession of Gordon N. Ray). Pound's first try was Cecil Dorrian, London representative of Oliver Morosco, Burbank Theatre, Los Angeles, an organization in which Pound had a "personal, unprofessional acquaintance." In the next letter Pound also mentions *Ulysses* for the first time, though not by name. Joyce had projected his book in 1906 and begun it in 1914, while he was putting the finishing touches on *A Portrait*. The mention of a new magazine refers to early negotiations with John Quinn, the New York lawyer, art patron, manuscript collector, and friend of the Yeatses. Quinn admired Pound's work and through him became interested in the vorticist painters; he later aided Pound in seeking American publishers. The search for a new review did not bear fruit until Pound became associated with *The Little Review* in 1917.

27 August 1915   *5, Holland Place Chambers, Kensington. W.*

Dear Joyce: Pinker says (writes) that your play has gone to Cecil Dorrian.

This letter is to say that there seems a chance of a monthly magazine that can pay contributors. I have spent the day writing a prospectus designed to entrap American dollars, in response to a New York cablegram.

I put your name down in a prominent place among the probable contributors. Do send whatever you have, to me direct, and then if the scheme falls through I can pass 'em on to Pinker.

I want a sort of "Mercure de France", only better.

I wonder if apart from your creative work you would care to take a "rubric", i.e. one of the monthly chronicles of books in some language or other, or if any contemporary literature interests you enough to bother with, or which?

At any rate you might send me a full list of works, of essays already written or of subjects on which you would care to write.

In essay writing I should want matter rather than theories "about it and about", but I think about anything you cared enough about to write would be "available" some time or other.

Do you know of anyone whom you think ought to be roped in to cooperate. I've made out a list containing about all the intelligent men I know of (and some that are only partially so). Still the more people's ideas I have before me the better.

Something must come of it sooner or later, I think.

41

I should think your continuation of the Portrait of the Artist might be serialized, in rather larger chunks than the Egoist has managed.

I've a deal of letter writing to get on with, so enough for the moment.

yours ever
Ezra Pound

6 September 1915   *5, Holland Place Chambers, Kensington. W.*

Dear Joyce: Pardon the bloody apparition of this page, but the other half of the type-ribbon is tired.

I am glad the committee has coughed up something, I could have done nothing with 'em if it had not been for Yeats' backing. He has had an amusing correspondence with Gosse in which Gosse complains that neither you nor W. B. Y. have given any definite statement of loyalty to the allies (it being a mathematical impossibility that it should ever have occurred to either of you that such a statement would be expected . . . etc.) Any how Yeats has pacified him, and he, Gosse, has passed on your name to someone who may (? ? ? possibly) know of something you could do in Switzerland. However I think you'd calm G's mind and comfort him if you sent him a note full of correct, laudable, slightly rhetorical (but not too much so) protestations of filial devotion to Queen Victoria and the heirs of her body.

Damn the syndicate anyhow, still if C[ecil]. D[orrian]. has refused the play I suppose it will only bring you glory and not cash. I have a blind faith in the knowledge of these curious people who think *exactly* like the multitude, with the exception that they know they do, that they are conscious of the multitudinous banality of their perceptions.

I am writing Pinker for the play, which I expected C. D. to send on to me. Tho' god knows what I can do with it. The Drama league in Chicago might put it on, or it might be done at some art theatre in America, or Drama might print it, all of which things are highly uncertain.

No, your books haven't been wholly useless even cashicly as without 'em we could have extracted nothing from the committee and £75 is "all that anyone gets for a novel". The public demand for a work being in inverse ratio to its quality, one exists by chance and [a] series of ignominies. La Gloire becomes, only after a long time, a

42

commercial asset. It insures one's being rejected by the editor instead of by the office boy.

Even if I get a magazine (it would be monthly) there wont be floods of gold in it. Still there'd be something. I think you are right about not wanting to do a rubric and you are certainly better employed reading your own stuff than you would be in reading Papini [7] or the young italians, who seem all tarred with the futuristic taint, i.e. spliced cinematography in paintings and diarrhoea in writing.

The other disadvantage of reading or criticizing one's contemporaries is that those whom you do not praise form themselves into a sort of *lourd* and semiconscious vendetta, and those whom you do praise fly into rages when you find a gleam of hope in the works of anyone else, and then we have paragraphs about "pontif litteraire" and "however prominent a literary personage, his own creative work" etc. etc.

On the whole it is amusing for anything which casts the human psychology on the screen or makes it act visibly from ascertainable motives is of interest bacteriologically. However you are better out of the teapot and its tempests. IF the magazine does materialize you shall write pretty much anything you like for it, and even old McClure (proprietor of a popular American magazine) [8] once advised me never to do anything I did not like, as he never had, and one only did such things badly.

I enclose the silly clippings, perhaps they will pass the censor in this form. I dont think there is anything seditious on the reverse sides of 'em. As the New Age was printed in Feb. and the St Louis paper [9] some time ago I doubt if the news can be of any assistance to any military commander more especially as it concerns only ourselves. The stuff is certainly not worth your writing to the papers direct in order to have the back numbers sent you. I perceive I have used a phrase in what I think is middle high german, meaning "I do ye to wit", but otherwise my article and letter contain nothing to which the censorship need take exception.

I dont suppose the magazine will start till Jan 1st. even if Quinn is successful in raising the money.

Now that Brzeska has been killed, pour la patrie, my criticism

[7] Giovanni Papini, Italian *avant-garde* writer and polemicist, one of the original futurists.

[8] S. S. McClure, pioneer American editor and publisher, founder of McClure's syndicate and *McClure's Magazine.*

[9] "The Non-Existence of Ireland," above pages 32–33, and "Affirmations: Edgar Lee Masters," *Reedy's Mirror,* St. Louis, Mo., which was removed from Pound's series because it praised *vers libre,* a form *The New Age* had condemned.

has found a market for his sculpture. It is some comfort to know that the market would have been there just the same if he survived and that he would have had a chance to work free of encumbrance if he had come back, but there is a deal of irony in it all.

This letter is of indecent size, so I stop before it gets any worse.

yours ever
Ezra Pound

[Between 6 and 12] September 1915
5, Holland Place Chambers, Kensington. W.

Dear Joyce: I have just read the splendid end of "The Portrait of the Artist", and if I try to tell you how fine it is, I shall only break out into inane hyperbole.

I think the Chapter V. went straight to the Egoist, or came when I was away and had to be forwarded at once , , , anyhow I have been reading it *in* the paper.

I have been doing nothing but write 15 page letters to New York about the new magazine and my head is a squeezed rag, so don't expect le mot juste in this letter.

However I read your final instalment last night when I was calm enough to know what I was doing, and I might have written then with more lucidity.

Anyhow I think the book hard, perfect stuff. I doubt if you could have done it in "the lap of luxury" or in the whirl of a metropolis with the attrition of endless small amusements and endless calls on one's time, and endless trivialities of enjoyment (or the reverse).

I think the book is permanent like Flaubert and Stendhal. Not so squarish as Stendhal, certainly not so varnished as Flaubert. In english I think you join on to Hardy and Henry James (I don't mean a resemblance, I mean that there's has been nothing of permanent value in prose in between. And I think you must soon, or at least sooner or later get your recognition.

Hang it all, we dont get prose books that a man can *re*read. We don't get prose that gives us pleasure paragraph by paragraph. I know one man who occasionally buries a charming short chapter in a long ineffective novel . . . but that's another story.

It is the ten years spent on the book, the Dublin 1904, Trieste 1914,

44

that counts. No man can dictate a novel, though there are a lot who try to.

And for the other school. I am so damn sick of energetic stupidity. The "strong" work . . . . balls! And it is such a comfort to find an author who has read something and knows something. This deluge of work by suburban counter-jumpers on one hand and gut-less Oxford graduates or flunktuates on the other . . . . . bah! And never any intensity, not in *any* of it.

The play has come, and I shall read it as soon as I can be sure of being uninterrupted. .

Later

I have just finished the play.

Having begun it (cliche) I could not (cliche) leave off until (cliche)

Yes, it is interesting. It won't do for the stage. (No, it is unsuitable for the "Abbey", as mebbe ye might kno'aw fer yourself, Mr J'ice).

It is exciting. But even [*crossout:* it] read it takes very close concentration of attention. I don't believe an audience could follow it or take it in, even if some damd impracticable manager were to stage it.

Not that I believe any manager would stage it in our chaste and castrated english speaking world.

Roughly speaking, it takes about all the brains I've got to take in [the] thing, *reading.* And I suppose I've [*crossout:* got] more intelligence than the normal theatre goer (god save us)

I may be wrong, the actual people moving on a stage might underline and emphasise the meaning and the changes of mood but . . . . . .

. . . . . again count in the fact that I "dont go to the theatre", that is to say I'm always enraged at any play (I don't know that I'm *bored*) I have cheap cinema amusement and then I get wroth at the assininity of the actors or the author etc. etc. I get a few moments pleasure and long stretches of annoyance. And now my wife dont care much about late hours . . . . . still I never did go much . . . it always cost money which I couldn't afford. At least I

45

like comfortable seats, which I occasionally get free, and I'm not devotee enough to stand in a shilling line waiting for a board in the gallery.

My whole habit of thinking of the stage is: that it is a gross, coarse form of art. That a play speaks to a thousand fools huddled together, whereas a novel or a poem can lie about in a book and find the stray persons worth finding, one by one seriatim. (so here I am with a clavichord—beside me, which I cant afford, and cant reasonably play on [1] .... here I am chucked out of the Quarterly Review for having contributed ithyphallic satirical verse to "BLAST" ......

and if I had written this letter last night (2 a.m.) just after finishing the "Portrait", I should have addressed you "Cher Maitre".

Now what would he want to write for the stage for
? ? ? ? ?
Can one appeal to the mass with anything requiring thought? Is there anything but the common basis of a very few general emotions out of which to build a play that shall be at once

        A. a stage play
        B. not common, not a botch.

There is no union in intellect, when we think we diverge, we explore, we go away.
When we feel we unite.

Of course your play is emotional. It works up quite a whirl of emotion, and it has, undoubtedly, form. I dont think it is nearly as intense as "The Portrait", at least I dont feel it as much.

My resultant impression is one of a tired head. (Count that I have written out three thousand words of complicated business plan .. been down town and bought two modern pictures for another man ... played a bit of tennis ..... well it's not more than any one in your theatre audience might have done. ...

I might have come to your mss. with a fresher mind ... ma che ...

All through the first act I kept doubting the fitness for the stage ..... for though I hate (oh well, not hate) the theatre I cant help reading a play with constant thoughts about its fitness for the stage

---

[1] Pound's Arnold Dolmetsch clavichord; like the Gaudier-Brzeska bust it followed him from London to Rapallo and then to Brunnenburg.

(habit contracted when I was supposed to be doing a doctor's thesis on "The functions of the *gracioso* in the Plays of Lope de Vega") [2]

Without re-reading, I should say that the first spot in the play where it would in any way gain by being staged is the exquisite picture of Robert squirting his perfume pump.[3]

That is to say or to quote "character" is comedy. [*crossout: Emotion is*] Tragedy is emotion. I may be wrong. The thing might carry. The Stage-Society might give it a try out.

I so loathe the Granville Braker[4] tone . . . . . . ma che . . . .

Whether one would want to see those detestable people acting it . . . . .

mind you . . . there's no telling what they mightn't do, or what they mightn't take to . . . . (if it were castrated . . . . . . the virginal Shaw would want it castrated . . . . . they're all vegetarians.

It will form an interesting ¼ volume when you bring out your collected works.[5] When you are a recognized classic people will read it because you wrote it and be duly interested and duly instructed, ... but until then I'm hang'd if I see what's to be done with it.

The prudery of my country (i.e. all of it that isn't lured by vulgarity.) The sheer numbers to which a play must appeal before it is any use to a manager.

Bed room scenes where the audience can by tittivated, eroticised . . . excited and **NOT** expected to think . . . . . . balcony full . . . dress circle ditto . . . boxes ditto . . . .

Ibsen is no longer played. If there were an Ibsen theatre in full blast I dare say your play could go into it . . . . ma che . . . .

I shall end this and send it by the midnight post.

I shall read the play again and see if I can think of anything.

Lane's manager writes ((With regards to Mr Joyce's novel, we are very glad to know about this, but Mr Lane will not deal with an

[2] Pound had gone to Europe in 1906 with a traveling fellowship from the University of Pennsylvania. Since the fellowship was not renewed he did not write the thesis but instead accepted a teaching post at Wabash College, Crawfordsville, Indiana, which he held from September to Christmas, 1907.

[3] Stage direction to the beginning of Act II, as Robert waits for Bertha to arrive at his lodgings.

[4] A pun or a typographical error? Harley Granville-Barker, playwright, actor, and Shakespeare critic.

[5] This sentence and the "Dear" of the salutation are both typed in red; they are Pound's only "experiments" in these letters with this form of typewriter emphasis.

agent. If, however, either you or Mr Joyce likes to send the MS. here we shall be very glad indeed to consider it)).

Don't bother to write to Pinker, I will get the ms. from him and take it round to Lane. Lane is publishing my memoir on Brzeska, so I am in touch with him.

(of course it's pure bluff their talking about not dealing with an agent. They all do . . . at least I believe they do . . . . . Secker is a * * * * * . . . publishes Abercrombie and that gang of stiffs . . .[6]

I must stop this if it is to go tonight.

yours
Ezra Pound

Pound's letter of September 6–12, his most theoretical and volatile of the correspondence, was written while he was in the very middle of struggling with the first drafts of *The Cantos*. His "rag-bag" for the modern world "to stuff all its thought in," a "new form" of "meditative, Semi-dramatic, semi-epic story," [7] was conceived in the spirit of Dante's *Divina Commedia* and Whitman's *Leaves of Grass*, and begun as a successor to Browning's *Sordello*. It was based on his vorticist or abstract "form sense," on his work during 1915 with the Japanese Noh plays, and on the idea behind his "L'Homme Moyen Sensuel" of modeling a series of satires on Byron's *Don Juan*. He would draw on the methods of the imagist lyric, of drama, of narrative poetry, and perhaps of the realistic novel and the cinema, to create a synthetic form capable of including the whole scope of the modern consciousness. By Christmas 1915 he had written drafts of at least five cantos, the first three of which appeared in *Poetry*, 1917, in a form different from that of the present final versions. But he had not solved the problem of how to include novelistic realism and history in a modern literary work, especially a poem. Could he continue, using Browning's dramatic

[6] A reference to the Georgians and Lascelles Abercrombie. A story is told in many versions about how Pound challenged Abercrombie to a duel for advising young poets to abandon realism and study Wordsworth (some versions say Milton). Abercrombie, it is said, took the challenge seriously and became frightened when told Pound was an expert fencer (Pound had been trying to get Yeats into condition by teaching him the art). But Abercrombie took advantage of the challenged party's right to choose the weapons and proposed that they bombard each other with copies of their unsold books. Soon thereafter, the story goes, Abercrombie paid a visit to Yeats; greeted by Pound at the door, he fled. That apparently closed the menacing incident, and two bards were preserved.

[7] "Three Cantos, I," *Poetry*, X, 3 (June 1917), pages 113, 117.

method to present his "visions," he asked in the original *Canto* I, or
would he have to "sulk and leave the world to novelists"? He is wres-
tling with this question in the following essay, which he wrote
fresh from his letter to Joyce and sent to *The Drama*, Chicago,
where it appeared in February 1916. His increased enthusiasm for
Joyce's work, especially *A Portrait*, led him to assert in April 1916,
in his survey of new poetry since 1912: "James Joyce, by far the
most significant writer of our decade, is confining himself to prose." [8]

MR. JAMES JOYCE AND THE MODERN STAGE [9]

A Play and Some Considerations

Two months ago I set out to write an essay about a seventeenth
century dramatist. As I had nearly finished translating one of his
plays into English, my interest in him must have been more than
that of a transient moment. His own life was full of adventure. The
play had a number of virtues that one could quite nicely mark out
on a diagram. It was altogether a most estimable "subject"; yet,
when I began to ask myself whether my phrases really corresponded
to fact, whether it was worth while causing a few readers to spend
their time on the matter, I was convinced that it was not. I believed
that old play and the author had fallen into desuetude from perfectly justifiable causes. I agreed to let the dead bury their dead,
and to let other people write about the drama, and I returned to
some original work of my own.

Last week I received a play by Mr. James Joyce and that argumentative interest, which once led me to spend two years of my life
reading almost nothing but plays, came back upon me, along with a
set of questions "from the bottom up": Is drama worth while? Is the
drama of today, or the stage of today, a form or medium by which
the best contemporary authors can express themselves in any satisfactory manner?

Mr. Joyce is undoubtedly one of our best contemporary authors.
He has written a novel, and I am quite ready to stake anything I
have in this world that that novel is permanent. It is permanent as
are the works of Stendhal and Flaubert. Two silly publishers have
just refused it in favor of froth, another declines to look at it
because "he will not deal through an agent"—yet Mr. Joyce lives on
the continent and can scarcely be expected to look after his affairs

[8] "Status Rerum—the Second," *Poetry*, VIII, 1 (April 1916), pages 38–43.
[9] *The Drama*, Chicago, VI, 2 (February 1916), pages 122–132.

in England save through a deputy. And Mr. Joyce is the best prose writer of my generation, in English. So far as I know, there is no one better in either Paris or Russia. In English we have Hardy and Henry James and, chronologically, we have Mr. James Joyce. The intervening novelists print books, it is true, but for me or for any man of my erudition, for any man living at my intensity, these books are things of no substance.

Therefore, when Mr. Joyce writes a play, I consider it a reasonable matter of interest. The English agent of the Oliver Morosco company has refused the play, and in so doing the agent has well served her employers, for the play would certainly be of no use to the syndicate that stars *Peg o' My Heart;* neither do I believe that any manager would stage it nor that it could succeed were it staged. Nevertheless, I read it through at a sitting, with intense interest. It is a long play, some one hundred and eighty pages.

It is not so good as a novel; nevertheless it is quite good enough to form a very solid basis for my arraignment of the contemporary theatre. It lays before me certain facts, certain questions; for instance, are the excellences of this play purely novelist's excellences? Perhaps most of them are; yet this play could not have been made as a novel. It is distinctly a play. It has the form of a play—I do not mean that it is written in dialogue with the names of the speakers put in front of their speeches. I mean that it has inner form; that the acts and speeches of one person work into the acts and speeches of another and make the play into an indivisible, integral whole. The action takes place in less than twenty-four hours, in two rooms, both near Dublin, so that even the classical unities are uninjured. The characters are drawn with that hardness of outline which we might compare to that of Dürer's painting if we are permitted a comparison with effects of an art so different. There are only four main characters, two subsidiary characters, and a fish-woman who passes a window, so that the whole mechanics of the play have required great closeness of skill. I see no way in which the play could be improved by redoing it as a novel. It could not, in fact, be anything but a play. And yet it is absolutely unfit for the stage as we know it. It is dramatic. Strong, well-wrought sentences flash from the speech and give it "dramatic-edge" such as we have in Ibsen, when some character comes out with, "There is no mediator between God and man"; I mean sentences dealing with fundamentals.

It is not unstageable because it deals with adultery; surely, we have plenty of plays, quite stageable plays, that deal with adultery. I have seen it in the nickel-plush theatre done with the last degree of sentimental bestiality. I admit that Mr. Joyce once mentions a garter, but it is done in such a way . . . it is done in the only way . . . it is the only possible means of presenting the exact social tone of at least two of the characters.

"Her place in life was rich and poor between," as Crabbe says of his Clelia; it might have been done in a skit of a night club and no harm thought; but it is precisely because it occurs neither in fast nor in patrician circles, but in a milieu of Dublin genteelness, that it causes a certain feeling of constraint. Mr. Joyce gives his Dublin as Ibsen gave provincial Norway.

Of course, oh, of course, if, *if* there were an Ibsen stage in full blast, Mr. Joyce's play would go on at once.

But we get only trivialized Ibsen; we get Mr. Shaw, the intellectual cheese-mite. That is to say, Ibsen was a true agonist, struggling with very real problems. "Life is a combat with the phantoms of the mind"—he was always in combat for himself and for the rest of mankind. More than any one man, it is he who has made us "our world," that is to say, "our modernity." Mr. Shaw is the intellectual cheese-mite, constantly enraptured at his own cleverness in being able to duck down through one hole in the cheese and come up through another.

But we cannot see "Ibsen." Those of us who were lucky saw Mansfield [1] do the *Peer Gynt*. I have seen a half-private resurrection of *Hedda*. I think that those are the only two Ibsen plays that I have ever had an opportunity of seeing performed, and many others must be in like case. Professionals tell us: "Oh, they have quickened the tempo. Ibsen is too slow," and the like. So we have Shaw; that is to say, Ibsen with the sombre reality taken out, a little Nietzsche put in to enliven things, and a technique of dialogue superadded from Wilde.

I would point out that Shaw's comedy differs essentially from the French comedy of Marivaux or De Musset,[2] for in their work you have a very considerable intensity of life and of passion veiling itself, restraining itself through a fine manner, through a very delicate form. There is in Shaw nothing to restrain, there is a bit of intensity in a farce about Androcles, but it is followed by a fabian sermon, and his "comedy" or whatever it is, is based solely on the fact that his mind moves a little bit faster than that of the average Englishman. You cannot conceive any intelligent person going to

[1] Richard Mansfield, American actor noted for his roles in the plays of Shakespeare, Molière, Rostand, Shaw, Ibsen, etc.; he introduced Ibsen to America.
[2] Pierre Marivaux (1688–1763) and Alfred de Musset (1810–1857), French comic dramatists.

51

Mr. Shaw for advice in any matter that concerned his life vitally. He is not a man at prise with reality.

It is precisely this being at grips with reality that is the core of great art. It is Galdos, or Stendhal, or Flaubert, or Turgenev or Dostoevsky, or even a romanticist like De Musset, but it is not the cheese-mite state of mind. It is not a matter of being glum; it can be carried into the most tenuous art.

The trouble with Mr. Joyce's play is precisely that he *is* at prise with reality. It is a "dangerous" play precisely because the author is portraying an intellectual-emotional struggle, because he is dealing with actual thought, actual questioning, not with clichés of thought and emotion.

It is untheatrical, or unstageable, precisely because the closeness and cogency of the process is, as I think, too great for an audience to be able to follow . . . under present conditions.

And that is, in turn, precisely the ground of my arraignment.

All of this comes to saying: can the drama hold its own against the novel? Can contemporary drama be permanent? It is not to be doubted that the permanent art of any period is precisely that form of art into which the best artists of the period put their best and solidest work.

That is to say, the prose of the *trecento* was not so good as Dante's poetry, and, therefore, that age remains in its verse. The prose of the Elizabethan period was at least no better than Shakespeare's plays and we, therefore, remember that age, for the most part, by drama. The poetry of Voltaire's contemporaries was not so good as his prose and we, therefore, do not remember that period of France by its verses. For nearly a century now, when we have thought of great writers, we have been quite apt to think of the writers of novels. We perhaps think of Ibsen and Synge. We may even think of some poets. But that does not answer our problem.

The very existence of this quarterly and of the Drama League means, I take it, that an appreciable number of people believe that the drama is an important part of contemporary art . . . or that they want it to be an important or even great art of today.

It is a very complex art; therefore, let us try to think of its possibilities of greatness first hand.

Acting

I suppose we have all seen flawless acting. Modern acting I don't know, I should say flawless *mimetic* acting is almost as cheap and plentiful as Mr. A. Bennett's novels. There is plenty of it in the market. A lot of clever, uninteresting people doing clever, tolerable plays. They are entertaining. There is no reason to see any one in particular rather than any other one or any six others. It is a time of commercial efficiency, of dramatic and literary fine plumbing.

But great acting? Acting itself raised to the dignity of an art?

Yes, I saw it once. I saw Bernhardt; she was so wobbly in her knees that she leaned on either her lover or her confidant during nearly all of the play, *La Sorcière,* and it was not much of a play. Her gestures from the waist up were superb. At one point in the play, she takes off a dun-colored cloak and emerges in a close-fitting gown of cloth of gold. That is all—she takes off a cloak. That much might be stage direction. But that shaky, old woman, representing a woman in youth, took off her cloak with the power of sculpture.

That is to say, she created the image, an image, for me at least, as durable as that of any piece of sculpture that I have seen. I have forgotten most of the play; the play was of no importance.

Here was an art, an art that would have held Umewaka Minoru,[3] great acting.

Speech

But it is impractical? Perhaps only a crazy, romantic play would give a situation of abnormal tragedy sufficient to warrant such gestures? And so on.

I noticed, however, one other thing in that Bernhardt performance, namely, that the emotional effect was greater half an hour after I had left the theatre than at any time during the performance. That, of course, is a "secret of Bernhardt's success."

Maybe, but it is due to a very definite cause, which the practical manager will probably ridicule. It is possible, by the constant re-iteration of sound from a very small bell, to put a very large room in a roar, whose source you cannot easily locate. It is equally possible by the reiteration of a cadence . . . say the cadence of French alexandrines, to stir up an emotion in an audience, an emotion or an emotional excitement the source of which they will be unable to determine with any ease.

That is, I think, the only "practical" argument in favor of plays in verse. It is a very practical argument . . . but it may need the skill of Bernhardt to make it of any avail.

[3] Umewaka Minoru restored and preserved the art of Noh in Japan. He was Ernest Fenollosa's principal source for his study of that drama.

I might almost say that all arguments about the stage are of two sorts: the practical and the stupid. At any rate, the rare actor who aspires to art has at his disposal the two means; that is, speech and gesture. If he aspires to great art, he may try to substitute the significant for the merely mimetic.

The Cinema

The "movie" is perhaps the best friend of the few people who hope for a really serious stage. I do not mean to say that it is not the medium for the expression of more utter and abject forms of human asininity than are to be found anywhere else ... save possibly on the contemporary stage.

Take, for example, the bathos, the *bassesse*, the consummate and unfathomable imbecility of some films. I saw one a few weeks ago. It began with a printed notice pleading for the freedom of the film; then there was flashed on the screen a testimonial from a weeping Christian, a "minister of a gospel," who declared that having had his emotions, his pity, stirred by a novel of Dickens in his early youth, had done more to ennoble his life, to make him what he was than any sermons he had ever heard. Then we had some stanzas from a poem by Poe (Omission: we had had some information about Poe somewhere before this). Then we had some scenes out of a Poe story in before-the-war costume; then the characters went off to a garden party in quite modern raiment and a number of modern characters were introduced, also a Salome dance in which the lady ended by lying on her back and squirming (as is so usual at an American garden party). Then the old before-the-war uncle re-appeared. There were a few sub-plots, one taken from a magazine story that I happened to remember; later there came Moses and the burning bush, a modern detective doing the "third degree," Christ on Golgotha, some supernatural or supernormal creatures, quite nondescript, a wild chase over the hills, the tables of the law marked, "Thou shalt not kill," some more stanzas from a lyric of Poe's, and a lady fell off, no, leapt off, a cliff. There had been some really fine apparitions of the uncle's ghost somewhere before this, and finally the murderer awakened to find that he had been dreaming for the last third of the film. General reconciliation!

This film, you will note, observes the one requirement for popular stage success; there is plenty of action ... and no one but a demi-god could possibly know what is going to come next.

Nevertheless, the "c'mat" is a friend to the lovers of good drama.

54

I mean it is certainly inimical to the rubbishy stage. Because? Because people can get more rubbish per hour on the cinema than they can in the theatre, *and* it is cheaper. And it is on the whole a better art than the art of Frohman, Tree and Belasco.[4] I mean to say it does leave something to the imagination.

Moreover, it is—whether the violet-tinted aesthete like it or not—it is developing an art sense. The minute the spectator begins to wonder why Charles Chaplin amuses him, the minute he comes to the conclusion that Chaplin is better than X——, Y—— and Z——, because he, Chaplin, gets the maximum effect with the minimum effort, minimum expenditure, etc., etc., the said spectator is infinitely nearer a conception of art and infinitely more fit to watch creditable drama than when he, or she, is entranced by Mrs. So-and-So's gown or by the color of Mr. So-and-So's eyes.

On the other, the sinister hand, we have the anecdote of the proud manager of "the Temple of Mammon" (as a certain London theatre is nicknamed). It was a magnificent scene, an oriental palace *de luxe*, which would have rivalled Belasco's, and the manager, taking a rather distinguished dramatist across the stage, tapped the lions supporting the throne with his gold-headed cane and proudly said, "Solid brass!"

Is it any wonder that the simple Teuton should have supposed this country ripe for invasion?

Well, benevolent reader, there you have it. The drama, the art of Aeschylus and of Shakespeare, the art that was to cast great passions and great images upon the mind of the auditor! There is the "drama" staged for the most part by men who should be "interior decorators" furnishing the boudoirs and reception rooms of upper-class prostitutes, there is the faint cry for art-scenery with as little drama as possible, and there is the trivialized Ibsen, for Shaw is the best we get, and all Shaw's satire on England was really done long since in a sentence quoted by Sterne:

"Gravity: A mysterious carriage of the body to cover the defects of the mind."

Even so, Shaw is only a stage in the decadence, for if we must call Shaw trivialized Ibsen, what shall we say of the next step lower, to-wit: prettified Shaw?

What welcome is this stage to give the real agonist if he tries to

[4] Charles Frohman and David Belasco, the leading producers of the American theater, noted for their lavish productions. Sir Herbert Beerbohm Tree dominated the British theater between 1885 and 1915 as a producer and a noted character actor, especially of Shakespeare.

write "drama"? These problems are your problems, gracious reader, for you belong to that large group whose hope is better drama.

Also, in your problem plays you must remember that all the real problems of life are insoluble and that the real dramatist will be the man with a mind in search; he will grope for his answer and he will differ from the sincere auditor in that his groping will be the keener, the more far-reaching, the more conscious, or at least the more articulate; whereas, the man who tries to preach at you, the man who stops his play to deliver a sermon, will only be playing about the surface of things or trying to foist off some theory.

So Mr. Joyce's play is dangerous and unstageable because he is not *playing* with the subject of adultery, but because he is actually driving in the mind upon the age-long problem of the rights of personality and of the responsibility of the intelligent individual for the conduct of those about him, upon the age-long question of the relative rights of intellect, and emotion, and sensation, and sentiment.

And the question which I am trying to put and which I reform and reiterate is just this: Must our most intelligent writers do this sort of work in the novel, *solely in the novel*, or is it going to be, in our time, possible for them to do it in drama?

On your answer to that question the claims of modern drama must rest.

12 September 1915 *5, Holland Place Chambers, Kensington. W.*

Dear Joyce: Again you will get the fag ends of my mind. But I have spent the morning doing about 2000 words on you and your play and the state of the theatre . . I shall try to get it (the article) printed in an American Quarterly called "the Drama". It may stir up something, if not a manager, at least a publisher.

Don't be alarmed, I have not given away the plot of the play or even indicated anything about it. I have dragged in a few remarks on the virtue of the novel (more or less what I wrote you). "The Drama" is highly specialized and only takes articles on drama and the stage. They've printed my translations (i.e. "Fenollosa and me,) of the Japanese classical plays. If they swallow the article they might even be lured on to printing "The Exiles", but I am afraid it is a bit too outspoken for them ... however they'd give a good price if they took it ..... supposing you finally despaired of getting it performed.

At any rate it is a large well printed magazine and an article in it on you can do no harm to the prospects of getting a publisher for your stuff.

Pinker was very optimistic, said it might take [*crossout:* time] [*longhand:* a good while] but that he would get you going *some*time. I am letting him keep the novel to try on some other house before I bag it and carry it to Lane.

Pinker asked if it would be possible to suggest deletions, and I told him CERTAINLY NOT! ! I may also have disappointed him slightly in my estimation of the texture of Conrad's mind. However . . . . .

I wonder were you able to bring your books, i.e. your library from Trieste, or if I have anything that would be of any use to you, or if the post will take books for neutral countries.

I once did a bad translation of Guido Cavalcanti [5] of which I have a spare copy, it has the text with it and that might entertain you if you're not fed up with the period, or a Corbière or a Catullus or a stray volume of Stendhal (though I dare say they are all more accessible in Switzerland than here) or a stray leaf of my own earlier imbecilities, vanitatis causa,

I have just sent to the press another contemporary anthology, [6] I'm afraid it's not a very rich haul, but you shall have it to throw away when it's printed.

I am having a volume of my own in the spring . . . having refrained for some years.

I have just made a fine haul of old greek books, including the Emperor Julian who is, I believe, fairly rare, but I wont offer you the loan of him until means of transportation are surer.

I cant go on with my discussion of your play because I have

---

[5] *The Sonnets and Ballate of Guido Cavalcanti,* 1912.

[6] *Catholic Anthology 1914–1915,* 1915, was Pound's effort to differentiate the new poets from those of Amy Lowell's *Some Imagist Poets,* which had usurped Pound's designation and "diluted" the movement. Pound printed Yeats, Eliot, Masters, Bodenheim, Sandburg, Williams, himself, and others.

[7] *Exiles,* New York: The Viking Press, 1951, page 44:

ROBERT, *gravely:* I fought for you all the time you were away. I fought to bring you back. I fought to keep your place for you here. I will fight for you still because I have faith in you, the faith of a disciple in his master. I cannot say more than that. It may seem strange to you . . . Give me a match.

RICHARD, *lights and offers him a match:* There is a faith still stranger than the faith of the disciple in his master.

ROBERT: And that is?

RICHARD: The faith of a master in the disciple who will betray him.—Act I.

exhausted my compositiory faculty in the essay .. for the day at least.

"The master's trust in the disciple" etc

stand out

as a rememberable sentence.[7] and .. and

No it's no use

I must keep off the subject.

It is 3.30 on a fine day and I have been typing since I got up, rather late, but still I must get a breath of air or I shall expire.

yours ever

Ezra Pound

23 October 1915   *5, Holland Place Chambers, Kensington. W.*

Dear Joyce: There's nothing faintly resembling news. The damn photographer who promised me some prints of his last effort hasn't sent 'em. And I am damn sure I'm not going to pay for 'em. I enclose a job lot. A recent snap shot which represents me as a chinless diplomat from the Balkans. A photo of a portrait painted by a jew in Paris four years ago. He has used part of his own face and part of mine. The resoluteness with which some people believe that all beauty is made in their own image . . . . . !

I also include a clipping from a paper with my mug on it. I believe the representative element in this last is rather greater than that in the other photos. I leave the printed matter to distinguish me from Mr P. Collier on the obverse. The photo is already some years old *ma che*.

"Drama" says they will try to get my article on you into the Nov. number, but can't promise to do so. The number was already in the press when they got my mss . . . . speriamo . . . If it don't go in Nov. it will go in Feb. (they are a quarterly publication.)

Michio Itow is going to give some performances of Noh dancing, in proper costume, next week. That is all that's on in the "awt-woild". Proper japanese daimyo dress reconstructed by Du Lac and Ricketts. etc. very precious. Itow is one of the few interesting japs I have met. They usually seem lacking in intensity. There is another pleasant one here who plays a huge bamboo flute.[8]

[8] Michio Itow, a performer of the traditional Japanese dance then living in London, danced in Yeats's experimental dramas, which were inspired by the Noh plays. On April 2, 1916, Itow and Edmond Dulac, the artist, illustrator, and stage designer, helped stage Yeats's *At the Hawk's Well* in Lady Cunard's drawing room. Charles De Sousy Ricketts, artist and eminent stage designer, was denominated by Yeats "the magician."

The illustrations for my book on Brzeska are being very well done . . . which is a comfort in the midst of a lot of petty intrigue about his remains. This mornings problem is the question of whether Mr . . . . will try to hold up a gift to the nation because of £7/10 which he hasn't earned but *might* earn. *E cosi va la ruota.* Probably Mr . . . . is a most virtuous man and the whole affair a mistake. etc. etc. etc.

I will go down to Pinker again about the novel as soon as I finish my second article on DeGourmont.[9]

By the way, the beastly studio in which the snap shot is taken is NOT my normal habitat. Eliot rented it once for a fortnight. Neither he nor I is nor am responsible for the phase of neo-impressio-blottist art displayed on its edges.

yours ever
Ezra Pound

In November 1915 efforts to find a publisher for *A Portrait*, which had finished running in *The Egoist* in September, intensified. It had been rejected in May by Grant Richards, Joyce's publisher (if he could be said to have one). Martin Secker rejected it in July and Herbert Jenkins in October (Pound wrote to Joyce later that Secker "thought the Portrait a good bit of work but didn't believe it would pay"). When Joyce instructed Pinker to withdraw the manuscript from Duckworth and send it to the French publisher Louis Conard, both Pinker and Pound advised against it. In November Miss Harriet Weaver offered to have *The Egoist* publish it, but she could not find a printer who would set it (under British law not only the author and the publisher but also the printer are liable to prosecution). Pound and Pinker continued to seek a commercial publisher. Joyce's instructions and his absorption in the fate of his book, as though neither a war nor frontiers existed, were characteristic; he always remained, like his Mr. Dooley-ooley-ooley-oo, *au dessus de la mêlée.*

27 November 1915   *5, Holland Place Chambers, Kensington. W.*

Dear Joyce: I forget where things had got to, when I last wrote, at any rate, when I last called up Pinker he had not given up hopes of Duckworth, with whom the mss. then was.

---

[9] Remy De Gourmont, an acquaintance of Pound's and a lasting influence on his thought and work, had just died. Pound wrote commemorative articles in *The Fortnightly Review*, London, December 1, 1915, and in *Poetry*, January 1916.

Werner Laurie, via Mrs Hueffer, has promised to read the mss, under our recommendation and has written to Pinker for it, and is to see it if Duck. rejects it. Lane is interested, but Pinker is not ready to let me take it to Lane until he has finished with D. and W. L.

It would be better, if possible, to publish in England. France is very much occupied with a war, news of which may have reached you.

However, as to publishing in Paris: I have recently met an intelligent french woman, Mlle. de Pratz, she is a friend of Laurent Tailhade's, and of Judith Gautier,[1] & niece of a former premier, and I think, from the way she spoke of Gide, that she knows him also.

I gave her the files of the Egoist and she called your novel "stupendous", she knows the new publisher indirectly, the one who is doing the french [*insert:* equivalent of the] Tauchnitz, and will recommend the book to him, either directly or through some one who knows him better . . . . I can have her send on the incomplete text from the Egoist, at once if you like . . . . . . but I still think you'd better get english publication if possible . . . . .

I think there is very decent chance that you will. Laurie wont mind your frankness. And Lane's manager told Lewis last week that there was no use bothering about such matters.

I doubt very much if the "Mercure" would print an english text. That firm is very sound commercially and they have never yet done a translation of any english book that has not *had* a big sale. [*longhand:* They don't move much out of their track.]

At present they are wholly engaged in discussing the war. I don't think Jean [*longhand:* de Gourmont] [2] would be much use. I doubt if anyone in France would pay the least attention to anything not concerned with the war. Gide is probably busy. however , , , , ,

I have had three cables from Quinn, in one of which he says he has been canvassing for the magazine "with fair hopes of success".

My small anthology is out. I will send you a copy the next time I get down to Mathews . . . . . for the sake of a couple of poems by Eliot, I

[1] Pound had met the French poet Laurent Tailhade in Paris in 1913 and admired his urbane modernist satire. Judith Gautier, daughter of Théophile Gautier, was a poet, novelist, and woman of letters noted for her adaptations from the Chinese and Japanese.

[2] Jean De Gourmont, brother of Remy, poet, novelist, and contributor to the *Mercure de France*.

doubt if the rest of it will in any way entertain you, but its the best there is. (oh well, perhaps not, there are a few things, one or two authors whom I had to include against my admiration . . . however its not so bloody dead and dull as "Georgian poets")

I am pleased with the way Lane is doing my "Gaudier Brzeska", the illustrations good, etc. . he will have it out in Jan or Feb.[3]

I am ploughing through Roscoe's "Leo X", Italy of that time as seen by provincial england in 1805.[4] The Borgias couldn't possibly have been *so* wicked or their contemporaries would have been *much* more shocked. etc.

Ebbene.

yours
Ezra Pound

12 January 1916   *Stone Cottage, Coleman's Hatch, Sussex*

Dear Joyce: I am very much surprised to hear that you have not yet heard from Miss Weaver. I thought she would have settled the matter and written to you, and probably have sent the cash.

I understand that if Pinker hasn't, or hadn't disposed of the novel last friday, or perhaps it was the friday before, (I forget, and can't find her letter,) The Egoist definitely was going to publish and to send you £50 at once.

I shall of course write [*longhand:* have written] to her by this same post. I dare say you will have heard from her by the time this reaches you.

//////////

Re/the poems. I have absolutely no connections in England that are any use. There is no editor whom I wouldn't cheerfully fry in oil and none who wouldn't as cheerfully do [*crossout:* me] the same [*crossout:* favour, *longhand:* by me.] The English review tried to

---

[3] Pound's *Gaudier-Brzeska,* a memoir that includes Brzeska's writings, a selection of his letters, photographs of his sculpture, portraits, and drawings, and essays by Pound on vorticism, was published in April 1916. Pound still possesses a large collection of Brzeska's sculpture and drawings, which are impressively exhibited at Brunnenburg.

[4] William Roscoe, *The Life and Pontificate of Leo the Tenth. With a dissertation on the character of Lucretia Borgia,* London: C. Daly, 1840. It was later revised by his son, Thomas Roscoe; Pound probably read the Bohn Standard Library edition, 2 vols., 1876–1883.

cheat me in 1912. Since then I have [*longhand:* printed no where in England save] a few poems printed in Monro's magazine,[5] but he has stopped printing until the end of the war. The New Age don't pay for poetry.

[*longhand:* Thats all.]

I am down here in the country because I can't afford London, am behind in accounts, and hope to catch up. You only enclosed two poems. [*longhand:* not 3 as you say.] There will be, I think, no trouble about having "Flood" printed by "Poetry" with probably no more delay than is implied by sending the mss. to Chicago.

If you want me to send the things to Chicago, I wish you would send [*insert:* to me] also whatever other poems you have. It is rather important that *all* of them should be typed as one can *not get proofs* from our friends in Chicago. Again I can't *promise* anything about their actions. I told them long since that I wanted some poems from you. And I *suppose* they will print a reasonable proportion of what I send them, and decently soon.

I think it will be best for me to send on your two poems to Chicago at once. (today), [*longhand:* I ask them to remit at once if they can.] If you or Pinker can place the poems in England, that will be all right. Tell Pinker the American rights are engaged. Also send me whatever other poems you have and I will forward them on receipt.

I doubt if I shall be in London for another month. I haven't the spare car fare.

I hear from America that there is fair chance of my magazine's coming off. In which case I shall probably get my fare paid to New York, and have to go over to make arrangements. This is all very uncertain. The publication would begin in the autumn. I dont know whether they would let me have some money in the spring to make advance purchases with. I don't even know what you have that I could use. I should want, I think, some of some prose you once wrote of, and the continuation of the "Artist" when it is ready. But that's all nebula yet.

Eight years ago I had a professorship in a backwood's college and thought I was settled for life with no necessity of writing stuff that would sell. At the end of four months they fired me because I had

[5] Harold Monro, proprietor of The Poetry Bookshop, published *Poetry Review,* which printed poems and reviews by Pound in 1912.

given food to a female who was broke and starving on the other side of the hall in my boarding house. She wouldn't have "tempted" Caliban in the height of his first spring rut. ma che! [*insert:* at any rate my innocence of that period was not excited.] [6]

It probably goes to show that peace is not for us. I have never had a steady job since, [*longhand:* though I have had easy seasons.]

You at any rate, if you have to come back to London and take up journalism, will have at least given proof of your prose mastery and the public can only blame itself if they do not give you conditions under which you can give them more work of the first quality.

Well, I [*crossout:* will write] have written to Miss Weaver. And to Chicago. This last needn't delay any possible sale Pinker can make in England. Also *do* send me the other poems, so that I can get as large a cheque as possible from Chicago.

yours ever
Ezra Pound

Pound sent Joyce's poems to Miss Monroe immediately with the request: "Can you manage to pay him *at once?* . . . He is a writer who should be kept up. And it is the war that has put him out of his job in Trieste (this last is NOT an aesthetic reason). . . . It is an outrage that he shouldn't have got something from his books by now. Which isn't our fault. Ma che." Miss Monroe apparently waited for the others Pound had asked Joyce to send, for not until May 1917 did *Poetry* publish "Simples," "Tutto É Sciolto," "Flood," "A Flower Given to My Daughter," and "Night Piece," all as a group.

Pound's attention now turned fully to the effort to find a publisher for *A Portrait* and to his "book war"; as he told William Carlos Williams in 1920, he had had "the whole stinking sweat of providing the mechanical means for letting through the new movement, i.e., scrap for the mot juste, for honest clear statement in verse." Early in the year the novel was refused by Duckworth and Werner Laurie (although Pound had told Joyce "Laurie won't mind your frankness," Laurie responded that it was "a very clever book but it is too naughty for me to publish"); it had no better luck with

---

[6] Pound was fired from his teaching post at Wabash College in 1907 when his two maiden landladies reported this incident to the president and the trustees. The story has been told in several versions, all attesting to Pound's chivalry, and has become a part of the Pound myth; it has even been cited as the cause for his leaving America for cosmopolitan Europe.

Heinemann or with John Lane. Pound set the tone for 1916–1917 in his outrage at the Duckworth rejection. It was actually a "double" rejection. Herbert J. Cape had written to Pinker on December 3, 1915, that although he thought Joyce a very able writer, *A Portrait* was rather discursive and the point of view was not an attractive one. He hoped that Joyce would put his manuscript aside and begin something else, which he expressed interest in seeing. Pinker submitted it again to Duckworth in January 1916; this time Cape offered to consider the book once more if Joyce would revise it along the lines suggested by his reader, Edward Garnett, whose opinion he enclosed:

James Joyce's 'Portrait of the Artist as a Young Man' wants going through carefully from start to finish. There are many 'longueurs.' Passages which, though the publisher's reader may find them entertaining, will be tedious to the ordinary man among the reading public. That public will call the book, as it stands at present, realistic, unprepossessing, unattractive. We call it ably written. The picture is 'curious,' it arouses interest and attention. But the author must revise it and let us see it again. It is too discursive, formless, unrestrained, and ugly things, ugly words, are too prominent; indeed at times they seem to be shoved in one's face, on purpose, unnecessarily. The point of view will be voted 'a little sordid.' The picture of life is good; the period well brought to the reader's eye, and the types and characters are well drawn, but it is too 'unconventional.' This would stand against it in normal times. At the present time, though the old conventions are in the background, we can only see a chance for it if it is pulled into shape and made more definite.

In the earlier portion of the MS. as submitted to us, a good deal of pruning can be done. Unless the author will use restraint and proportion he will not gain readers. His pen and his thoughts seem to have run away with him sometimes.

And at the end of the book there is a complete falling to bits; the pieces of writing and the thoughts are all in pieces and they fall like damp, ineffective rockets.

The author shows us he has art, strength and originality, but this MS. wants time and trouble spent on it, to make it a more finished piece of work, to shape it more carefully as the product of the craftsmanship, mind and imagination of an artist.[7]

These communications, relayed by Pinker, aroused Pound's indignation against British society and the British publishing system. They would tolerate and print a generation of allegedly realistic writers like H. G. Wells, Arnold Bennett, John Galsworthy, George Bernard Shaw, and G. K. Chesterton, or a writer of romance like Elinor Glyn. They had no trouble with the entertainment currently being offered in the music halls, whether the ferocious raw humor of a comedian like George Robey or the titillations of a French singer like Gaby Deslys. But they balked at a Joyce. Pound fulminated to Pinker (the letter is at Yale) and informed Joyce. He returned to *The Egoist* in March, after nearly a year's absence, with an outburst in his *Blast* vein; he was prompted also by publishers' refusals of Wyndham Lewis's *Tarr*, a book Pound admired for its author's energy and which he had persuaded Miss Weaver to serialize in *The Egoist*.

30 January 1916   *Stone Cottage, Coleman's Hatch, Sussex*

Dear Mr Pinker: I have read the effusion of Mr Duckworth's reader with no inconsiderable disgust. These vermin crawl over and be-slime our literature with their pulings, and nothing but the day of judgement can, I suppose, exterminate 'em. Thank god one need not [*longhand:* under ordinary circumstances] touch them.

Hark to his puling squeek. Too "unconventional". What in hell do we want but some change from the unbearable monotony of the weekly six shilling pears soap annual novel. [*longhand:* and the George Robey-Gaby mixture]

"Carelessly written", this of the sole, or almost sole piece of contemporary prose that one can enjoy sentence by sentence and re-read with pleasure. (I except Fred. Manning's "Scenes and Portraits" (pub. Murray, 1910.) [8]

It is with difficulty that I manage to write to you at all on being presented with the Duckworthian muck, the dungminded dung-

[7] Ellmann, *James Joyce,* pages 416–417, and *Letters of James Joyce,* II, pages 371–372.

[8] Frederic Manning, Australian poet and miscellaneous writer; Pound explored the genre of his *Scenes and Portraits,* imaginary, mythopoeic, philosophical conversations, in 1917–1918.

beared, penny a line, please the mediocre-at-all-cost doctrine. You English will get no prose till you [*crossout:* extet] enterminate this breed . . . . .

to say nothing of the abominable insolence of the tone.

I certainly will have nothing to do with the matter. The Egoist was willing to publish the volume, Lane would have read it a while ago.

I must repeat my former offer, if this louse will specify exactly what verbal changes he wants made I will approach Joyce in the matter. But I most emphatically will not forward the insults of an imbecile to one of the very few men for whom I have the faintest respect.

Canting, supercilious, blockhead . . . . I always supposed from report that Duckworth was an educated man, but I can not reconcile this opinion with his retention of the author of the missive you send me.

If you have to spend your life in contact with such minds, God help you, and

do accept my good will and sympathy in spite of the tone of this note.

God! "a more finished piece of work".

Really, Mr Pinker, it is too insulting, even to be forwarded to Joyce's friend, let alone to Joyce.

And the end . . also found fault with . . . again, Oh God, O Montreal . . . .

Why can't you send the publishers readers to the serbian front, and get some good out of the war . .

Serious writers will certainly give up the use of english altogether unless you can improve the process of publication.

In conclusion. You have given me a very unpleasant quarter of an hour, my disgust flows over, though I suppose there is no use in spreading it over this paper. If there is any phrase or form of contempt that you care to convey from me to the reeking Malebolge of the Duckworthian slum, pray, consider yourself at liberty to draw on my account (unlimited credit) and transmit it.

Please, if you have occasion to write again, either in regard to this book or any other. Please do not enclose publisher's readers opinions.

Sincerely yours
Ezra Pound

[*longhand:* Jan 30, 1916.—They pour out Elinor Glyn & pornography after pornography.

=====

but a piece of good writing they hate.

P.S.

I am reminded that Landor had equal difficulty in getting published—yet he is the best mind in your literature.

———

as for altering Joyce to suit Duckworth's reader—it would [be] like trying [*crossout:* to fit the ve]—fit the Venus de Milo into a piss-pot.—a few changes required.]

31 January 1916   *Stone Cottage, Colman's Hatch, Sussex*

Dear Joyce:

I sent you a post card scribble on receipt of poems a few days ago. I am a little worried because with the Egoist fork-up I think I have come about to the end of my connections. I mean to say when that lot and the Royal fund's remainder is gone I don't see what more there is to be worked. If the Stage Society put on your play, they wont *pay*, they just give a man a chance of an audience. It is worth getting for a new dramatist. Of course the R. fund may renew their donation, however I can't be sure. I told 'em you ought to have a pension. Yeats says pension is dam'd difficult as it is a parliamentary grant, and [*longhand:* the general grant for pensions] cant be increased without fuss. Your work is a damd sight more valuable than De La Mare's, ma che! ! he has been very dutiful and assiduous and has never given the slightest offense to the tenderest and most innocuous persons. Then again I am only a "pore ignorant furriner" and these are not really my concerns. The magazine seems the only chance, and I put no reliance in it, not till it is actually begun.

Pinker, it seems, has not delivered your mss. to Miss Weaver but taken it to Duckworth. I had a note saying they would probably take it IF you would alter etc.—would I approach you on the delicate question.

I said if they'd send me an exact list of the changes required I would consider it.

Pinker then sent me the "Opinion" of D's reader, which I consider both stupid and insolent. I replied that if they wished to fit the Venus de Milo into a piss-pot it would require *some alteration* [*long-hand:* and that they need not look to me for assistance.] I added a couple of pages of commiseration to Pink. on having to come into contact with such animals. I hope it will do him some good.

I have had a row with Lane over a new book by Lewis . . . . which the Egoist is now going to run as a serial.

Of course if one could find a publisher who would make an advance it would be worth it. If the Egoist publish you now, I don't suppose they'll be able to make any further advance. Though they might be able to fork up something (I doubt it) later.

Sooner or later we *must* have publisher, free, like the Mercure in Paris. Judging from Lewis' troubles and yours I think none of the commercial houses will *ever* be any use, and perhaps the sooner the Egoist leads off the sooner we can get a public organized to fight the accursed library octopus.

That Rotten American magazine that (I think) finally printed two Dubliners (? ? ? ? ? ? did it), anyhow it pays less and less, and I have no longer much to do with it . . . . . . even supposing you had any short stories. Still Pinker ought to do *something*, he had visions of a career *jadis*.

The remaining question is, have you any readers, "connections", wires, or *anything* here that I can electrify. It is very often easy to do for another what one couldn't possibly do for one's self. I once even got a man a job reviewing books. Not that I suggest this as a future for you, but if you think of anything, for god's sake suggest it for my invention is at about the end of its tether.

Yeats has hopes or illusions about the reorganized "Athenaeum". I think they are "reinstating the spirit of 1870" or profess to be doing some noble deed of that sort.

I don't keep up a "connection", for I have never found the organized world of publication much use, they usually try to get one under the hatches and then stop the bread and water ration.

The New Age would I think give you a guinea a week for an article of about 1200 words, for a time. I usually put their readers in a rage, and can only pay my rent out of their pocket intermittently . . . . at distressingly rarer intervals . . . even so. However despite our difference in aim, Orage has been a good friend to me when I most needed one.[9]

The commissioner general then reported to Xerxes that the land would provide so much fodder.

C'est une ideé: You had better write direct to the Yale University press, New Haven, Conn. U.S.A. don't mention me, but say you have heard of their work, want a catalogue, or something of that sort. Their catalogue may suggest some point of contact. I have just proposed 'em scholastic, or semi-scholastic book on troubadours. They print creative work too.

Another show with which I have iracified is the North American Review, Franklin Sq. New York . , they might be of some use to you.

I tried to send you the small anthology, but the book shop hadn't a license and I haven't been near Elkin.[1]

yours
E. Pound

P.S. Of course I should be glad if you came to London, even if you do detest it. I am not in the least sure that you'd make anything by it. Lewis will be called up with the next lot of men and the intelligent population of the metropolis will thereby be reduced $\frac{1}{4}$ or $\frac{1}{3}$. [*longhand:* The suggestion is purely a selfish one]

MEDITATIO [2]

I

Thoughts, rages, phenomena. I have seen in the course of the morning new ecclesiastical buildings, and I know from the events of

[9] Alfred R. Orage (1873–1934), Guild socialist, literary critic, and editor of *The New Age* (1907–1922) and *The New English Weekly* (1931–1934), was one of Pound's chief mentors and benefactors. Pound's articles in *The New Age,* 1911–1921, are an important record of his intellectual development during the London and war years. At Orage's death Pound paid several tributes to his achievements and to his social, political, and economic thought, also recalling gratefully: "he did more to feed me than anyone else in England, and I wish somebody who esteems my existence wd. pay back whatever they feel is due to its stalvarrdt sustainer. My gate receipts Nov. 1, 1914–15, were 42 quid 10 s. and Orage's 4 guineas a month thereafter wuz the SINEWS, by gob the sinooz," *Letters,* May 30, 1934.

[1] A license required for sending printed matter abroad during wartime hampered Pound's efforts to keep Joyce informed about literary developments and about the way his work was being received. "Elkin" is Elkin Mathews.

[2] *The Egoist,* III, 3 (March 1, 1916), pages 37–38. Reprinted as "Meditations," etc., in *Pavannes and Divisions,* 1918, where the subtitle "Anent the Difficulties of Getting 'A Portrait of the Artist as a Young Man' Printed in England" replaced roman numeral "I".

the last few months that it is very difficult to get the two most remarkable novels, written in English by our generation, published "through the ordinary channels."

Yet it is more desirable that a nation should have a firm literature than that paste-board nonentities should pour forth rehashed Victoriana on Sundays. Waste! Waste, and again, multiplicitly, waste!

O Christian and benevolent reader, I am not attacking your religion. I am even willing to confess a very considerable respect for its founder, and for Confucius and Mohammed, or any other individual who has striven to implant a germ of intelligence in the soil of the circumjacent stupidity. And I respect him whatever his means and his medium, that is, say, whether he has worked by violent speech, or by suave and persuasive paragraphs, or by pretending to have received his instructions, and gazed unabashed upon the hind side of the intemperate and sensuous J'h'v, on the escarps of Mount Sinai.

Because we, that is to say, you and I and the hypothetical rest of our readers, in normal mood, have no concern with churches, we generally presume that all this pother has been settled long since, and that nobody bothers about it. It is indeed a rare thought that there are thousands of prim, soaped little Tertullians opposing enlightenment, entrenched in their bigotry, mildly, placidly, contentedly entrenched in small livings and in fat livings, and in miserable, degrading curacies, and that they are all sterile, save perhaps in the production of human offspring, whereof there is already a superabundance.

Perhaps 10 per cent. of the activities of the Christian churches are not wholly venal, *mais passons!* And the arts, and good letters, serious writing?

"Oh, you go on too much about art and letters!"

"Bleat about the importance of art!!!" Yes, I have heard these phrases. And very annoying people will "go on about" art.

"In no country in the world do the authorities take such good care of their authors." There are various points of view. There are various tyrannies.

"We are going to have an outbreak of rampant puritanism after the war."

"We shall have a Saturnalia!"

There are various points of view. The monster of intolerance sniffs like a ghoul about the battlefields even. Flammarion [3] or some-

70

one said that the sun was about to explode on, I think it was, February the fifth of this year. The end of the world is approaching. Perhaps.

At any rate I am not the first author to remark that the future is unknowable, or at least indefinite and uncertain. Concerning the past we know a little. Concerning "progress," how much?

It is about thirty-nine years since Edmond de Goncourt wrote the preface I quote.

> Thirteen years ago my brother and I wrote in an introduction to "Germinie Lacerteux":
>
> "Now that the novel is wider and deeper, now that it begins to be the serious, passionate, living great-form of literary study and of social research, now that it has become, by analysis and psychological inquiry, the history of contemporary ethics-in-action (how shall one render accurately the phrase 'l'histoire morale contemporaine'?), now that the novel has imposed upon itself the studies and duties of science, one may again make a stand for its liberties and its privileges."

There ends his quotation of what they had set down in "the forties."

Now in one's normal mood, in one's normal existence, one takes it for granted that De Goncourt's statement is simple, concise, and accurate. One does not meet people who hold any other view, and one goes on placidly supposing that the question is settled, that it is settled along with Galileo's quondam heresy.

If a man has not in the year of grace 1915 or 1916 arrived at the point of enlightenment carefully marked by the brothers De Goncourt in A.D. 1863, one is not admitted to the acquaintance of anyone worth knowing. I do not say that a person holding a different view would be physically kicked downstairs if he produced a different opinion in an intelligent company; our manners are softened; he would be excreted in some more spiritual manner.

In December, 1876, Edmond de Goncourt added, among others, these following sentences:

> In 1877 I come alone and perhaps for the last time to demand these privileges for this new book written with the same

[3] Camille Flammarion (1842–1925), French astronomer, popularizer of astronomy, and student of the unknown.

71

feeling of intellectual curiosity and of commiseration for
human sufferings.

It has been impossible, at times, not to speak *as a physician,
as a savant, as a historian.* It would be insulting (*injurieux*) to
us, the young and serious school of modern novelists, to forbid
us to think, to analyse, to describe all that is permitted to
others to put into a volume which has on its cover "Study," or
any other grave title. You cannot ask us at this time of day to
amuse the young lady in the rail-road carriage. I think we have
acquired, since the beginning of the century, the right to write
for formed men, without the depressing necessity of fleeing to
foreign presses, or to have, under a full republican regime, our
publishers in Holland, as we did in the time of Louis XIV and
Louis XV.

Well, there you have it. We were most of us unborn, or at least
mewling and puking, when those perfectly plain, simple and, one
would have supposed, obvious sentences were put together.

And yet we are still faced with the problem: Is literature possible
in England and America? Is it possible that the great book and the
firm book can appear "in normal conditions"? That is to say, under
the same conditions that make musical comedy, Edna What's-her-
name, Victoria Cross, Clement Shorter,[4] etc. etc., so infernally possible among us!

It seems most unlikely. Of course, five hundred people can do any
mortal thing they like, provided it does not imply the coercion of a
large body of different people. I mean, for instance, five hundred
people can have any sort of drama or novel or literature that they
like.

It is possible that the *Mercure de France* has done much to make
serious literature possible in France "under present conditions."
The Yale University Press in America claims that it selects its
books solely on their merit and regardless of public opinion (or
perhaps I am wrong, "regardless of their vendibility" may be the
meaning of their phrase as I remember it).

And England?

"Oh, Blink is afraid to face the Libraries, I thought so." "The
Censor," etc. etc. "We don't think it necessary to superintend the
morals of our subscribers." "You can have it by taking a double
subscription."

[4] Clement King Shorter, journalist and editor, known for his work on the
Brontës.

Let me say at once that I make no plea for smuttiness, for an unnecessary erotic glamour, etc. etc. I have what I have been recently informed is a typically "French" disgust at the coarseness of Milton's mind. I have more than once been ridiculed for my prudery.

But if one can't, *parfois*, write "as a physician, as a savant, as a historian," if we can't write plays, novels, poems or any other conceivable form of literature with the scientist's freedom and privilege, with at least the chance of at least the scientist's verity, then where in the world have we got to, and what is the use of anything, *anything?*

During 1916, after his return from Sussex in March, Pound was temporarily inundated not only with Joyce's affairs but with the affairs of other artists. The vorticist painters Wyndham Lewis, Edward Wadsworth, Frederick Etchells, and William Roberts had entered the army, leaving Pound in charge of showing, promoting, and selling their work: "I appear," he said, "to be the only person of interest left in the world of art, London." His typical week was like the one he described to Kate Buss on March 9, just after his return:

> My occupations this week consist in finally (let us hope) dealing with Brzeska's estate; 2, getting a vorticist show packed up and started for New York; 3, making a selection from old father Yeats' letters, some of which are very fine (I suppose this will lap over into next week), a small vol. to appear soon; 4, bother a good deal about the production of Yeats' new play.

For Joyce he proposed in a letter to Miss Weaver (March 17) that he himself would paste into *A Portrait* whatever words the printers refused to set; he was also negotiating for an American publisher, seeking a producer for *Exiles*, and again trying to dig up funds for Joyce's living expenses. He was also at work on a new and larger book on the Noh plays and was preparing Fenollosa's "The Chinese Written Character as a Medium for Poetry." During the summer Iris Barry received in Pound's letters almost a book of instructions in poetry. His typical valediction was "P.S. Pardon haste of this note but I *am* really hurried." He vented his typical complaint when he wrote to Lewis, while acting as a go-between with Quinn, "My position is a little embarrassing as I have constantly to approach you in the paternal, admonitory, cautionary, epicierish bloodguttily IN-artistic angle" (at Cornell).

16 March 1916   *5, Holland Place Chambers, Kensington. W.*
                    [*longhand:* back permanently]

Dear Joyce: I will try to get time to look into your affairs in a few days. I have never been so hurried in my life, as during these weeks just after return to town, with all sorts of accumulations.

Of course you *ought* to be here on the spot. It is next to impossible to conduct a career by post.

I can't accelerate America. I have printed no verse, or practically no verse in England for years. I had one scrap in the dying number of "Poetry and Drama", [*longhand:* Dec 1914] [5] but we have never been paid for that. That was over a year ago. Yeats is in a row over his last verses printed here. One simply is NOT in the gang here that have control over the publication offices.

If all printers refuse to do your novel I shall tell Miss Weaver to print it with blank spaces and then have the deleted passages done in typewriting on good paper and pasted in. If I have to do it myself.

My proof reading is out of the question. I am incapable, even if I had time. The last book I was put on, had to go back to the shop and be unbound and some pages reprinted. My proofreading anyone would only lead to a fracas.

The only decent news I have, is a vague statement of Yeats' that Wheelan [6] liked your play, believed it would act, was trying to persuade the Stage Society to do it.

Wheelan is something or other, I dont really know what, save that he is "in with" Barker or someone of that sort. I dont know that this bit of news is worth *anything*.

I will certainly let you know the minute I receive any news or anything of use. One is wholly at the mercy of American editorial convenience. I want my cheque for that article that they promised to print in Feb. . . . . . they may have kept it over till May number . . . . . and then again the mails are subject to delay.

[5] "Dead Iönè," *Poetry and Drama*, London, December 1914; reprinted as "Ione, Dead the Long Year" in *Personae*, 1926.

[6] Frederick Whelan, a member of the Council of Management of the Incorporated Stage Society. *Exiles* was sent to the Society in January but was returned in July. Submitted again in 1917 at the request of another member, T. Sturge Moore, it was again rejected.

I will write to the cheapest typist I know about the price of proof reading.

hastily
E Pound

At the end of March Pound wrote to John Marshall, a New York publisher, who agreed to bring out *A Portrait* instead of Pound's projected *This Generation.* Marshall sent Joyce £10, apparently an advance. Another check was on its way from John Quinn, but Joyce did not get it until August, for Quinn's bookkeeper had been ill and had neglected to send it. Quinn wrote to Joyce on August 11 (at Cornell) that he was sending a new £10:

> I offered to stake Pound in a certain matter and he declined it, but he did suggest that I stake you to this extent. I am not generally in the staking business and the number of demands that have been made on me during the war from all quarters for advances and loans has been very great, more than I could meet, and I have had to shut down. But I send this with pleasure. Really it is because I am interested in your work.

At the same time Pound sought a grant from The War Emergency Fund of The Incorporated Society of Authors, Playwrights & Composers.

But in the meantime Pound's first collection of poetry since 1912, *Lustra,* also encountered the English printer. Elkin Mathews's reader, and then Mathews himself, balked at some of the poems in Pound's manuscript, even though they had been printed in periodicals. The printer refused to set certain passages. Pound wrote to Iris Barry in May:

> The scrape is both serious and ludicrous . . . . It is part printer and part Mathews. . . . The printers have gone quite mad since the Lawrence fuss [*The Rainbow* had been prosecuted in 1915]. Joyce's new novel has gone to America (AMERICA!) to be printed by an enthusiastic publisher. Something has got to be done or we'll all of us be suppressed, à la counter-reformation, dead and done for.

Pound argued with Mathews spiritedly and eloquently that serious poetry must use the serious language in which all "classics" had been written; broadening his perspective, he produced a definitive manifesto in which he formulated his theoretical position fully, lucidly, and powerfully (Appendix A). At this point Pound's and Joyce's positions became identical and the struggle became not only theirs but the well-known struggle for realism in modern literature.

1 June 1916   *5, Holland Place Chambers, Kensington. W.*

Dear Joyce: The enclosed [*first longhand:* £5 will be paid you from me.] [*second longhand:* I find that I do not enclose the money order.] is an advance from a private member of the relief committee. It will be deducted from the grant they make you.

I think you will probably get two cheques of £10 each from America, one of them from Marshall. (though this may not reach you for several weeks. I have filled out the committee's blanks as well as I could, although I naturally could not say what your salary had been before the war etc. etc. Can you send me an estimate of what it costs you, your wife and the two (it is two?) children to live in Zurich at present (naturally, not with luxury but in a clean place, *devoid of bugs,* and also how the food prices are likely to rise, or how they have risen.

I do a good deal of my own cooking, and I suppose you and your wife can manage that sort of thing. Would it be an advantage if you could take an unfurnished place and furnish it (I have made most bits of furniture save beds, one MUST buy beds.) I mean by this would a certain amount of cash down for furniture enable you to save something on the next years expenses, supposing you are to be in Zurich for a year?

Could you go to a village in the country, where life would be cheaper, IF you had a guarantee of supplies for the next year and didn't feel obliged to look for work that you cant find?

Various young writers here have done so.

yours
E. Pound

21 June 1916   *5, Holland Place Chambers, Kensington. W.*

Dear Joyce: The enclosed shows results of relief committee.[7] I imagine this grant can be renewed quarterly without much fuss. I

[7] Pound's letter is typed on the back of the enclosure that follows.

am not absolutely certain, but dont worry. I shall of course send them your address at once.

From your letter with details of prices I could not make out quite *what* it costs the four of you to live. I wish you would send me a round figure. £2 per week is £104 per year. Do tell me how much more you need, per week or per month. and I will try another line.

Marshall is to print the novel *unabridged.* I understand that Miss Weaver sent him the passages that the printer here had cut out, so he had the whole thing to judge by. And he said he agreed with me perfectly both as to the value of the book and the sense in printing it as you wrote it.

I am having a fine row over my own poems "Lustra". They promise me that the whole question of printers being able to hold up works of literary merit shall be raised in the house. So our troubles may lead to "good in the end".

Do tell me if Quinn's cheque or Marshalls has arrived from N.Y., or tell me when.

yours ever
E.P.
<u>over</u>

[*longhand:* Dear Joyce: You will by now have heard from the committee direct. I sent this days ago—but the censors held it up because I put in a photo—which is now *contra mores.*]

yrs
E. Pound

Enclosure

The Incorporated Society of Authors, Playwrights & Composers

14 June 1916

1, Central Building, Tothill Street, Westminster, S.W.

Ezra Pound Esq.

Dear Sir: Mr. James Joyce's papers were placed before the Administrative Committee of the War Emergency Fund and they have decided to make him a grant of £2. a week for 13 weeks. As however it would be a trouble and expense to send this out weekly I have been authorised to send it out in three instalments. The first instalment I shall make as soon as possible per cheque if you will be kind enough to give me Mr. Joyce's address as it does not appear to be amongst his papers.

Yours truly,
G. Herbert Thring [Secretary]

22 July 1916   *Harrod's Royal Exchange, Brompton Road, S.W.*

[longhand]

Dear Joyce: I am just sending you £20. from an anonymous donor. You might write a brief letter to the anonymous in my care.

The gift was unexpected.

Luck pursues your novel. Marshall has had a domestic calamity & given up his publishing ghost. I don't think it need worry you as I believe Huebsch of New York has made an equal firm, offer. (possibly at a smaller royalty, but with solider funds. behind him.

I have told Pinker to close with it.

Marshall seems blameless—wife collapsed with consumption & he with emotion.

Trust the £20 will cover incidental delay.

yours hastily
E Pound

[Between 1 and 7] August 1916

5, Holland Place Chambers, Kensington. W.

Dear Joyce: Lady Cunard [8] is your very good friend, she has been trying to stir up ***** to publish you. She got the little beast to read the Portrait for himself, and he has professed an admiration for "Death" in Dubliners.

Lady C. has even gone the length of inviting the pig to see her a couple of times and enduring the sight of his face while she tried to instill sense into his soapy kurranium.

Result is that he "would consider" publishing the Portrait with the Sequel, if the sequel could be inspected "within reasonable time". He dont think the Portrait would pay by itself.

[8] Lady Maud Alice Burke Cunard, famous London hostess and patroness of the arts.

78

I haven't much faith in him. BUT if he could be made to publish is he, [*sic:? he is*], I believe, a "good publisher".

I think I wrote you that I met Secker by chance a month or so ago. He said he thought the Portrait a good bit of work but didn't believe it would pay.

Of course I am not waiting for *****, but if he could be started at the same time as Huebsch in New York, it would be a help. How much of Ulysses is done?

Dont for god's sake hurry it. BUT if it is fairly shaped up you might send on a draft or synopsis or something.

I hope you have by now rec'd the £20 I sent on to you last week, or rather the saturday of the week before last.

If by any chance you should get into direct communication with ***** DONT indicate that you arc a friend of mine, BUT remember that you are a friend or acquaintance of Lady Cunard. My name is no help in "that quarter". [*longhand:* or ghetto.]

[*longhand:* You are getting about as much reputation as if you were already published, but glory is a damd inedible substance— not that being in print does of necessity serve one's exchequer either. as I, the writer hereof, can testify.]

yrs
E. P.

16 August 1916   *5, Holland Place Chambers, Kensington. W.*

Dear Joyce: I was surprised to receive this a.m. some VERY good news re some sort of grant or pension. It is not yet settled and of course one can't be certain until a thing IS settled. However the addresses on the stationery are as good as could be wished.

George Moore has been backing you. What I heard concerning his remarks on your youth may have been exaggerated. His letter to the secretary, or what ever it is that has this matter in charge was very firm. Said there was "NO question about your literary qualification" for pension, and that your life had for years been a model. (I do not remember the phrasing of the latter statement). Any way it was a jolly good recommendation. Dubliners is getting read by the right people (even if they do all read the same copy).

Hope this will make up for delay over the "Portrait".

Hope something will come of it.

yours
E. P.

In August, the Asquith government granted Joyce a £100 Civil List pension. Pound had spoken to Yeats, who had such a pension, and then had had Lady Cunard lend Joyce's books to Asquith's secretary, Edward Marsh, leader of the Georgians and editor of volumes entitled *Georgian Poetry* for 1911–1912, 1913–1915, and 1918–1919. Marsh was impressed and asked Yeats's and George Moore's opinions. Moore assured Marsh that Joyce's politics were unobjectionable and asserted that although some of *Dubliners* was "trivial and disagreeable" the book was the work of "a clever man" and "The Dead" near perfection. He concluded: "P.S. I am sure that from a literary point of view Joyce is deserving of help." [9] Pound gave all the credit to the others, but Joyce wrote to Yeats on September 14: "I have every reason to be grateful to the many friends who have helped me since I came here and I can never thank you enough for having brought me into relations with your friend Ezra Pound who is indeed a wonder worker." [1]

Marsh had met Pound at T. E. Hulme's evenings in 1912 and had wanted to print "The Ballad of the Goodly Fere" and "Portrait d'une femme" in his first anthology. But since Pound was bringing them out himself he asked if Marsh wouldn't consider something more modernistic or something from *Canzoni*. Marsh became disaffected, and both he and Pound soon felt that they represented irreconcilable groups. To add to their literary differences, Pound had published in *Blast*, II, July 1915, "Our Contemporaries," a satiric poem about Rupert Brooke, who had just died at Gallipoli. Criticism of Pound's bad taste was widespread. He defended himself to Harriet Monroe (October 12 and December 1, 1915), explaining that the poem, written before Brooke's death, contained nothing derogatory but was "a complaint against a literary method" (the note printed with the poem read in part: "Malheureusement ses poèmes ne sont remplis que de ses propres subjectivités, style Victorien de la 'Georgian Anthology'"). *Blast* had been scheduled to come out in December 1914, and in April Pound had been working on an appreciation of Brooke, whom he considered the best of the Georgian group; he claimed that he was a better defender than "friends who have taken to writing sentimental elegies about . . . 'Rupert's mobile toes.'" Pound admitted, however, that the poem had appeared at an inopportune moment.

[9] *Letters of James Joyce,* II, pages 380–381.
[1] *Letters of James Joyce,* I, page 95.

1 and 2 September 1916 *5, Holland Place Chambers, Kensington. W.*

Dear Joyce: I did not write to you when I heard that there was to be official recognition of your scriptorial lustre, because I wanted you to have a pleasant surprise.

I did not write before the grant was official, or at least I wrote only indefinitely. I had heard that the Prime Minister had in conversation expressed his personal willingness to sanction the grant but I thought it ill became me to take his name in vain until the matter was definitely decided.

The people you should thank if you are thanking people are Lady Cunard, 20 Cavendish Sq. W̲. who bought your books and lent them to Marsh.
Marsh=Edward Marsh, 10 Downing St., Whitehall S.W. He is in some way in charge of these grants. I dont know exactly what his position is. He was Churchill's private secretary, and is now some sort of Parliamentary or other sort of secretary, and writes from the Prime Minister's address. I should by all means write to him, graciously. He thinks you are a "man after his own heart". He has expressed admiration of your writing.
   You can say that you hear from me that he has been instrumental (or some more human word , , , ,) that he has recommended you to the P.M.'s notice, or given great and decisive assistance, or whatever bloody and classic turn you can give it.

Geo. Moore lives at 121 Ebury St. London S.W.

Yeats also wrote a strong letter of recommendation, but he was in France and I don't know but what the grant was made before his letter was rec'd., still you might thank him, and certainly assume that he helped. He did help, whether that particular letter was rec'd. W. B. Y. 18 Woburn Blds. Euston W.C.

I really don't know what is going on in N.Y. Marshall has disappeared with his sick or dying wife, that's all I know. Huebsch has told someone he would publish the book. Whether he has got a complete mss. or not I don't know. I think Miss Weaver will see it through.

81

Lady Cunard is having another whack at *****, on the strength of the govt. recognition of your work. I doubt if it will help. Still he has not (so far as I know) returned the mss. to Miss Weaver, so he may still be in the running.

At any rate it is my seventh day and I am resting.

You might however send on the extra copy of that damn play. I am to meet Knoblauch [2] sometime, and perhaps he would see his way to a stage version. From the point of view of career nothing better could happen to you, I think, both for cash and connection. No play is acted as it is written, and you could always have your original version used when the thing is printed.

I have succeeded in selling a lot of pictures in New York, by Lewis, Wadsworth, Etchells and Roberts. So they are no longer on my mind either. I shall devote the next six months entirely to my own interests. (Which will do them no good whatever.) All life's blessings except loose change seem to have been showered upon me, it behooves me to remedy that deficiency AT ONCE.

At any rate I hope Huebsch will be regularized before you get to the end of the present grant. Write Marsh a letter that will give him a chance to reply if he is so inclined.

He was a great friend of Rupert Brooke's. He has brought out two anthologies called "Georgian Verse". He says, or said that he has been trying for years to ruin my career and that it is no use, that I am now more firmly established than ever. (By which he probably means that I have had three digestable lunches and have been seen on a free front seat at the opera between Balfour and a duchess. Glories which do not add in the least to my income. Perhaps in some way they contribute to "establishment" in the parliamentario-secretarial world.

I have done nothing of importance for ages. I have written about 2000 words in a sort of story or portrait, thick, brown and Indian.[3]

---

[2] Edward Knoblock, American-born playwright and novelist. Pound wrote to Iris Barry in August: "I hear he is the Gawd of the British theatre." At this time *The Drama,* Chicago, became interested in *Exiles* through Pound, and Pound asked Pinker to send it to them.

[3] "Jodindranath Mawhwor's Occupation," *The Little Review,* May 1917.

MacMillan are doing a Japanese Play book, a good deal bigger than the small one at Cuala.[4]

A new magazine called "Seven Arts" [5] will probably be glad to print anything you do for a while. i.e. as long as they last. I shall try your play on them if Drama don't take it. Have you ANY short things AT ALL?

I am going on with the Fenollosa stuff, the Chinese part. Have found an eighth century Jules Laforgue: Wang Wei, or Omakitsu. I am delighting in Brantôme.[6]

There was once a young writer named Joyce
Whose diction was ribidly choice,
And all his friends' woes were deduced from his prose
Which never filled anyone's purse

These lines can be regarded as a limerick only in certain parts of New York, in the halls of the University of the City of N.Y. etc. etc. where I assure you the rime "-urse" and "oice" falls upon the ear with perfect exactness.

yours
Ezra Pound

6 September 1916   *5, Holland Place Chambers, Kensington. W.*

Dear Joyce: Despite my affection for the British Empire there are times when I desire to wring the necks of its official representatives.

The enclosed [7] was sent you some days ago on receipt of your letter. BUTTTTT I put a four page announcement of my book printing with the Cuala press in it, HENCE it is returned with the censors notice.

How laudable and lovely is the zeal of the zealous.

[4] Macmillan published *"Noh," or Accomplishment. A Study of the Classical Stage of Japan by Ernest Fenollosa and Ezra Pound* in 1917. The Cuala Press book was *Certain Noble Plays of Japan,* 1916, with an introduction by Yeats.

[5] *Seven Arts* was dedicated to what Van Wyck Brooks called "America's Coming of Age," a native self-consciousness which did not appeal to Pound's cosmopolitanism. The *Seven Arts* group included Brooks, Robert Frost, James Oppenheim, Waldo Frank, Randolph Bourne, Paul Rosenfeld, and Louis Untermeyer; *Seven Arts* ran from November 1916 to October 1917, when it merged with *The Dial.*

[6] Pierre di Bourdeilles, Abbé and Seigneur de Brantôme, sixteenth-century French courtier and soldier. A native of Périgord, he left a valuable account of his life and times.

[7] Doubtless the previous letter.

All I have to add is that I have met Knoblauch, and not been at strife, and that he will look through your play. SO please send me the second mss. of it as soon as you get this, and also an authorization for a stage version if Knoblauch chooses to take it up.

yours ever
Ezra Pound

13 November 1916   *5, Holland Place Chambers, Kensington. W.*

Dear Joyce: I have no news to impart. Knoblock seems to have vanished. Most agreeable when I met him, but busy, genuinely busy.

Neither have I heard from "Drama". The swine promised to print something of mine months ago, but I have had no word from them either about that or "Exiles".

My income for the year ending Oct 31, reached the low water mark of £48, and I am scrabbling to recoup.

Cadging for penny a line reviewing, etc. etc. Necessitas dura mater etc. .

I have free stalls at the Opera as compensation. I am, as I think I said, translating a Massenet libretto, which will pay part of my debts, but by no means start me in the ways of opulence.

Hackett,[8] whom you mention, is known to me only by name. He does something or other in New York, and I am yearly in less intimate contact with the wrong side of the Atlantic.

I wish you'd come to London, for nerves and various reasons, but I suppose it is out of the question, etc. etc.

I have, thank god, at last finished the last proofs of the Macmillan book on the Classical Stage of Japan. All the years publications will bring in something in the far distant future. But now my days are dotted with reviews. I seem to get one job out of a paper which professes itself delighted, promises more work and does NOT send it. On the whole it amuses me, though I dont know that it is of much interest to anyone else. Still without it I should not realize that that societies gather and recommend the [*crossout:* clothing] closing of all brothels in Burmah, "Rangoon and other stations".

Of course IF you came to London now you would find work easy to get, for the simple and brutal reason that all staffs are depleted and so many men gone to the front.

[8] Francis Hackett, literary editor of *The New Republic,* New York.

I wish to God the Italians would get into Trieste. I dont suppose you could go back to your job there, even if they did ? ? ? ? at least not till the lines had advanced decently beyond it and life somewhat resumed its normal outline.

Oh well. Hope this will find your nerves restored. I'll write the instant I get any news. Best regards to your wife and your descendants.

yours ever
Ezra Pound

Photographs that Joyce sent shocked Pound about what Pound later called Joyce's "pathological eyes." An episode was about to begin that resulted in Pound's diagnosis and a long-distance consultation with Dr. George Milbry Gould, Philadelphia ophthalmologist.

20 December 1916   *5, Holland Place Chambers, Kensington. W.*

Dear Joyce: Thanks for the photo. It is a bit terrifying. I suspect your oculist of believing that your astigmatism is harmonic and not inharmonic. Hence the lines of eyestrain in the forehead. I'd like to see your glasses prescription. I had a rather alarming experience with my own eyes about ten years ago. Hence my quasi scientific diagnosis at a distance and on so little evidence. Three or four American oculists preceded by Gould were at work on this problem at that time. Gould a very interesting chap who has done a book on Lafcadio Hearn [9] and another on genius and eye-sight.

It might be worth while my writing to him, if your eyes are still worrying you. (Unless he has died in the interim.) He'd be interested in your work, and from that in your eyes. The other men are not, so far as I know interested in literature.

At any rate you let me know what glasses you are wearing.

As personal presentation I like the smaller photo better. The last one is more Orestes than Odysseus.

I am on the whole feeling more cheerful. Perhaps a fatal sign. First thing I did after feeling that luck was turning, was to loose my

---

[9] The American poet and novelist (1850–1904). Like Ernest Fenollosa, Hearn was one of Pound's American precursors in introducing the Orient into modern western literature.

purse (with very little in it.) I have, thank god, finished my libretto and some cash is due me. It is also due to others as soon as I get it, but still there is a return of cheer in feeling the paper. I had five pounds in my pocket yesterday. NOT gains, but merely the last reserve which is being disbursed on the strength of the fact that something is supposed to be coming in. It is at least certain that I cant make less during the coming year than I have during the year past.

Oh Lord. There are still letters to answer. and I must quit this and get at 'em.

[longhand: Xmas.]

Your Xmas post card just arrived on the hour. Thanks for the same and our best wishes to you, your spouse and offspring.

I believe I am weathering the winter fairly well, though I've never before had to stand so much english climate without a recess in the South , .

I dont know that there's much news. The attacks on "Lustra" are in full swing and rather venomous. "Drunken helot" seems to be the preferred epithet for me at the moment.

It is at least more emotional than "traitor to the Imperium of poesy" with which the Nation began years ago. The reviewatorial mind is however a curious thing, (not *curieux*). Its choice of insult so limited, so seldom searching.

The Observer and the Chronicle are exceptions but their favour was limited by the rush for Xmas space. The Chronicle presumably contributed a compliment without opening the book. The Observer had manifestly enjoyed the contents though he did not think his Aunt Matilda would.

However 200 copies had gone off some time ago without Fleet St's. assistance. That may be an exaggeration, the Times column of grave but civil disapproval of everything save the Chinese stuff may have sold some.

With all good wishes for 1917 and the hope that Either you will reach England or that I shall see you on the way to Italy.

yours ever
Ezra Pound

Pound's amusement at "Drunken helot" referred to Arthur Waugh's review "The New Poetry," in the October *Quarterly Review,* London, in which he questioned the poetic methods of *Georgian Poetry* (1911–1912 and 1913–1915), then heaped scorn on Pound's *Catholic Anthology 1914–1915,* a work of "literary Cubists" which threatened "anarchy" and " 'red ruin' ". He concluded: "It was a classic custom in the family hall, when the feast was at its height, to display a drunken slave among the sons of the household, to the end that they, being ashamed at the ignominious folly of his gesticulations, might determine never to be tempted into such a pitiable condition themselves" (page 386). Waugh had cited examples from Pound's verse and from Eliot's "The Love Song of J. Alfred Prufrock." Pound took occasion to reply in his June 1917 review of *Prufrock and Other Observations* in *The Egoist,* "Drunken Helots and Mr Eliot."

As 1917 opened, Pound and Miss Weaver were preparing their campaign to call attention to the English edition of *A Portrait.* Pound had received a letter on November 14, 1916, in which Joyce had asked, among other things, that Pound do an article or a preface for the edition. Pound wrote to Miss Weaver on the same day: "Of course I am ready to do an article or preface BUT I think I have written so much about him that it would be much more advantageous to have some other critic turned loose." He suggested that she ask Edward Marsh to do the article since his appreciation would reach a different and new circle of people and would do more good than anything by Pound could. If Marsh declined, she could procure a set of testimonials from H. G. Wells, himself, Marsh, George Moore, and anyone else she could think of. His article in *Drama* had been the strongest kind of statement he could make and she could quote from it; he was willing to write another piece, but other methods should be tried before the readers of *The Egoist* had to hear any more "Me on Joyce."

Instead of testimonials they decided to get *A Portrait* reviewed as widely as possible; the extracts from the reviews could be compiled for further advertising. Later in November Pound suggested that Miss Weaver write to Wells and William Archer (Joyce had known Archer); Pound would ask Arthur Clutton-Brock to review the book for *The London Times.* Joyce had also suggested, perhaps jokingly, perhaps because it would dramatize his own penury, that Pound's limerick of September 2, 1916, be used in the advertising.

Miss Weaver forwarded the suggestion. Pound replied on January 22, 1917:

> The limerick Joyce asked me to use was my limerick on him, a very poor bit of doggerel, rhyming "Joyce" with "purse" (the latter pronounced "poice" in the manner of the N. Y. Bowery). I don't think his request was serious; if it was so, it [was] merely a bit of amiability on his part. At any rate the limerick won't fit a serious manifesto.
>
> His limerick on me shows that an amiable feeling exists between author and reviewer, and that also would weaken the force of my note.

Limerick or no limerick, when the English edition appeared on February 12, 1917, Pound's review launched it. (As his letter to Miss Weaver shows, he had wanted to name names of Joyce's detractors, but was persuaded to settle for "a few sheltered, and therefore courageous, anonymities.") Pound kept Joyce informed about the campaign and in June printed in *The Egoist* a selection of extracts from the press (see pages 118–120).

JAMES JOYCE [1]

At Last the Novel Appears

It is unlikely that I shall say anything new about Mr. Joyce's novel, *A Portrait of the Artist as a Young Man*. I have already stated that it is a book worth reading and that it is written in good prose. In using these terms I do not employ the looseness of the half-crown reviewer.

I am very glad that it is now possible for a few hundred people to read Mr. Joyce comfortably from a bound book, instead of from a much-handled file of EGOISTS or from a slippery bundle of type-script. After much difficulty THE EGOIST itself turns publisher and produces *A Portrait of the Artist* as a volume, for the hatred of ordinary English publishers for good prose is, like the hatred of the *Quarterly Review* for good poetry, deep-rooted, traditional.

Since Landor's *Imaginary Conversations* were bandied from pillar to post, I doubt if any manuscript has met with so much opposition, and no manuscript has been more worth supporting.

[1] *The Egoist*, IV, 2 (February 1917), pages 21–22.

Landor is still an unpopular author. He is still a terror to fools. He is still concealed from the young (not for any alleged indecency, but simply because he did not acquiesce in certain popular follies). He, Landor, still plays an inconspicuous rôle in university courses. The amount of light which he would shed on the undergraduate mind would make students inconvenient to the average run of professors. But Landor is permanent.

Members of the "Fly-Fishers" and "Royal Automobile" clubs, and of the "Isthmian," may not read him. They will not read Mr. Joyce. *E pur si muove.* Despite the printers and publishers the British Government has recognized Mr. Joyce's literary merit. That is a definite gain for the party of intelligence. A number of qualified judges have acquiesced in my statement of two years ago, that Mr. Joyce was an excellent and important writer of prose.

The last few years have seen the gradual shaping of a party of intelligence, a party not bound by any central doctrine or theory. We cannot accurately define new writers by applying to them tag-names from old authors, but as there is no adequate means of conveying the general impression of their characteristics one may at times employ such terminology, carefully stating that the terms are nothing more than approximation.

With that qualification, I would say that James Joyce produces the nearest thing to Flaubertian prose that we have now in English, just as Wyndham Lewis has written a novel which is more like, and more fitly compared with, Dostoievsky than is the work of any of his contemporaries. In like manner Mr. T. S. Eliot comes nearer to filling the place of Jules La Forgue in our generation. (Doing the "nearest thing" need not imply an approach to a standard, from a position inferior.)

Two of these writers have met with all sorts of opposition. If Mr. Eliot probably has not yet encountered very much opposition, it is only because his work is not yet very widely known.

My own income was considerably docked because I dared to say that Gaudier-Brzeska was a good sculptor and that Wyndham Lewis was a great master of design. It has, however, reached an almost irreducible minimum, and I am, perhaps, fairly safe in reasserting Joyce's ability as a writer. It will cost me no more than a few violent attacks from several sheltered, and therefore courageous, anonymities. When you tell the Irish that they are slow in recognizing their own men of genius they reply with street riots and politics.

Now, despite the jobbing of bigots and of their sectarian publishing houses, and despite the "Fly-Fishers" and the types which they represent, and despite the unwillingness of the print-packers (a word derived from pork-packers) and the initial objections of the Dublin publishers and the later unwillingness of the English publishers, Mr. Joyce's novel appears in book form, and intelligent readers gathering few by few will read it, and it will remain a permanent part of English literature—written by an Irishman in Trieste and first published in New York City. I doubt if a comparison of Mr. Joyce to other English writers or Irish writers would much help to define him. One can only say that he is rather unlike them. *The Portrait* is very different from *L'Education Sentimentale*, but it would be easier to compare it with that novel of Flaubert's than with anything else. Flaubert pointed out that if France had studied his work they might have been saved a good deal in 1870. If more people had read *The Portrait* and certain stories in Mr. Joyce's *Dubliners* there might have been less recent trouble in Ireland. A clear diagnosis is never without its value.

Apart from Mr. Joyce's realism—the school-life, the life in the University, the family dinner with the discussion of Parnell depicted in his novel—apart from, or of a piece with, all this is the style, the actual writing: hard, clear-cut, with no waste of words, no bundling up of useless phrases, no filling in with pages of slosh.

It is very important that there should be clear, unexaggerated, realistic literature. It is very important that there should be good prose. The hell of contemporary Europe is caused by the lack of representative government in Germany, *and* by the non-existence of decent prose in the German language. Clear thought and sanity depend on clear prose. They cannot live apart. The former produces the latter. The latter conserves and transmits the former.

The mush of the German sentence, the straddling of the verb out to the end, are just as much a part of the befoozlement of Kultur and the consequent hell, as was the rhetoric of later Rome the seed and the symptom of the Roman Empire's decadence and extinction. A nation that cannot write clearly cannot be trusted to govern, nor yet to think.

Germany has had two decent prose-writers, Frederick the Great and Heine—the one taught by Voltaire, and the other saturated with French and with Paris. Only a nation accustomed to muzzy writing could have been led by the nose and bamboozled as the Germans have been by their controllers.

The terror of clarity is not confined to any one people. The

90

obstructionist and the provincial are everywhere, and in them alone is the permanent danger to civilization. Clear, hard prose is the safeguard and should be valued as such. The mind accustomed to it will not be cheated or stampeded by national phrases and public emotionalities.

These facts are true, even for the detesters of literature. For those who love good writing there is no need of argument. In the present instance it is enough to say to those who will believe one that Mr. Joyce's book is now procurable.

At about this time Pound was completing negotiations with *The Little Review*. He had written to editress Margaret Anderson early in 1917:

> *The Little Review* is perhaps temperamentally closer to what I want done? ? ? ? ? ?
> DEFINITELY then:
> I want an "official organ" (vile phrase). I mean I want a place where I and T. S. Eliot can appear once a month (or once an "issue") and where Joyce can appear when he likes, and where Wyndham Lewis can appear if he comes back from the war.
> DEFINITELY a place for our regular appearance and where our friends and readers (what few of 'em there are), can look with assurance of finding us.

The Little Review was an alternative to publishing in England. Pound had been contributing little to English periodicals, and he had given up on *Poetry*, which, moreover, did not publish fiction and would therefore not be able to print anything like *Ulysses*. A new front was about to open; he was ready to try making New York instead of London the home of his cenacle and the *avant-garde*, and therefore the literary capital of the English-speaking world.

9 February 1917   *5, Holland Place Chambers, Kensington. W.*

Dear Joyce: I would have taken your play to Yeats on Monday only I was in bed with nose. Endless, perpetual nose, flowing and swilling, cough, chuff, sneeze, weather. I will let him see it [*longhand:* the play] as soon as possible. He *says* "If it's any good we'll do it at the Abbey".

They damn well wont, of course. They gibbed at a one act farce of mine on account of *indecency*. However I'll take it to him. Knoblock has disappeared completely. Old Sturge Moore [2] praises your play and says the Stage Society should do it. <u>So</u> they damn well should.

Clutton Brock has promised to ask the Times for the "Portrait" for review. He apologizes for his age.

/ / /

There at last seems a chance that I will get at least the corner of a magazine. Seriously I want you to send on any short stuff you have, and that you can afford to sell (magazine rights only) for £2 per thousand words. Anything you have in your desk.

It has always struck me that you could do a unique series of "portraits", 1000 to 2000 words, Priests in Padua. Students in Dublin, etc. God knows where you have been and what you have gazed upon with your [*crossout:* myopic] microscopic [*crossout:* eye], remarkable eye.
    Rough drafts of parts of Ulysses, if they wouldn't interfere with later serial publication of the whole.

At any rate I think the chance of something's at last coming off, is good enough to make it worth your while sending any odd stuff you possess.

I dont believe much in the "7 Arts", nor do I think their format is big enough to take "Exiles" but I'll send it on to them if Yeats doesn't take it.

How long will your subsidy hold out? What month was it granted you?

Short stories, I should try to pay £5. unless you can get more elsewhere. At any rate mark a price on whatever you can send and I'll try to meet it.

Yours in the midst of many contrivings
Ezra Pound

---

[2] T. Sturge Moore, British lyric poet and man of letters, a friend of Yeats and Pound.

12 February 1917   *5, Holland Place Chambers, Kensington. W.*
[*crossout:* Savile Club, 107, Piccadilly. W.]

[*longhand*]

Dear Joyce: Behold the characteristic epistle—of William, smeared
—yea well smeared at the back, & folded with true Celtic zeal & fum-
ble, using 2 sheets of someone else's club's paper, & thus providing me
with this unusually elegant bit of stationery—folded up & enclosed
in his missive. I preserve the traditional folds—which as you observe
do not cross the paper at right angles with paper's own edges.

———

I still dont believe the Abbcy will do it; but the iron appears to be
warming.

I will take him the mss. this evening.

In the meantime—this for Ulysses' historic collection of autographs.

====

Yeats has not read a novel for years—which is a compliment if you
are a mind so to take it.

yours ever
Ezra Pound

I have lost your new address. hope this will reach you.

Enclosure

11 February 1917   *Savile Club, 107, Piccadilly. W.*

My Dear Ezra: I have almost finished "A Portrait of the Artist". I
think it a very great book—I am absorbed in it.

If you have the play bring it tomorrow night. If at all possible
the Abbey should face a riot for it.

Yrs
W. B. Yeats

93

Yeats read *Exiles* but did not reply to Joyce. On August 26, 1917, after Joyce had made an inquiry, Yeats wrote him that since *Exiles* was too far from the folk drama and a type of work the Abbey had never played well, he had not recommended it.[3]

With the next letter Pound enclosed a review of *A Portrait* that had appeared in *The Times Literary Supplement* on March 1. The H. G. Wells review mentioned appeared in *The Nation*, London, on February 24, and on March 10 in *The New Republic*, New York. Wells praised *A Portrait* but noted a "cloacal obsession."

1 March 1917   *5, Holland Place Chambers, Kensington. W.*

[longhand: London Eng.]

Dear Joyce: I enclose the Times review, and hope the censor will pass it.

I should think it was by Brock, evidently written when ill or tired.

Wells has done a page in the Nation. He IS a bloody damn fool, but a full page from him ought to do a good deal of good to your sales.

My own poor thing in the Egoist will already have reached you. I found it very hard to treat the same subject for a fourth time. Result: I haven't treated it, I have just put down 1000 words or thereabouts.

It is the only novel in todays Times that is treated separately. The others are lumped as "New Novels" and get half a col. each.

The Dublin Express has given half a col. to my Japanese plays, and I have written them to say that the Portrait is worth reviewing. Mrs. Jo Cambell [4] has taken a copy to the Emerald Islet.

wearily and in haste

Ezra Pound

NOTE to CENSOR

Enclosure is a review of a novel written by the addressee to whom I am sending or endeavouring to send it.

Ezra Pound

---

[3] This letter and the above enclosure are at Cornell; they are printed in *Letters of James Joyce*, II, pages 388, 405.

[4] Probably the wife of Joseph Campbell, Irish poet and playwright connected with the Abbey Theatre.

On February 22 Slack, Monro, Saw & Co., Solicitors, informed Joyce that an anonymous client had instructed them to pay him £50 quarterly. Joyce suspected Pound's hand in it, but it was Miss Weaver, acting independently. She made further grants in 1919 and 1920; Joyce did not learn her identity until shortly after the 1919 sum had been announced to him. The grant coincided with an improvement of Joyce's eyes. Pound, relieved and gratified at both temporary ameliorations, cited Guido Cavalcanti's sonnet "A Guido Orlandi," in which Cavalcanti imagines that a figure of his lady in the church of San Michele in Orto heals those sick in body and spirit and makes "those with crooked eyes see straightway straight" (Pound's translation).

13 March 1917   *5, Holland Place Chambers, London W.8.*

[*longhand:* note new form of address]

Dear Joyce: The niggers in my country say certain things are "good for sore eyes".

"E gli occhi orbati fa vedere scorto"

says noster Guido in another and different context. I am very glad your orbs are again enlightened. And also very glad about the £200. I was feeling very uncertain of my own powers in raising the financial wind.

Battara's [5] last letter was rather illegible. I couldn't make out how much it was, 100, 700, 300. With my usual caution I had put it at £100 and given due thanks to the gods. [*insert:* I couldn't even make out whether it was "sure" or "proposed."]

The Manchester Guardian has given you the best review yet, and there is a priceless page by Boyd [6] in New Ireland, recognizing your ability, and ending with a bit of "rael foine owld Oirish orrratory" about young men not realizing the cultural advantages of the city of Dublin as compared with other less favoured metropoles.

He found the Dublin brothels less cheering. His review will give you pleasure. I myself have enjoyed it

Yeats is pleased that Lady Gregory has pronounced it a model autobiography, and that she is not put off by the "unVictorian"

[5] Someone who helped Joyce write his letters during his eye troubles?

[6] Pound published extracts from the review by Ernest Boyd, Irish critic, essayist, and historian of the Irish revival, in "James Joyce and His Critics," below, pages 119 and 120. Joyce wrote Boyd twice thanking him for his article.

language. She had liked parts of "Dubliners" but been worried by the "freedom of speech".

An intolerable bitch called *****, some relation of the minister, says "it is true of life in Belgium".

A bit hard on "Eire soul of the Nations" ? ? ? ? but interesting as praise of the book.

Eliot, whose opinion I value next to my own, also approves, and is trying to get the book for review from some paper or other.

yours ever.

Ezra Pound

[*longhand*: this is in answer to your card of 6/3/17]

Note to censor

I feel this letter is rather cryptic. It relates mostly to the reviews of Mr Joyce's novel "A Portrait of the Artist as a Young Man."

In the middle of March 1917 Joyce's eye troubles recurred; his isolation in Zurich and his financial difficulties precipitated a quixotic series of exchanges. In January he had suffered an attack of glaucoma and synechia, diseases of the eye which, if untreated, lead to blindness.[7] He sought treatment in several ways. Most obviously, he put himself under the care of a doctor; but he also, as he so often did, turned to Pound. Pound, dismayed by the appearance of Joyce's eyes in his photographs, had suggested that it might be worthwhile to write Dr. George Milbry Gould. Pound considered Dr. Gould (1848–1922), ophthalmologist, prolific writer on medical subjects, biographer, essayist, and poet, Joyce's chief hope. Not only had Gould, a refractionist, helped Pound, but he saw a connection between eyestrain and genius, which made him irresistible to Pound. Gould had written incessantly in support of such theories and had gone further to contend that eyestrain is the cause of numerous physiological disorders. He had studied past writers in order to show that medical facts "Like flashes of lightning of the past storm . . . reveal for an instant the whole landscape of their time and work and suffering." [8] In one of his six volumes of studies Gould argues that near absence of eyesight caused Lafcadio Hearn to become "the poet of myopia" (Pound had been on the verge of calling Joyce "the novelist of myopia," but had caught himself and substituted the microscope). Gould also wrote a full biographical,

[7] Ellmann, *James Joyce*, pages 426, 430–431.
[8] *Biographic Clinics,* Philadelphia: P. Blakiston, Son, & Co., 1903, Vol. I, page 12.

medical, and literary study, *Concerning Lafcadio Hearn* (1908).

Joyce's imagination had apparently been intrigued by the idea of a poetical ophthalmologist. Pound had neglected to write to Gould, or to his collaborator, Dr. Walter Lytle Pyle, but in mid-March, having taken seriously Pound's perhaps only half-serious offer, Joyce wrote to ask if Pound had heard from Gould and enclosed some "letters" apparently describing his symptoms and sufferings. Pound did three things: he himself, as the man of many devices, prescribed; he also suggested that Joyce consult an osteopath in case the origin of his malady was not merely local; and he sent Joyce's letters "toward" Gould—via John Quinn. Thus Quinn, along with another set of ocular opinions, entered the picture.

Quinn had admired *A Portrait* and had helped arrange for Huebsch to publish it in New York. He now tried to help a fellow Irishman in distress. As Joyce's various difficulties became aggravated, an urgent three-cornered correspondence developed between Zurich, New York, and London. Joyce wrote to Pound and Pound wrote to Quinn enclosing Joyce's letters. Quinn responded to Pound enclosing notes, reviews, and other correspondence. Then Pound responded to Joyce. While communications proceeded at the mercy of the wartime post, Joyce's eyes became worse and worse and his lack of funds more and more pressing. Finally the three correspondents began to resort to cables; as business and glaucoma intensified, Joyce and Quinn began to write to each other direct; at last, when Joyce became unable to write, Nora Joyce took his place. Between March and August, when Joyce was finally forced to submit to an operation, the long-range consultations about his eyes became mixed up with the launching of the renovated *Little Review*, with the "Hackett affair," an imbroglio involving Quinn and two brother Irishmen about the opinions of *A Portrait* and the purchase of some proofsheets, and with Quinn's efforts to find a publisher for *Exiles*. To avoid confusion, it is convenient to summarize here the exchanges relating to Joyce's eyes.

At the end of April Joyce's eyes took a turn for the worse and his doctor talked of operating. Joyce demurred. Grasping for straws he once again sought Gould's opinion, now via Nora. Pound replied that the urgency of Joyce's case precluded waiting for Gould's advice, and that in any case there had been a delay because Quinn had consulted his own eye experts ("Gould's enemies," Pound called them). Nevertheless, since Joyce apparently wanted Gould's opinion, Pound said that he would write to Gould direct. He wrote at once. Meanwhile

Quinn had definite opinions of his own about experts and eye specialists. He wrote to Nora on May 25 (the letter is at Cornell) warning her about relying on the alleged expertise of friends, regardless of their good-will, or on distant diagnoses:

. . . I am sorry that Joyce has glancoma [*sic*]. That is a serious thing. I have talked to a physician friend of mine here who is accustomed to making decisions in medical matters. Of course, neither he nor I knew how pressing the matter was or whether there was time to wait to hear Dr. Gould's opinion. Glancoma is a serious thing. Now, Mrs. Joyce, please remember this: that I have had a very great deal of experience in picking out specialists in medicine as well as in law. In fact some day, if I have the time, I will write an essay on the idea of the specialist. Most of the people spend more time in getting the right tailor or the right barber or getting the right restaurant than they do in getting the right doctor. Zurich is a good sized city and there ought to be a good specialist in Switzerland somewhere. All I can do is to urge Joyce as strongly as I could to get the best eye specialist or two of them that he can possibly get in Switzerland. Tell him not to take the advice of any casual friend as to what specialist to get; not the advice of the British Consul; not the advice of any priest or personal friend of his; not the advice of any casual acquaintance in a boarding house; but the advice of the head of a hospital as to whom the best specialist is. Not the advice of an ordinary casual doctor; not the advice of an average professional man; but the advice of an expert as to what eye expert to get. There must be just as good eye experts in Switzerland as there are in New York City or in Philadelphia or in Dublin. Of course, I don't know how urgent it is. I don't want to go against Pound's recommendation of Dr. Gould. But I have a profound mistrust of a man three thousand miles away advising on a condition that may be as acute or as critical or painful as glancoma may be, if it is a deep seated glancoma. If Joyce was my brother and if I couldn't go to him, I would write just as I am writing to you, and that is to have him get the best expert on eyes, or to put it another way, the man who is doing the best eye work, now in Switzerland. This was my personal feeling when I read your letter. It is also the advice of the eminent general practitioner whom I have talked to about the matter. If, for example, I had to advise some person here, I would not take the advice of any lawyer or priest or best friend of mine. I would call up a high class physician or one or two of the heads of the leading hospitals here. I would ask them who is now doing the best eye work in New York City. I would get the names of two or three of the best men. Then I would decide among those two or three, from age, experience, qualifications, which one of the two or three leaders in New York City was the best for the particular case, and would recommend the patient to go there. Some such procedure is what your husband should follow or what should be followed for him. I can't make this too strong. . . .

(Quinn's letter can be read as an indirect reply to Pound's prescription.)

Joyce, however, persisted. He sent Quinn "the facts," apparently trying himself to describe and elaborate on the diagnosis of his Zurich doctor and to suggest remedies. Quinn submitted Joyce's data to an ophthalmologist of his own choice, "one of the best eye experts in New York or America," Dr. John R. Shannon, another Irishman, and sent Joyce an opinion on July 7. At that point the affair collapsed into comedy. Shannon had written to Quinn of Joyce's "facts": "Your quotations must in some way be incorrect, for atropine is not used in Glaucoma—indeed, is absolutely contra-indicated. The reference to 'cohesion in the eye' and 'a vertebral operation' are unintelligible to me" (at Cornell). "The stylist" was no more a universal expert than Pound himself; the language of vision does not necessarily include ophthalmology. Shannon recommended two Zurich specialists. Gould, whose opinion Pound finally received and sent on, also prescribed on-the-spot treatment, perhaps the very operation which Joyce had been trying to avoid. Meanwhile Joyce's eyes had been obeying laws of their own and on August 18 he suffered a severe attack. His Zurich ophthalmologist finally decided that he must operate and Joyce underwent surgery on August 24.

According to Dr. Edward E. Hart, an ophthalmologist now practicing in Ithaca, New York, Pound's prescriptions may not have been entirely relevant to Joyce's ailment, but his descriptions and his terms were clear and reflect as good optical knowledge as was then available. Dr. Gould had received the first Doyne Medal of the Ophthalmological Congress in London; *Gould's Medical Dictionary*, first published in 1904, is still a standard reference work.

17 March 1917   *5, Holland Place Chambers, London W.8.*

[*longhand:* new style for Postal address]

Dear Joyce: I have culpably put off writing to Dr. Gould. Couldn't find address, couldn't remember his initials, etc. etc. the labour of composing a letter that would sufficiently stir up his interest, AND be brief, and sufficiently clear etc. etc. plus the difficulty of prescribing across the atlantic. AND the uncertainty after eight years if he was still alive, and in case of death how to get the letter forwarded to Dr Pyle, etc. I having no hold on Pyle.

HOWEVER lets get to business. I put on glasses at age of five or six, at about twenty I found (no need to be circumstantial) that an inharmonic astigmatism was supposedly driving toward blindness (probably very remote) and also twisting my spine.

The astigmatism was very slight, I think the cylindrical cut in my glass is only .25. One optician left it out altogether. Another put in both axes at 90 degrees.

The discovery that astigmatism is inharmonic is, I believe more or less Gould's own. At least, eight years ago, only he and two pupils were taking count of it in Philadelphia.

I never know where I am with English doctors and I have never been to an oculist on this side of the atlantic. I dont know whether they are still in the XVIIIth. century or not.

Time was, I believe, when they used to sort of strike an average between the astigmatisms of both eyes and thereby leave neither relieved.

That is to say, in my case, I was being [*crossout:* driven] plagued by two cylindrical grooves set thus

In my lenses. But when Gould suddenly twisted the left cylinder into this position

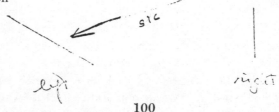

I suddenly felt "a weight lifted", and have had practically no bother since. I have reduced my general glasses to 1.37, and have a pair about 1.75 for *protracted* reading.

Cylinders for astigmatism about .25 put in at above mentioned angles. [*longhand*: axes 145 & 90, I think.]

The man who took me to Gould, himself a doctor, had had a much worse time, and felt he owed his eyesight to Gould and to the same simple means of correcting strain.

You make no mention of any astigmatism, yet it must almost surely be present in eyes so distorted as yours, also one eye is worse than the other according to your last note.

At least it can do you no harm to try cylindrical lenses, such as you should find in any opticians test room, twisting them about in the double grooved frames to see if they give any relief.

I doubt if any 6.5 eye can be perfectly spherical in its distortion, or in its lens. Still it may be.

I dont much believe in [*longhand*: habitually] squirting drugs into anything so sensitive as the eye.

One other thing you can try, before being operated on, IS there a trained osteopath in Zurich? Atrophy of the deltoid and biceps shows that the trouble is not necessarily local and confined to the eye. I know an increasing number of people whom "regular" physicians have bungled, who have been cured and renovated by having a vertebra set right side up and thus relieving blood or nerve pressures.

In the mean time, I will today send on your letters to, or toward, Dr Gould, with a request to forward them to Pyle, if he is unable to tackle it. Just what he did for Lafcadio Hearn I dont know, but he kept him going a long while and [*insert*: at least] prevented blindness. BUT Hearn, I think, lived with him for some months. I suppose it is out of the question for you either to come here or go to America ? ? ? ?

Unfortunately I have not any of Gould's books here. The last I remember seeing was a pamphlet on a man who could see a whole

101

page of print at a glance, one eye doing the rim and the other the middle of the page.

Well, I will write to Gould at once. Try squinting through cylindrical lenses (put on over the spherical ones, [*longhand:* which] probably [*longhand:* may be] of a lower curvature than 6.5), and if there is an osteopath (not a quack but one who has taken his proper degree after four years training like the training of other doctors) let him consider your vertebrae.

That's all I can think of, at the moment. I will now desist and write to Gould.

I dont know that there is much news to interest you. My book of Japanese plays has been well reviewed. I dont like them so well as the Chinese stuff in Lustra, though they may be just bad enough to get some circulation.

I have begun an endless poem, of no known category. Phanopoeia [9] or something or other, all about everything. "Poetry" may print the first three cantos this spring. I wonder what you will make of it. Probably too sprawling and unmusical to find favour in your ears. Will try to get some melody into it further on. Though we have not *ombra* and *ingombra* to end our lines with, or poluphloisbious thallassas to enrich the middle feet.

dina para thallassa poluphloisboio, I think it is, the attempted anglicization does not look well.

/ / /

I think I wrote that the Manchester Guardian had done "The Portrait" better than anyone. The Editor of the New Statesman says he has read it twice and that it is the best novel he has seen. He proposes to review it. A brief notice in "The Future" stating that it [*insert:* "Portrait"] is about to appear.

A chap named Rodker [1] has writ a short novel, badly, but with some stuff in it.

---

[9] "Phanopoeia" ("light-" or "image-making," with "melopoeia" and "logopoeia" one of Pound's "kinds of poetry") is Pound's original, provisional title for his long poem. He also used the title for a vorticist poem, Φανοποεία (*The Little Review,* November 1918; "Phanopoeia," *Personae,* 1926).

[1] Pound's friend John Rodker, British poet, novelist, and critic; Pound considered his *Adolphe,* 1920, one of the valuable developments from *Ulysses,* along with William Carlos Williams's *The Great American Novel,* 1923 ("Dr Williams' Position," 1928, *Literary Essays,* p. 397). Rodker was connected with *The Egoist* and The Egoist Press, which tried to publish *Ulysses* in England in 1922; as publisher of The Ovid Press he brought out several of Pound's works.

Hope to be able to send you Eliot's poems before many weeks elapse.[2]

Yes. And thank you for the autographed copy of The Artist. The civilities forsake me. It came just as I was in the middle of something or other, and I was about to forget I hadn't already thanked you for it.

I have a new copy of Dubliner's, as your first copy went out propaganding and never came home. I have two copies of the Artist and so can keep one of them chained to the baptismal font.

About hallucinations. NO medico ever knew anything about the matter. Apply to an alcoholic flagellant in holy orders. Or a vertebraist, as suggested above.

Enough of this.

yours ever

Ezra Pound

28 March 1917   *5, Holland Place Chambers, Kensington. W.8*

Dear Joyce: Rec'd your money order for 10/. I forget how much the cable was, but I think I owe you 3/ change, which I will send along with the £20 when it arrives.[3]

NOW serieusement. My magazine seems on the point of materialization. The magazine, or section of it to be placed in my charge, is ready, and only awaits Quinn's sanction. As he has offered me as much cash before for similar purpose, and much more for purposes only slightly different, I dont think he is likely to balk now.

I am sending over the stuff for the May number, this week. A story of mine, or rather sketch of Indian life, some excellent imaginary letters by Lewis, and something from Eliot, which I have not yet seen.

I want SOMETHING from you, even if it is only 500 words.

The "Little Review" has something like 3000 subscribers of the sort who read and buy books. They have a puff of you in the last number, promising long review in April. I think from purely practical point of view it will do you no harm to "keep in touch with" their readers. Remind them of your existence, at least six times a year.

---

[2] *Prufrock and Other Observations*, 1917.
[3] Payment by Quinn for proofsheets of *A Portrait* (see below, April 1917, pages 106–111 passim, also Appendix B).

I dont want, at any price, to interfere with the progress of "Odysseus", but you must have some stray leaves of paper, with some sort of arabesques on them.

Anything you like. [*crossout:* And also name your own rates, if you can keep within reach attainable limits.] There can't be much at a time, as the format is small. From 500 to 3500 words, is about the limit. Though I [*crossout:* should] could print a story up to 6000 words if you had one. 1000 to 2500 will be about the regular size.

I'd like to start the May number with all of us in it.

If you haven't, absolutely haven't anything, will you send me a note, of general good wishes, saying you are ill, but hope to send something soon. [*longhand:* Assurances of votre concurrence.]

Dont mention the matter yet to Miss Weaver if you are writing to her, as I shall not tell her until I have actually rec'd confirmation from Quinn,

I am sending the manuscripts to him, now, to be passed on by him to the printers, IF he approves.

I shall propose to do a criticism of your critics in the Egoist, as soon as there are a few more of them to criticize.

Yeats still has "Exiles". I did not see him Monday, as several of us were dining together and we did not finish in time to go on to his "evening". If he doesn't take it, I think the best thing to do will be to send it to Huebsch in New York.

Good luck, and get your eyes in order as soon as may be.

yours ever, with regards to Madame and the next generation.

Ezra Pound

Joyce's answer to Pound's request for "SOMETHING" has survived. (*Letters of James Joyce*, I, pages 101–2) With his letter Joyce enclosed the following note, which appeared in *The Little Review* in June (page 26):

I am very glad to hear about the new plans for The Little Review and that you have got together so many good writers as contributors. I hope to send you something very soon—as soon, in fact, as my health allows me to resume work. I am much better however, though I am still under care of the doctor. I wish The Little Review every success.

Dear Pound: Many thanks for yours of 26th ult. [*sic:* 28th] which arrived only this morning. Owing to the delay and the fact that I have nothing ready, I am sending you an accompanying note, as you wish. I sent three pieces of verse in December, I think, to *Poetry* (Chicago) through my agent, but heard nothing more of them. If they have not been and will not be published, would you take them in reversion? As regards stories I have none. I have some prose sketches, as I told you, but they are locked up in my desk in Trieste. As regards excerpts from *Ulysses,* the only thing I could send would be the Hamlet chapter, or part of it—which, however, would suffer by excision. If there is anything else I could do—perhaps a simple translation or review—will you tell me? I shall be glad to do it, though I am quite sure that, with your usual friendliness, you exaggerate the value of my poor signature as a 'draw'. I have been thinking all day what I could do or write. Perhaps there is something if I could only think of it. Unfortunately, I have very little imagination. I am also a very bad critic. For instance, some time ago a person gave me a two-volume novel to read, *Joseph Vance.* I read it at intervals for some time, till I discovered that I had been reading the second volume instead of the first. And if I am a bad reader I am a most tiresome writer—to myself, at least. It exhausts me before I end it. I wonder if you will like the book I am writing? I am doing it, as Aristotle would say, by different means in different parts. Strange to say, in spite of my illness I have written enough lately.

As regards my novel, it seems that it has now come to a standstill. I did not see any review in the *New Statesman.* Mr Boyd sent me a notice from the *New York Sun,* about 2,000 words, by Mr Huneker,[4] very favourable. Miss Weaver sent me also other American notices but they seem to have fallen out of the envelope somewhere on the way. By the way, I think you ought to type your letters to me without cancellings of any kind. Perhaps that delayed your last letter.

As I wrote you, the Stage Society wishes to reconsider my play, *Exiles.* I shall ask my agent to submit it also for publication in London and New York this autumn. I wish I could hear of a good dramatic agent in America who would take it up. Perhaps it would

4 James Gibbons Huneker (1860–1921), American musician and critic.

be more successful than *A Portrait of the Artist*. I send you a limerick thereon:

There once was a lounger named Stephen
Whose youth was most odd and uneven.
　　He throve on the smell
　　Of a horrible hell
That a Hottentot wouldn't believe in.

In spite of the efforts of the critics of the *Times* and *Manchester Guardian* to galvanize the book into life, it has collapsed or is about to collapse—possibly for lack of inverted commas. I should like to hear what Yeats says about *Exiles*.

I am rather tired for I have been correcting misprints in my novel. There are nearly four hundred. No revise was sent to me. This in view of a possible second edition during the century. The announcement on the last page of *The Egoist* is a pious exaggeration—so Miss Weaver writes.[5]

In any case I am better. Please write to me about your review. I shall go on writing, thanks to the kindness of my unknown friend and also of Mr Quinn.

I hope you are well. My wife and noisy children thank you for your good wishes. From me, *ogni bene!*

In the midst of Joyce's eye troubles and the final negotiations for *The Little Review* came the volatile "Hackett affair." At almost the same time, on April 18, that Joyce's letter arrived, Pound received from Quinn a fat packet of documents. Quinn had become angry at a review of *A Portrait* entitled "Green Sickness" by Francis Hackett of *The New Republic*. He became further enraged at Francis's brother E. Byrne Hackett, a New Haven book dealer, who, Quinn thought, had tried to profit from Quinn's purchase of the proofsheets of the American edition, four pages of which Joyce had altered in his own hand. After some negotiations with Byrne Hackett, Quinn, to aid Joyce, had cabled Joyce offering him $100 for the sheets. Joyce had authorized Pound to accept and Pound had responded, "Joyce accepts. Money to be sent via me." But then Quinn, annoyed that Joyce had not answered directly, and incensed at the Hacketts, "volcanoed" in New York, pouring forth an indig-

---

[5] *The Egoist* had announced in January that *A Portrait* would be published in March; it had, of course, already appeared in February.

nation that the Irish apparently reserve for the Irish. Attorney Quinn's fat packet included his letter of March 27, which explained the Hackett "infamy," and, as exhibits to be sent on to Joyce, Francis Hackett's review, a review by Quinn himself written for *Vanity Fair*,[6] and the correspondence with Byrne Hackett relating to his effort to purchase the proofsheets. (For Quinn's letter and the correspondence with Byrne Hackett, see Appendix B.) Upon receiving Joyce's and Quinn's letters, Pound, the hard-beset middleman, wrote Joyce a note enclosing the two reviews and promising to forward the rest of Quinn's letter after he had deciphered it and sorted it out. On the same day, Pound wrote to Quinn discussing Quinn's attack on Francis Hackett and explaining why he differed with the judgments Quinn had expressed in his own article (the sections of this letter relating to Joyce are printed here). Finally, on April 19, Pound sent to Joyce the letter he had received from Quinn and the correspondence with Byrne Hackett, along with his own comments on them.

A letter from Miss Weaver to Joyce of October 16, 1916 (at Cornell), explains who the Hacketts were and evidences their goodwill toward Joyce:

I have a letter ... from Mr. Byrne Hackett to whom Mr. Pound wrote originally and who brought your book to the notice of Mr. Huebsch. He writes that he considers Mr. Huebsch the best of the younger American publishers and by best he means the most imaginative honourable and resourceful. I gather that Mr. Hackett keeps a bookshop in connexion with the Yale University Press. He says that in his capacity of bookseller he will do all in his power for the success of the book and he also feels sure that his brother, who is literary editor of the New York *New Republic*, will review the book "at length and with discrimination." This should be a help for I think the journal has a large circulation. Mr. Hackett asks to be remembered to you though he thinks it quite likely that you will have no recollection of him. He says he was at Clongowes when you were but was an altogether obscure member of "first junior" at that time. He was unhappy at the school.

Before the incident of the proofsheets, Joyce had written to Byrne Hackett by way of Huebsch to thank him for his help. After

[6] "James Joyce, A New Irish Novelist," *Vanity Fair*, New York, May 1917.

the incident Huebsch, who had "the unpleasant task of standing between the two [Quinn and Hackett] while trying to serve your interests without taking sides in the controversy" cautioned Joyce "you should not in any way misjudge Mr. Hackett, who is honorable both in act and intent, and whose enthusiasm for your work has been effectively directed" (May 14, 1917, at Cornell). Quinn's rage and Pound's banter should be read against this background.[7]

18 April 1917 *London*

Dear Quinn: *The New Republic* has come. The title "Green Sickness" and the paragraph on "mortal sin" seem to me the two backhanders in the thing. Perhaps in less degree the phrasing, "never even thought of *plot* or importance of consulting the reader."

This latter paragraph and the one on Wells give Hackett away and should not harm Joyce.

The title is a dig. Some of the other things you have marked don't seem to me vicious. His saying that the novel is "unpleasant" is balanced by the next paragraph which says it has beauty and intensity (which is more than most reviewers would do, especially if they were disappointed novelists instead of being disappointees in other walks of litterchure).

I don't much like the opening sentence. However, the tribe of Gosse all think the public has to be apologized to for the existence of genius *in any form*. . . .

I am rereading your article on Joyce. Do send copies to official circles. Possibly to the English ambassador in Washington. It ought to do more good than anything else I have seen on Joyce. Good also to me, *The Egoist*, Picasso, etc.

Re what you say of the book's being most intelligible to Irish Catholics, did I write you that a female married to a Belgian said the whole thing was just as true of Belgium as of Ireland (with, of course, necessary substitutions in the matter of Parnell, etc.)?

I am neither Irish nor Catholic, but I have had more mediaeval contact than most, through Dante and my Provençal. I have read a 12th Century Provençal sermon about hell—same model as the one in *The Portrait*, same old hoax.

I don't put myself up as a sample of how the book will strike most people. But I do think Joyce has done his job so well and so thoroughly that he conveys the *milieu* of the book, and that an Irish

[7] For Joyce's replies to Quinn, *Letters of James Joyce*, II, pages 394–396.

Catholic with local knowledge has very little advantage over the outsider with good grounding in literature when it comes to understanding *The Portrait*.

(That sentence is written nearly as badly as some of Hackett's.) This may not be so. My uncle-in-law couldn't understand parts of the conversation, or at least found them difficult. And he is extremely well read. It may be my having read Dante and a few paragraphs of Richard St. Victor, and Guido Cavalcanti, that makes me so much readier to take in the novel than some other people seem to be.

I wonder if he *has* read Balzac many times. I read about a dozen books of Balzac's ten years ago, but I can't read him now.

I also wonder if he has read Flaubert and the de Goncourts, or if his hardness isn't a direct development from the love of hardness bred by reading Dante, or possibly in his case, Aquinas. (I have not read Aquinas, but I have looked through a good book of scholastic logic, by something-Agricola.)

His hardness is more like *La fille Elisa* [8] than anything of Balzac's, I think. . . .

Perhaps you'll be good enough to forward Joyce's question about his eyes to Gould, with the other data I sent you. That is, if Gould is still alive. Vide the end of Joyce's long letter enclosed.

More later.

18 April 1917   *5, Holland Place Chambers, Kensington. W.8*

Dear Joyce: Your letter and limerick arrived ten minutes ago. I am in the hell of a rush. Will transmit Quinn's £20 to or towards you today or tomorrow. They also have just arrived.

I enclose two press notices of your novel. Or rather one clipping and the proofs of Quinn's article. I have a long duplicate copy of a lot of his correspondence, swearing death and destruction to the whole Hackett family. I will forward it as soon as I can sort it out.

The underlinings in the New Republic articles are his, and put there to show me that F. H. is a swine etc.

Will answer your letter at leisure.

yours ever
Ezra Pound

[8] A monograph on prostitution and the penitentiary by Edmond de Goncourt, 1877.

Nobody can object to the sentiments on the back of the second page of Hacketts review of you, anyhow.

19 April 1917   *5, Holland Place Chambers, London W.8.*

Dear Joyce: From your excellent limerick, I judge that you are at any rate, feeling better. I mailed you a brief note in haste yesterday, containing two long American press cuttings. Both ought to sell copies of the Portrait. Especially Quinn's. You will see that he is very diffident about his unusual action [*longhand:* in writing it.]. I don't think he has ever burst out as a critic before. (The New Statesman review is also out, but I have not seen it. Miss Weaver writes me that it is "useful".

I will send the £20 tomorrow, as I couldn't get the bank to cash the draft at once.

/ / /

The long enclosed correspondence of Quinn and Hackett is a little obscure on hurried reading, but if one perseveres one discovers the facts.

1. Two days ago I got the enclosed cablegram from Quinn, saying he had had a "good letter from you" and that I was to disregard his allusion to you in his letter.
2. Letter arrived yesterday. He couldn't understand why you had replied via me instead of direct. . I have written him, that I supposed you thought it a courtesy to me. ? ? ? ? as I had introduced you to him.

Also he had not realized how long it takes letters to reach America, and had been irritated by not hearing from you.

The cable puts all that right, and you need not worry. I would not forward his letter if I did not think that you would be able to understand.

He is the busiest man in America, or one of the busiest, and as old father J. B. Yeats wrote long ago "the biggest hearted and most irascible". He isn't really irascible, but [*crossout:* too] impetuous.

It appears that Hackett having got your page of manuscript, and having no damn'd right to it whatever, tried amiably to collect a percentage of 50% on the sale of it to [*crossout:* him] Quinn.

110

With that fact in mind, the correspondence between Quinn and Hackett becomes lucid, more lucid than if one begins to read the correspondence without having a clear grip on the fact aforesaid.

Quinn has flayed Hackett. More completely was not Marsyas flayed of Apollo. He sends us the hide of the said Hackett, nicely dried, cured and burnished, that we may hang it upon our walls as a trophy.

> The ex-Irlandais that hight Hackett
> Attempted to purloin Joyce's jacket
>> But the Godly J. Quinn
>> Forestalled him in sin
> And purloined Hackett's hindpart to smack it.

I do not use these classic forms with your ease and felicity, but as Camoens says, it at least has the merit of relating to real events. The flaw being in the forced and poor rhyme on "jacket".

[*crossout:* Alia]
Aliter

> In a life so lacking in condiment
> I confess I am smitten with wonderment
>> At the curious neatness,
>> At the "lightness and sweetness"
> With which Q. has smacked Hackett's fundiment.

I hope to hear definitely that the magazine is settled. I wish I could put all my eggs into that one basket and not have to send stuff to anything else. And also that I could make the format big enough to hold "Ulysses", We must hope hard, and perhaps by the time "Ulysses" is complete, there may be pages enough. It is always well to desire the miracle.

The Duchess of Marlborough [9] is charming, diffident, or at least sensitive, and I liked her very much, so much that I shouldn't hesitate to tell her it was her duty to God and literature pay for the printing of another 16 pages a month . . . . IF I ever see her again. One can not ask such things of imbeciles. I dont know who else there

[9] Consuelo Vanderbilt, daughter of William Kissam Vanderbilt of New York, Duchess of Marlborough 1895–1921.

is. I know a few people would [*sic:?* who] would help, and a few of good will.

/ / /

Yes. Thanks for your note saying you will collaborate in the review. Did I say "thank you" yesterday. If not accept the delayed acknowledgement.

I have forwarded your letter to me, to Quinn, as I had sent on the other letter about your eyes to him. He being nearer Gould than I am. If Gould is dead, we can count on Quinn's doing all that can be done toward getting expert opinion.

I hope to send you Eliot's poems in a few weeks. He has burst out into scurrilous french during the past few weeks, too late for his book, which is in the press, but the gallicism should enrich the review. He is "just as bad" as if he had been to Clongowes. But it is perilous trying to manipulate a foreign language.

I feel Lewis' definition of me as a "pantechnicon" becoming daily more apt. I hope however to do, still, a few decent things of my own. If those brutes in Chicago would only get on with my long poem, I would send that also for your perusal. Very shaggy, and lacking in Gautier's perfection of neatness. Helas, Helas and yet again "Vae, vae rustici." (rustico?) It IS dangerous trying to use a foreign tongue that one never knew save in a sloppy, lopsided fashion.

I seem to have been playing on this keyboard since 9. p.m. Tuesday. It is now Thursday. Basta.

yours ever
Ezra Pound

Quinn agreed to back *The Little Review*, and the two-year tenure of the "pantechnicon" began with the May 1917 issue. Quinn and three of his friends staked the magazine to $1600 a year for two years, and Pound to $750 a year ($300 for his editorial duties, $450 for contributors). In a May letter Pound explained to Margaret Anderson his policy on patronage and his determination to use Quinn's money only as artists absolutely needed it:

> The point is that if I accept more than I *need* I at once become a sponger, and I at once lose my integrity. By doing

the job for the absolute minimum I remain respectable and when I see something I want I can ask for it. I mean to say, as things stand I can ask for money when Joyce finishes his next novel or if Hueffer ever gets his *real* book finished.

If I began by blowing 1500 dollars and did no more than I shall now do with 750 I should feel a mucker and there would be nothing ahead.

My whole position and the whole backing up of my statement that the artist is "almost" independent goes with doing the thing as nearly as possible without "money."

Pound's position, to which he stuck, sounds fresh and heroic fifty years later.

Pound accepted the post of London editor with an editorial and was represented by a pseudonymous adaptation from Jules Laforgue and his satirical sketch "Jodindranath Mawhwor's Occupation." Joyce was represented by his note of April 9, Eliot by a satirical piece, "Eeldrop and Appleplex," and Lewis by the first of his imaginary letters to Mrs. Bland Burn, which Pound later continued. But although he was now entrenched in *The Egoist* and *The Little Review*, these very successes, on the heels of his varied activities of 1916, produced in the "pantechnicon" misgivings about devoting so much energy to his extra-literary work. Lewis had written prophetically in *Blast*, II (July 1915, page 82), of American art: "when it comes, will be Mongol, inhuman, optimistic, and very much on the precious side, as opposed to European pathos and solidity." Pound, successor to the Red Indian, Poe, Whistler, Henry James, and Walt Whitman, is denominated "Demon pantechnicon driver, busy with removal of old world into new quarters. In his steel net of impeccable technique he has lately caught Li Po. Energy of a discriminating element." Lewis later extended his prophecy to include Pound in the category "revolutionary simpleton."

Pound was becoming acutely aware of his style and of conflicts in himself between modernism and passéism. The reference to Théophile Gautier recalls that Pound and Eliot were then using the tight quatrains of *Emaux et Camées* and the Bay State Hymn Book as antidotes to undisciplined *vers libre* (Pound probably began *Mauberley* in 1916). The reference in the next letter to the Irishman Stephen Dedalus's use of the Anglo-Saxon word "tundish," or candle-holder, which makes Stephen aware of the tyranny of the

113

English language over him and of the irony that he has a deeper sense of its tradition than does the prefect of studies, a native Englishman who has become a Jesuit convert, is a compliment to Joyce "the stylist" but also hints at an admiring envy. Pound had expressed dissatisfaction about the "shaggy," unmusical version of the three cantos which were about to appear in *Poetry*; in his May 18 letter he worries about not doing more original and contemporaneous work. These strains, which persist throughout 1917 and 1918, foreshadow more acute uncertainties about himself and his work during 1919–1920. Further cause for frustration was the paucity of new poetry, which is perhaps ironically reflected by his "*too large* vol. of 'poems since 1912' " (he was preparing an American edition of *Lustra*). Actually, it collected work from before 1911, and it included little new work since the London *Lustra* of 1916, except for the three cantos—which he revised even as they were appearing in *Poetry*.

7 May 1917   *5 Holland Place Chambers, Kensington. W.8.*

Dear Mrs Joyce: I am very sorry to hear that James' (it seems foolish to call him "Mr Joyce" to you, after so long a correspondence with him) eyes have gone bad again.

There wouldn't have been time to get Dr Gould's advice in any case, but there has been some delay, for Mr Quinn happened to know Gould's enemies, those who misunderstood his book about Lafcadio Hearn. I enclose Quinn's letter. His view of Gould is, I am quite convinced, wrong, and I have written to tell him so. I gather from it that Gould is still alive, however, and will write to him. I doubt if anyone could prescribe at such distance, but Gould is interested in literature and would, I think, do all he could.

My books are coming out in New York, not Chicago, so also the magazine. The fund's are assured for one year and I think for two. I hope we'll be able to print "Ulysses" when finished. It could appear both in the "Egoist" and in the "Little Review" and J. J. would get double fees.

I have a good set of Yeats' poems for the June number. The review will be sent you direct from America.

Miss Weaver had a bundle of the American press notices of "The Portrait". The book is certainly launched. I dont think anyone has been so well received since Butler's "The Way of ALL Flesh".

A book of this sort does not sell with whoop of a detective story, but it should go on selling. Jean de Bosschere [1] writes me a card after beginning to read it. As follows:

J'ai lu une centaine de pages de l'admirable livre de Joyce. Charles Louis Phillipe [2] n'a pas fait de mieux. Joyce le depasse par le style qui n'est plus *le* style. Cette nudite de tout ornement rhetorique, de toute forme ideomatique (malgré le plus stricte sévérité contre le detour ou l'esthetique) et beaucoup d'autres qualités fondementales font de ce livre l'oeuvre le plus sérieux en anglais que j'ai lu. Les soixante premiers pages sont incomparables.

Your husband's work will be appreciated where ever there is intelligence. Unfortunately the world is largely inhabited by imbeciles.

Miss Weaver is, I think, trying to get special permission to send some press notices. It is against the general regulations.

I dont know what the press can say that they haven't said already. So far as press notices can make a book, the "Portrait" is "made". And J. J. may derive what satisfaction he can from it. He knew the work was good, or at least he ought to have known, if he didn't. I wish he were here in London, but I know there is no use in urging it.

I shall go to the Lago di Garda after the war, unless I am destroyed, and I shall manage to pass through Zurich or Italy redeemed or wherever J. J. is at that time.

I dont know what other news there is. I am now "London Editor" of the Little Review. I hope Eliot will be made a Contributing Editor on the Egoist, as it would greatly strengthen the paper, and also give us two "organs" for the expression of such sense as we've got.

I hope James will get through the beastly operation with all possible luck. My wife joins me in sending best wishes to you, le pere de famille, and the offspring, (or possibly "springs", in the plural,) submit that point to the stylist. *I* had never heard of a "tundish."

Yours ever
Ezra Pound

14 May 1917   *5, Holland Place Chambers, Kensington. W.8.*

Dear Mrs Joyce: I hasten to enclose the letter from Mr Quinn. It explains itself.

[1] Jean De Bosschère, French artist, illustrator, and poet who had moved to London; he collaborated with Pound, wrote on Pound's poetry, and contributed to *The Little Review*.

[2] French novelist, author of *Bubu de Montparnasse* (1901) and other realistic novels about the sufferings of the poor.

115

I think James should take up any further American business through Mr Quinn.

I am writing this in great haste as I have a full day before me.

I am sorry the exchange on Quinn's cheque for £100 only came to 480 francs. It might have been a few more if it had gone direct from New York. But it is too late to worry over it.

I hope James is doing well.

Yours ever
Ezra Pound

Enclosure

28 April 1917   *31 Nassau Street, New York*

My dear Pound: I received your cable this morning reading as follows:

"Quinn, 31 Nassau Street, New York,
    Drop small Maynard.

Pound." [3]

Answer: "They are dropped."

I am sending Knopf a copy of your cable. So much for that.

I got a letter from Little, Brown & Company, Publishers of Boston, April 27. I enclose you a copy of it. You will see that they have read my article in Vanity Fair on Joyce and that they noticed the statement that he had written a play.

I prefer a New York publisher to a Boston. I hope Joyce has not committed himself to young Huebsch about his play. I suggest that you tip him a word of warning not to make any arrangement with any publisher without consulting me. God knows I don't want any more troubles or irons in the fire, but Joyce is worth while, is worth making an exception of.

I hope his eyes are better.

I send you a copy of this letter so you can send it to him if you wish. Huebsch does not specialize on plays. The best man for plays would be a man who would be anxious to get Joyce now that he has made a success with the portrait. If he would try the MacMillan

---

[3] Small Maynard & Co. of Boston had been Pound's American publisher since 1910; he shifted to Alfred A. Knopf for *Lustra*.

Company I could sweat terms out of them, but I am not advising, I am only suggesting.

Yours very truly
J Q

18 May 1917   *5, Holland Place Chambers, Kensington. W.8.*

Dear Joyce: I have written to Dr Gould direct. But heaven knows what he will be able to do at such a distance. He may perhaps know who is who among continental oculists, anyhow.

Your mss. of 1st. act is here, and I will forward it.

I have had a flurried week, correcting proofs of my *too large* vol. of "poems since 1912", and getting off stuff for July number of the magazine. Have another lot of Yeats, and Lady Gregory says there is a one act play of hers that we can have. Probably it is too long.

I am glad at least that you can see again, for a while any how.

I don't think any novel has had such a press as the Portrait, for god knows how long. Whether it is better to starve celebrated or uncelebrated must be left for the learned casuists to decide. The former is perhaps more dramatic (stasis, no kinesis,) the latter more depressing (squashis.)

I purchased the Dictionnaire de Bayle,[4] four huge folios for a guinea on Wednesday, it throws no light on the subject.

I brought it from Tottenham Court Rd. in a huge sacking sack to the amusement of several french jewesses and other females en passant.

Let us hope it will form a suitable cornerstone for the review. It accrues from the subscriptions lying loose in my pocket.

Also found six vols. of "Poètes François jusqu'à Malherbe", 5/ yesterday. Half vol. of troubadours whom I was seeking in vain.

I have found a cellist with an incapacitated arm, and hope to do another job on the 12 century music. Rummel and I brought out 12 reconstructed troubadour tunes five years ago.[5]

---

[4] Pierre Bayle, *Dictionnaire historique et critique,* 1695–1697, enlarged 1702.

[5] *Hesternae Rosae,* 1912, nine songs for which Walter Morse Rummel did the musical arrangements and Pound the English renderings. Two songs by Arnaut Daniel were supplied by Pound from manuscripts in the Milan Library; the next paragraph suggests that Pound had obtained others as well. "Unfinished and rejected books" probably refers to work on Daniel that had appeared in "I Gather the Limbs of Osiris," *The New Age,* 1911–1912; Pound had doubtless expanded this material for a book by Swift & Co., with whom he had signed a ten-year con-

117

I have my own unfinished and rejected books, and also Miss Hullah's [6] unfinished work and reproductions of the milan mss. to go on. Destroyed a lot of my own notes four years ago when Swift and Co. failed (at which time I was damn glad NOT to have to publish a book I had contracted to finish.).

Am at present swamped in scholarly works, and feeling dam'd ignorant.

The Little Review will be sent you from America. I hope you'll find some entertainment in it.

I suppose I ought to do "original work", ma che. As Vildrac said to me some years ago, speaking as if of some unheard of and lunar form of existence "Ce serait très agréable passer sa vie en faisant ces études comme ça."

Some of the Provençal music and word consonance is exquisite. Even my dialogues for the Review are "passéist" in the extreme.[7] I hope to send you Eliot's little book in a week or so.

I hope the warm weather will really solve your eye trouble.

With best wishes

Ezra Pound

This sottisier, the criticism of Joyce's critics promised in Pound's letter of March 28, appeared in the June 1917 *Egoist*.

JAMES JOYCE AND HIS CRITICS [8]

Some Classified Comments

Caution: It is very difficult to know quite what to say about this new book by Mr. Joyce.—*Literary World*.

Drains: Mr. Joyce is a clever novelist, but we feel he would be really at his best in a treatise on drains.—*Everyman*.

Cleanmindedness: This pseudo-autobiography of Stephen Dedalus, a weakling and a dreamer, makes fascinating reading.... No clean-minded person could possibly allow it to remain within reach of his wife, his sons or daughters.—*Irish Book Lover*.

tract in 1911; they had published *The Sonnets and Ballate of Guido Cavalcanti* and *Ripostes,* but the firm had failed. Pound worked extensively on Daniel during 1917 but did not publish his work until *Instigations,* 1920.

[6] Probably Annette Hullah, writer on music, related to John Pyke Hullah (1812–1884), prominent nineteenth-century British musician and theorist who popularized music education.

[7] "An Anachronism at Chinon," in which Pound first published his invocation of the Rabelais-Joyce of *Ulysses, The Little Review,* June 1917, and "Aux Étuves de Weisbaden, A.D. 1451," July 1917.

[8] *The Egoist,* IV, 5 (June 1917), page 74.

OPPORTUNITIES OF DUBLIN: If one must accuse Mr. Joyce of anything, it is that he too wilfully ignores the opportunities which Dublin offers even to a Stephen Dedalus. . . . He has undoubtedly failed to bring out the undeniable superiority of many features of life in the capital. . . . He is as blind to the charm of its situation as to the stirrings of literary and civic consciousness which give an interest and zest to social and political intercourse.—*New Ireland.*

BEAUTY: There is much in the book to offend a good many varieties of readers, and little compensating beauty.—*New York Globe.*

The most obvious thing about the book is its beauty.—*New Witness.*

STYLE: It is possible that the author intends to write a sequel to the story. If so, he might acquire a firmer, more coherent and more lucid style by a study of Flaubert, Daudet, Thackeray and Thomas Hardy.—*Rochester (New York) Post-Express.*

The occasional lucid intervals in which one glimpses imminent setting forth of social elements and forces in Dublin, only to be disappointed, are similar to the eye or ear which appears in futurist portraits, but proves the more bewildering because no other recognizable feature is to be discerned among the chaos.—*Bellman* (U.S.A.). [*Editor's Note:* In the sentence quoted above, "lucid intervals" is to be parsed with "are similar" and "eye or ear" with "proves." The adjective "recognizable" is apparently pleonastic.]

REALISM: It is a ruthless, relentless essay in realism.—*Southport Guardian.*

To put the literary form of rude language in a book makes some authors feel realistic.—*Manchester Weekly Times.*

Mr. Joyce aims at being realistic, but his method is too chaotic to produce the effect of realism.—*Rochester (New York) Post-Express.*

Its realism will displease many.—*Birmingham Post.*

Mr. Joyce is unsparing in his realism, and his violent contrasts —the brothel, the confessional—jar on one's finer feelings.—*Irish Book Lover.*

The description of life in a Jesuit school, and later in a Dublin college, strikes one as being absolutely true to life—but what a life!—*Everyman.*

WISDOM: Is it even wise, from a worldly point of view—mercenary, if you will—to dissipate one's talents on a book which can only attain a limited circulation?—*Irish Book Lover.*

ADVANTAGES OF IRISH EDUCATION: One boy from Clongowes School is not a replica of all the other boys. I will reintroduce Mr.

119

Wells to half a dozen Irish "old boys" of whom five—Sir Arthur Conan Doyle is one—were educated at Roman Catholic schools and have nevertheless become most conventional citizens of the Empire. —*Sphere.*

COMPARISON WITH OTHER IRISH AUTHORS: The book is not within a hundred miles of being as fine a work of art as "Limehouse Nights," the work of another young Irishman.—*Sphere.*

There are a good many talented young Irish writers to-day, and it will take a fellow of exceptional literary stature to tower above Lord Dunsany, for example, or James Stephens.—*New York Globe.*

IMAGINATION: He shows an astonishingly un-Celtic absence of imagination and humour.—*Bellman* (U.S.A.).

RELIGION: The irreverent treatment of religion in the story must be condemned.—*Rochester* (*New York*) *Post-Express.*

TRUTH: It is an accident that Mr. Joyce's book should have Dublin as its background.—*Freeman's Journal* (Dublin).

He is justified, in so far as too many Dubliners are of the calibre described in this and the preceding volume.—*New Ireland.*

27 June 1917   *5, Holland Place Chambers, Kensington. W.*

Dear Joyce: At last a note from Dr. Gould. All he can say is that you "should have gone to some trustworthy ophthalamic surgeon and been treated perhaps operated upon". [*longhand:* which you have.] And that if it is not too late it would be well even now to see Sir Anderson Critchett, in London. At this day even it is possible that operation might save some remnant of vision".

Evidently I wrote while you were at your worst. I dont know anything more about Critchett. Gould's note has just come.

I should think your people in Zurich were probably all right. Your man has pulled you through the worst phase.

Gould's note would simply seem to encourage you to stand the operation if your Zurich man thinks it necessary. (I trust a good deal to old Eden having been ready to go to Zurich.)

Critchett is almost sure to be up to his ears in war cases.

[*longhand:* Have been writing ebulliently for days & feel like a dry sponge. Hence the brevity of this.]

Yours ever
Ezra Pound
Amitiés à madame.

[*longhand:* P.S. I don't know whether you get "Poetry" & the "Little Review". Poetry is serializing the first 3 cantos of my long poem—but I have since revised and cut out [*crossout:* 6 of] shortened 24 pages to 18—so would rather you judged it from the forthcoming £ [9] volume—if you can wade through it at all.]

yrs
E. P.

Pound's next letter is doubtless a reply to one of Joyce's "very poetical epistles," as he once called them, perhaps a version of his letter to Quinn of July 10 summarizing thirteen years of torture at the hands of publishers and the public. It must also have referred to Grant Richards's decision to publish *Exiles;* a contract was signed in August and the play was published in May 1918 by Richards in London and Huebsch in New York. The hope proffered that editor Henry Davray of the *Mercure de France* might review *A Portrait* is more encouragement than expectation; Pound asked Miss Weaver to send Davray a copy but told her he did not count on him.

17 July 1917   *5, Holland Place Chambers, Kensington. W.8.*

My Dear Job: You will establish an immortal record. At what period the shift of terminal sound in your family name occurred I am unable to state, but the -yce at the end is an obvious error. The arumaic -b, simply -b is obviously the correct spelling. Possibly an intermediate form Jobce can be unearthed, but the line of your descent from the patriarch is indisputable.

I did not in the least gather that the mss. of your play was for typing in New York. I supposed that it was solely to be sold to Quinn as a manuscript. He writes me that he has sent you an advance on it. I did not hurry to send on the second and third act, as he would presumably have accepted my receipt of them, and they could have gone with more surety later.

He now writes me ten pages of biography to the effect that he can not undertake to see the mss. typed and corrected. He is busier than even I knew, and I doubt if anyone would undertake such a responsibility. It would certainly be MUCH simpler to have the typescript duplicated here from the existing type-script.

Either Knopf or Huebsch saw the typescript of the play when it

[9] The American edition of *Lustra,* but also Pound's monogram for his name. See Introduction, pages 13–14. For Pound the man equals the book.

was in America, and declined it. I dont know which, and it means reading through 150 typesheets of Quinns correspondence to find out. I dare say he has written you direct.

At this moment I lift my typing fingers with extreme weariness. Only your letter is just here this a.m. and I dont want to delay answering as much of it as I can manage.

I am afraid the Little Review cant cope with music. At least not for a year or two. I dont think it is the right medium for publishing music. Maybe I can find out what is. I haven't been in touch with musicians for several years, but given time I might [crossout: cope wi] manage the matter.

Did I write you that I met Davray of the Mercure de France, and that he promised to review you in it when he gets leisure from his national work.?

/ / /

I wish I believed more in "Exiles", but damn it all, I dont think it up to the rest of your stuff. I dont of course know what infamous contract Richards lured you into. I think you had as well get the play printed on any terms you can get, (i.e. so long as it costs you nothing. There is a limit of author's tolerance of publishers' swindling.). Still I dont believe anybody will make anything [insert: cash] out of the play in book form. Or that it will build up your position, or help your next novel.

On the other hand it will ease your mind to have it in print, and off your chest.

I hope to God you wont try to read my beastly [insert: long] poem in "Poetry", I have revised the whole thing, and it is at least better than it was, and will appear in my American edition, which you will receive, if it, you, and I survive till late autumn.

As for mellifluous archaism, I am reduced to mistranslating Horace:

O cruel until now, mighty in Venus' gifts,
When unexpected falls thy feathery pride,
And all the locks, that hide
Thy shoulders now, be shent;
And colour that outdoes the Punic rose
Show but an ashen face, O Liguriné,
Thou shalt say,
To see thyself so altered in thy glass,
"Alas, the day!
"Why had I of these thoughts no trace

122

"In youth ; or why, today,
"These thoughts that have no face?" [1]

Has Miss Weaver sent you Eliot's booklet, and do you like it?
I must rouse myself and take this to the post.

Yours ever
Ezra Pound

15 August 1917   *5, Holland Place Chambers, Kensington. W.*

Dear Joyce: I am still buried in work. Museum and outpouring of articles and trying to finish prose book of criticisms, etc. etc.

The enclosed has just come. *I* haven't any other copy of "Exiles", compared or otherwise.

/ / / /

Re/your last letter, or the last I remember. I think you are a blind idealist believing in ubiquitous intelligence among men. How many intelligent people do you think there are in England and America?

If *you will* write for the intelligent, how THE HELL do you expect your books to sell by the 100,000? ? ? ? ? ?

I will write to Pinker, re/Exiles, and if there is a spare copy, it can go to N. York at once.

yours ever
Ezra Pound

[*longhand:* enclosed cablegram from Quinn]

Enclosure (cablegram)

15 AUGUST 1917

TO: EZRA POUND. 5 HOLLAND PLACE CHAMBERS. KENSINGTON. LDN.

ACTS TWO THREE EXILES RECEIVED PLEASE SEND COMPARED TYPED COPY QUICKLY SUGGEST CHANGE FULL OFT PAGE ONE SIX TWO KNOPFS EDITION LINE EIGHT [2] TO OFTEN DISLIKE WORD THRICE LINE ONE PAGE ONE SEVEN ONE SUGGEST CABLING ALTERNATIVE READING

JOHN QUINN

Joyce's anxiety about *Exiles* had by 1917 become an obsession. Pound had been helping to seek a producer or a publisher since 1915, when he had written "Mr James Joyce and the Modern

[1] Horace, *Carmina,* IV, 10.

[2] Quinn, turned literary critic, refers to Pound's "The Seafarer," "In icy feathers full oft the eagle screamed," *Lustra.* New York, 1917, page 162, and to "Salve Pontifex (A.C.S.)," "The wonder of the thrice encinctured mystery," page 171.

123

Stage." He had had flurries of correspondence with Pinker, as well as Joyce, and he had tried to interest the Oliver Morosco Company, Yeats, the Stage Society, and Arthur Knoblock in producing it; Pinker had been circulating the play in England, and Quinn in America. Throughout, there had been a shortage of typescripts. Quinn had bought Joyce's manuscript and Pound had forwarded it, piecemeal and with misunderstandings, but Quinn needed a typescript to show to publishers. When Quinn cabled Pound to send a "compared typed copy" and Joyce sent the cable that occasioned the following letter, Pound was in the midst of preparing a collection of his essays of 1913–1917, *Pavannes and Divisions* (published by Knopf in 1918, it included "Dubliners and Mr James Joyce" and "Meditatio"). Understandably, Pound neared the end of his patience—he once said that he had been born more patient than an elephant: "You mightn't think it, but when I lose patience something is LOST. It ain't that thur waren't any" (*Letters*, page 253). What Pound did not know was that Joyce had collapsed on August 18 from an attack of glaucoma.

Joyce commemorated the *Exiles* imbroglio with a limerick "written in dark":

John Quinn

There's a donor of lavish largesse
Who once bought a play in MS
    He found out what it all meant
    By the final instalment
But poor Scriptor was left in a mess.[3]

23 August 1917   *5, Holland Place Chambers, Kensington. W.*

Dear Joyce: I cant understand your telegram, and have just telegraphed you asking "WHAT do you want cash".

The cheap rates (4d and 4½ d. per word) to New York are "off". It is now a shilling a word, and that seems rather high until one has some conception of what is meant.

The telegram from you reads, as rec'd

"Cable Quinn confirm (sic. confrin) or remit you telegraphically nothing here remitting".

                                             Joyce.

[3] Herbert Gorman, *James Joyce,* illustrated with photographs, New York, Rinehart and Company, Inc., 1939, 1948, page 249. *Letters of James Joyce,* II, page 406.

I couldn't understand his cable to you either. Is the play being printed in New York? ? ? ? Or what the deuce do they want with corrections cabled? ? ? ? ? Pinker's office has just told me over the phone, that they know nothing about any American printing of it. Surely Grant Richards' sheets can be sent to America, or at least an American edition could be set up from them,

IF you merely want Quinn to send on the cash for mss. of play. I will cable him something comprehensible to that effect.

Its the "confirm or remit" that I can't "get".
Manuscript or cash or WHAT? ? ? ? ?

And what about the last "remitting" in your telegram. If you have nothing, What are you remitting? ? ?)

I am probably very stupid, but I do not understand.

If you are broke, WHY didn't you let me know you were *approaching* that state, and I would have acted with due palatial deliberation.

I have written to Yeats who is in France, re the copy of the play he had. BUT I thought it had gone to Stage Society.

Pinkers letter in reply to my question re/copies of mss. of Exile, merely said he had only one copy which he was showing to someone at your order.

Yours ploddingly
Ezra Pound

10 September 1917   *5, Holland Place Chambers, Kensington. W.*

Dear Mrs Joyce: I am relieved to hear that the operation has been, I presume, successful. At least you say there are no complications.

You will have rec'd the £10 telegraphed by the Egoist, and I suppose by now, at any rate, the £25 mailed from New York [longhand: on Aug. 20]. At any rate a letter posted there has [*insert:* on Aug. 25] reached me, so you should be getting Mr Quinn's cheque by the time you get this.

The Egoist is going to serialize Ulysses, that much you can tell James. So long as he gets paid fairly soon I don't suppose it matters what month the actual printing of the story begins. The Little Review [*crossout:* will] [*insert:* is ready to] hold down the American copyright for him, and print to synchronize with Egoist. All I can promise is £25 extra, but I can presumably pay that fairly early in the year. At least as soon as I get my second year's money for the Little Review. I also presume I can add another £25. At least I have offered for sale some old Spanish manuscripts. Autographs of King Ferdinand and Queen Isabella, dated 1492. Which ought to provide funds, even if I do not succeed in raising them in any other way.

Still I simply can not PROMISE. The things aren't sold *yet*. And I wont promise things that arent dead certain.

Still I think the chances of James getting £100 altogether for [*longhand:* serial rights to] "Ulysses" (or as much of it as printers will print) are fairly good.

The Little Review will have to add about 16 pages per month. Which means increase of printing bill, all of which I have to bear in mind.

The autographs sound like a fairy story, but they ain't. Also the magazine, despite its smallness, is beginning to be noticed seriously. Yeats, Hueffer, Arthur Symons, Lady Gregory, Lewis, Eliot, the editors, James problematically, DeGourmont (represented by a letter he wrote me shortly before his death) begin to make a fairly sound list of contributors.

I will, of course, let James know the moment there is a CERTAINTY of his getting £50 from the Little Review. That's the best I can do. The Egoist thinks March will suit them to start the serial, IF it is ready. But they or I or someone could *probably* send an advance as soon as the type-script arrives.

Can anything be done about sending a typed copy of "Exiles" to Mr Quinn. SOON? Or perhaps Grant Richards have got it set up and could send proof sheets? ?

Oh well. I hope the worst days are over. If I can get the review really established, I hope the few real authors will be permanently out of danger from starvation, at any rate.

I had a letter from the friend who helped with the first grant to James, she says she will try for another, but success is not by any means sure. Still he has made friends by his work, and he is not so isolated as he was a few years ago. So if his eyes can be got right, the future should not be impossible, but should steadily brighten.

I hope you are past the worst worry from the operation, and that children are well.

Sincerely yours
Ezra Pound

25 September 1917   *5, Holland Place Chambers, Kensington. W.8.*
[*longhand:* W.8 not S.W.]

Dear Mrs Joyce: I am relieved and very glad to hear that Quinn's cheque has arrived in time, and that you wont have further worry about it, or be delayed in getting off. I hope the Egoist cheques came in time to bridge over the wait.

And having the operation over must also be a relief, especially as I suppose it definitely settles the question of James' eyesight.

You needn't have bothered about the 5/. I wish I could be more flamboyant re/the Little Review and make stronger promises, but anyhow there'll be £25, and I think the rest of the fifty will turn up.

I am afraid there is small chance of a grant, however. Marsh says the government fund can only be applied on the same person once in three years.

Gosse has written a killing letter, professing his willingness to help, but stating that his connection ended when Asquith left office. He continues, verbatim

"I am unacquainted with the present Prime Minister"

I can hear Gosse's snuffy voice sniffing the syllables.

Yeats was in town for a day or so, but I haven't had the opportunity of talking to him of the matter.

I didn't make out from James' last letter whether Ulysses was so far finished that it would be ready with the New Year in spite of his operation, or whether the operation will have put it off for another three months.

Lewis' novel "Tarr" is to be published in America, I think our generation is getting a rather stronger grip on publishers "in general", and that the backbone of the opposition is weakening a bit.

I think there is also the chance of a collection of my prose being done. (including one or two of my notes on "The Portrait".)

I wonder have any copies of the Little Review reached you?? It should have been sent from New York.

Yeats has another book of poems in the press at Cuala, containing the 15 we have printed in the L.R.

I dont know that there's much else to be said. I am doing a series of satires on English Magazines,[4] and it is a fairly amusing lark, I dont know whether the solemn quarterlies or the "popular" weeklies are the more ludicrous.

Greetings to Giorgio and Lucia,

Ever yrs
Ezra Pound

Joyce finished the first chapters of *Ulysses* at Locarno, where he had gone to recover from his eye operation. He sent to Pound in December the first chapters of the work Pound later called "an epoch-making report on the state of the human mind in the twentieth century."

19 December 1917 [5]   (*London*)

Dear Joyce: Pages 1–17, in duplicate rec'd. Since you will get yourself reviewed in modern Greek and thereby suggest new spellings of the name Daedalus. All I can say is Echt Dzoice, or Echt Joice, or however else you like it.

The opening is echt Joice. There was a passage on page three that made me question it for a moment, but I cant, on rereading find anything wrong.

Then the going gets too serious for me to prattle into criticism. I think it is the only youth that has ever been written down. At least, if the thing has been done in French the nationality is too different for me to feel the same thing in the same way.

In one or two places your actual writing suggests De Gourmont to me. I say this neither as praise nor the reverse.

---

[4] "Studies in Contemporary Mentality," twenty installments, *The New Age*, August 1917 through January 1918. Pound later considered the series his Flaubertian *sottisier*, "Date Line," *Make It New*, 1934, pages 16–17; *Literary Essays*, pages 83–84.

[5] *Letters of James Joyce*, II, pages 413–414. The last four paragraphs are reproduced photographically in Patricia Hutchins, *James Joyce's World*, London: Methuen and Co., Ltd., 1957, page 118.

I wonder about the adjective 'merry' in 'merry over the sea' page 8. And the movement of the sentence. 'another now yet the same'.

Also 'fro' and 'glow' in paragraph 4 of that page, look like an accidental rhyme.[6]

I suppose we'll be damn well suppressed if we print the text as it stands. BUT it is damn wellworth it. I see no reason why the nations should sit in darkness merely because Anthony Comstock[7] was horrified at the sight of his grandparents in copulation, and there after ran wode in a loin cloth.

Your 17 pages have no division marks. Unless this is the first month's lot, instead of the first three months, as you wrote it would be, I shall divide on page 6. after the statement that the Sassenach wants his bacon. and at the very top of page 12.

Hope to forward a few base sheckles in a few days time. Wall, Mr. Joice, I recon your a damn fine writer, that's what I recon'. An' I recon' this here work o' yourn is some concarn'd litterchure. You can take it from me, an' I'm a jedge.

I have been doing ten and twelve hours a day on Arnaut Daniel, which some lunatick clerk in orders wants to private print in Cleveland Oo.[8] I have for the time being reduced myself chiefly to a rhyming dictionary of all the ornrey terminations in the language. Some of the stuff is at least better than the bloody mess I made of my first attempt, five years ago.

Lewis is to paint gunpits for the Canadian records. It will get him out of the firing line for a few months. Thank God.

Let me sink into slumber.

yours ever

EZRA POUND

Pound sent the first two episodes off to *The Little Review* with a eulogistic note. Margaret Anderson cited Pound in *The Little Review's* announcement in January that *Ulysses* would be serialized:

[6] The phrases are in *Ulysses,* page 11. They ultimately read: "Warm sunshine merrying over the sea." "I am another now and yet the same." "In the gloomy domed living-room of the tower Buck Mulligan's gowned form moved briskly about the hearth to and fro, hiding and revealing its yellow glow."

[7] Anthony Comstock (1844–1915), American crusader for moral rectitude and reform, responsible for postal laws against obscene literature (the "Comstock Laws"); "comstockery" became a butt for Shaw, Mencken, and others. Comstock founded the New York Society for the Suppression of Vice, which instigated the prosecutions of *Ulysses,* 1919–1921.

[8] Rev. C. C. Bubb, 2077 E. 36th St., Cleveland, Ohio. Pound sent a typescript to "Clark's Press," but it disappeared. "Arnaut Daniel" appeared in *Instigations,* 1920.

It is, I believe, even better than the Portrait.

So far it has been read by only one critic of international reputation. He says: "It is certainly worth running a magazine if one can get stuff like this to put in it. Compression, intensity. It looks to me rather better than Flaubert."

This announcement means that we are about to publish a prose masterpiece.

Pound was "*Ulysses* editor" for more than three years; he continued to receive it episode by episode through "Circe," 1921, before Shakespeare and Company published the famous first edition in 1922. Publication began in *The Little Review* in March 1918 and continued with few lapses until the issue of September-December 1920. In all, thirteen episodes and part of a fourteenth ("Telemachus" through "The Oxen of the Sun") were printed before *The Little Review* was enjoined from further printing because of "obscenity" in "Nausikaa." *The Egoist* managed to print five small selections from four episodes in 1919, but the English printer prevented further publication in England.

Pound had written to Mencken on January 18, 1918, "Joyce's new novel has a corking 1st. Chap. (which will get us suppressed), not such a good second one." His reaction to episode four, "Calypso," was influenced by the first suppression of *The Little Review*, November 1917, over the alleged indecency of Wyndham Lewis's story "Cantleman's Spring Mate." In deciding against *The Little Review* Judge Augustus Hand argued that while free expression can be countenanced in the classics because they have few readers, there is no certainty that modern works won't be read by all who smell pornography. Pound ridiculed Judge Hand's opinion in "The Classics 'Escape'" (March 1918), citing for the first of many times the central text of his protest, subsection 211 of the U.S. Penal Code, which lumps together "obscene" literature and information about contraceptives and abortion. "I confess to having been a bad citizen," he quipped acidly, "to just the extent of having been ignorant that at any moment my works might be classed in the law's eye with the inventions of the late Dr. Condom." He climaxed his scorn with his well-known epigram "Cantico del Sole" ("The thought of what America would be like If the classics had a wide circulation Troubles my sleep," etc.). Nevertheless, as an editor Pound had to be practical—especially when he had misgivings about Joyce's art.

PUBLISHED MONTHLY.
YEARLY SUBSCRIPTION 7/-

7-6-1918

THE LITTLE REVIEW

London Office :—5, HOLLAND PLACE CHAMBERS, W. 8.

Contributors 1917-18.
W. B. Yeats
Ford Madox Hueffer
Arthur Symons
Wyndham Lewis
James Joyce
T. S. Eliot
Lady Gregory
Arthur Waley
May Sinclair
" Jh."
Margaret Anderson
(EDITOR)
Ezra Pound
(*Foreign Editor*)

Books on art, poetry,
criticism of literature,
belles lettres received
for review.

No responsibility can
be accepted for un-
solicited manuscripts.

Good Friday [29 March] 1918, 12.07 a.m.
Dear Joyce: As I wrote this a.m. or yesterday, we have got your first installment into print. 30 copies have reached me here. I suppose we'll be suppressed. The Egoist printers wont set up the stuff at all. I dont mind suppression for the first chapter. Its worth it.

Section 4. has excellent things in it; but you overdo the matter. Leave the stool to Geo. Robey. He has been doing "down where the asparagus grows, for some time.

I think certain things simply bad writing, in this section. Bad because you waste the violence. You use a stronger word than you need, and this is bad art, just as any needless superlative is bad art.

The contrast between Blooms [*insert:* interior] poetry and his outward surroundings is excellent, but it will come up without such detailed treatment of the dropping feces.

Quinn is already in a rage over my reference to the late Doctor C. in the March number. Quinn, by the way, has been in hospital for a major operation, and we cant have him worried unnecessarily.

Perhaps an unexpurgated [*crossout:* work] text [*longhand:* of you] can be printed in a greek or bulgarian translation later.

I'm not even sure "urine" is necessary in the opening page. The idea could be conveyed just as definitely.

In the thing as it stands you will lose effectiveness. The excrements will prevent people from noticing the quality of things contrasted.

At any rate the thing is risk enough without the full details of the morning deposition.

[*crossout:* At any rate.] If we are suppressed too often we'll be suppressed finally and for all, to the damn'd stoppage of all our stipends. AND I cant have our august editress jailed, NOT at any rate for a passage which I do not think written with utter maestria.

[*longhand:* Hence these tears.]

Yrs.
Ezra Pound

131

Throughout his tenure as *Ulysses* editor Pound walked a tight-rope between editorial expediency and free expression. In defending Joyce against Quinn on April 3, several days after the foregoing letter, he stuck doggedly to his admiration of Joyce's realism: "I can't agree with you about Joyce's first chapter. I don't think the passages about his mother's death and the sea would come off with such force if they weren't imbedded in squalor and disgusts." On the other hand:

> I may say that I rec'd the fourth chapter some days ago, and deleted about twenty lines before sending it off to N.Y.; and also wrote Joyce my reasons for thinking the said lines excessive.

Still, however, "He does not disgust me as Wells does." Joyce wrote adamantly to Miss Weaver that the episode as published was not his full text and demanded that the excisions be restored before it should be printed in book form. (Huebsch was considering printing it. For Pound's deletions, see Appendix C.)

All things considered, however, Pound's conception of free expression was based solidly upon literary standards and upon his notions of mental, social, and artistic freedom. Although he exercised the blue pencil for a mixture of reasons, the perfection of art came first. He pressed his dialogue with Quinn in the same letter: [9]

> Getting back to Joyce. It still seems to me that America will never look *anything*—animal, mineral, vegetable, political, social, international, religious, philosophical or ANYTHING else—in the face until she gets used to perfectly bald statements.
>
> That's propaganda, if you like, but it seems to me something larger than the question of whether Joyce writes with a certain odeur-de-muskrat.
>
> The present international situation seems to me in no small measure due to the English and American habit of keeping their ostrich heads carefully down their little silk-lined sand-holes.

[9] *Letters,* page 138. The letters of April 3 and June 4, 1918, are mixed up. The first part of the April 3 letter should end with "more than that" in the paragraph that begins "Jules Romains" (page 133), continue with the paragraph beginning "If Griffin and Merrill" (page 137), and conclude with "time to breathe" (page 139). The June 4 letter should continue after "utterly French" (page 137) with the rest of the letter dated April 3 ("Duhamel, Chennevière," etc., to *"Pavannes,"* pages 133–134).

I wrote an article on the "situation" a couple of months ago. I am told it is intelligent but unprintable. Orage simply said, "You mingle with people who are far too interesting. You should go to the National Liberal Club and learn how ONE intelligent remark can blast a man's whole career."

Oh well, one can't go back over all that. I don't care a hang for one matter more than another. It is the whole habit of verbally avoiding the issue that seems to be injurious. However, I mustn't get fanatical over it.

Pound's essay on Joyce in his "Books Current" column, *The Future*, May 1918, expressed his considered literary judgment. The occasion was an important victory in the book war: a second edition of *A Portrait* in March, this time composed of English sheets set by English printers. Elkin Mathews had also issued a second edition of *Chamber Music*. In May *Exiles* appeared and all of Joyce's work was in print; Pound wrote a notice in his November column.

JOYCE.[1]

Despite the War, despite the paper shortage, and despite those old-established publishers whose god is their belly and whose godfather was the late F. T. Palgrave,[2] there is a new edition of James Joyce's "A Portrait of the Artist as a Young Man." [3] It is extremely gratifying that this book should have "reached its fourth thousand," and the fact is significant in just so far as it marks the beginning of a new phase of English publishing, a phase comparable to that started in France some years ago by the "Mercure."

The old houses, even those, or even *more* those, which once had a literary tradition, or at least literary pretensions, having ceased to care a damn about literature, the lovers of good writing have "struck"; have sufficiently banded themselves together to get a few good books into print, and even into circulation. The actual output is small in bulk, a few brochures of translations, Eliot's "Prufrock," Joyce's "A Portrait," and Wyndham Lewis' "Tarr" (announced), but I have it on good authority that at least one other periodical will

[1] *The Future*, London, II, 6 (May 1918), pages 161–163. Later in 1918 Pound altered his article in *Future*, added the section headed "ULYSSES," and printed them together in *Instigations*, 1920; reprinted *Literary Essays*, 1954.

[2] Sir Francis Turner Palgrave (1824–1897), critic, poet, and editor of *The Golden Treasury of English Songs and Lyrics* (1861), which formed the poetic taste of at least two generations; to Pound it was a staple of The Macmillan Company and a Chinese wall against modern poetry.

[3] "A Portrait of the Artist as a Young Man." Egoist Ltd., 4s. 6d. [E.P.].

start publishing its authors after the War, so there are new rods in pickle for the old fat-stomached contingent and for the cardboard generation.

Joyce's "A Portrait" is literature; it has become almost the prose bible of a few people, and I think I have encountered at least three hundred admirers of the book, certainly that number of people who whether they "like" it or not, are wholly convinced of its merits.

Mr. Wells I have encountered only in print. Mr. Wells says that Joyce has a cloacal obsession, *but* he also says that Mr. Joyce writes literature and that his book is to be ranked with the works of Sterne and of Swift. Mr. Wells' recent appearance [4] is rather in the *rôle* of the small boy of the following dialogue (most ancient):

"Johnnie, what are you drawing?"

"God."

"But nobody knows what he looks like."

"They will when I get through."

But let us pass over this. Mr. Wells had doubtless heard that Silas Hocking [5] had a bigger circulation than he, H. G. W., had attained. Before we get messed up with bishops, their souls, &c., Wells was mixed up with abdomenalia. His "New Machiavelli" could be read with alternate admirations and disgusts, but his style was always a bit greasy in comparison with the metallic cleanness of Joyce's phrasing. Wells is no man to babble of obsessions. But let it stand to his honour that he came out with a fine burst of admiration for a younger and half-known writer.

Still, from England and America there has come a finer volume of praise for this novel than for any that I can remember. There has also come impotent spitting and objurgation from the back-woods and from Mr. Dent's office boy, and, as offset, interesting comment in modern Greek, French and Italian.

Joyce's poems have been reprinted by Elkin Mathews, his short stories re-issued, and a second novel started in "The Little Review."

For all the book's being so familiar, it is pleasant to take up "A Portrait" in its new exiguous form, and one enters many speculations, perhaps more than when one read it initially. It is not that

[4] *The Soul of a Bishop,* "A Novel (with Just a Little Love in It) about Conscience and Religion and The Real Troubles of Life," 1918, in which Wells presented a clergyman's discovery of The New God. *The New Machiavelli,* 1911, was a novel about the Edwardian political world in which Wells had championed freer love.

[5] Silas Kitto Hocking, popular novelist and preacher who wrote "of what he knew for people he understood" (*D.N.B.*).

one can open to a forgotten page so much as that wherever one opens there is always a place to start; some sentence like—

"Stephen looked down coldly on the oblong skull beneath him overgrown with tangled twine-coloured hair"; *or*

"Frowsy girls sat along the curbstones before their baskets"; *or*

"He drained his third cup of watery tea to the dregs and set to chewing the crusts of fried bread that were scattered near him, staring into the dark pool of the jar. The yellow dripping had been scooped out like a boghole, and the pool under it brought back to his memory the dark turf-coloured water of the bath in Clongowes. The box of pawntickets at his elbow had just been rifled, and he took up idly one after another in his greasy fingers the blue and white dockets, scrawled and sanded and creased and bearing the name of the pledger as Daly or MacEvoy.

"1 Pair Buskins, &c."

I do not mean to imply that a novel is necessarily a bad novel because one can pick it up without being in this manner, caught and dragged into reading; but I do indicate the curiously seductive interest of the clear-cut and definite sentences.

Neither, emphatically, is it to be supposed that Joyce's writing is merely a depiction of the sordid. The sordid is there in all conscience as you would find it in De Goncourt, but Joyce's power is in his scope. The reach of his writing is precisely from the fried breadcrusts, as above, and from the fig-seeds in Cranley's teeth to the casual discussion of Aquinas:

"He wrote a hymn for Maundy Thursday. It begins with the words *Pange lingua gloriosi*. They say it is the highest glory of the hymnal. It is an intricate and soothing hymn. I like it; but there is no hymn that can be put beside that mournful and majestic processional song, the Vexilla Regis of Venantius Fortunatus.

"Lynch began to sing softly and solemnly in a deep bass voice:

'Impleta sunt quae concinit
David fideli carmine . . . .'

"They turned into Lower Mount Street. A few steps from the corner a fat young man, wearing a silk neck-cloth, &c."

On almost every page of Joyce you will find just such swift alternation of subjective beauty and external shabbiness, squalor, and sordidness. It is the bass and treble of his method. And he has his scope beyond that of the novelists his contemporaries, in just so far as whole stretches of his keyboard are utterly out of their compass.

And the conclusion or moral termination from all this is that the great writers of any period must be the remarkable minds of that period; they must know the extremes of their time; they must not represent a *social status;* they cannot be the "Grocer" or the "Dilettante" with the egregious and capital letter, nor yet the professor or the professing wearer of Jaeger or professional eater of herbs.

In the three hundred pages of "A Portrait of the Artist as a Young Man" there is no omission; there is nothing in life so beautiful that Joyce cannot touch it without profanation—without, above all, the profanations of sentiment and sentimentality—and there is nothing so sordid that he cannot treat it with his metallic exactitude.

I think there are few people who can read Shaw, Wells, Bennett, or even Conrad (who is in a category apart) without feeling that there are values and tonalities to which these authors are wholly insensitive. I do not imply that there cannot be excellent art with quite distinct limitations, but the artist cannot afford to be ignorant of his limitations; he cannot afford a pretence of such ignorance. The artist must also choose his limitations. If he paints a snuff-box or a stage scene he must not be ignorant of the fact that he is not painting a landscape, three feet by two feet, in oils.

I think that what tires me more than anything else in the writers now past middle age is that they always seem to imply that they are giving us all modern life, the whole social panorama, all the instruments of the orchestra. They have their successors in Lawrence and Gilbert Cannan.[6] Joyce is of another donation.

Joyce's earlier book, "Dubliners," contained several well-constructed stories, several sketches rather lacking in form. It was a definite promise of what was to come. There is very little to be said in praise of it which would not apply with greater force to "A Portrait." I find that whoever reads one book inevitably sets out in search of the other.

The quality and distinction of the poems in the first half of Mr. Joyce's "Chamber Music" (new edition, published by Elkin Mathews, 4A, Cork Street, W. 1, at 1s. 3d.) is due in part to their author's strict musical training. We have here the lyric in some of its best traditions, and one pardons certain trifling inversions, much

---

[6] Gilbert Cannan, considered in 1918 one of the strongest younger novelists; he was a friend of D. H. Lawrence and John Middleton Murry.

against the taste of the moment, for the sake of the clean-cut ivory finish, and for the interest of the rhythms, the cross run of the beat and the word, as of a stiff wind cutting the ripple-tops of bright water.

The wording is Elizabethan, the metres at times suggesting Herrick, but in no case have I been able to find a poem which is not in some way Joyce's own, even though he would seem, and that most markedly, to shun apparent originality, as in:

> Who goes amid the green wood
>   With springtide all adorning her?
> Who goes amid the merry green wood
>   To make it merrier?
>
> Who passes in the sunlight
>   By ways that know the light footfall?
> Who passes in the sweet sunlight
>   With mien so virginal?
>
> The ways of all the woodland
>   Gleam with a soft and golden fire—
> For whom does all the sunny woodland
>   Carry so brave attire?
>
> O, it is for my true love
>   The woods their rich apparel wear—
> O, it is for my true love,
>   That is so young and fair.

Here, as in nearly every poem, the motif is so slight that the poem scarcely exists until one thinks of it as set to music; and the workmanship is so delicate that out of twenty readers scarce one will notice its fineness. Would that Henry Lawes were alive again to make the suitable music, for the cadence is here worthy of his cunning:

> O, it is for my true love,
>   That is so young and fair.

The musician's work is very nearly done for him, and yet how few song-setters could be trusted to finish it and to fill in an accompaniment.

The tone of the book deepens with the poem beginning:

O sweetheart, hear you
        Your lover's tale;
A man shall have sorrow
        When friends him fail.

For he shall know then
        Friends be untrue;
And a little ashes
        Their words come to.

The collection comes to its end and climax in two profoundly emotional poems; quite different in tonality and in rhythm-quality from the lyrics in the first part of the book:

All day I hear the noise of waters
        Making moan,
Sad as the sea-bird is, when going
        Forth alone,
He hears the wind cry to the waters'
        Monotone.

The gray winds, the cold winds are blowing
        Where I go.
I hear the noise of many waters
        Far below.
All day, all night, I hear them flowing
        To and fro.

The third and fifth lines should not be read with an end stop. I think the rush of the words will escape the notice of scarcely any one. The phantom hearing in this poem is coupled, in the next poem, to phantom vision as well, and to a *robustezza* of expression:

I hear an army charging upon the land,
    And the thunder of horses plunging, foam about their knees;
Arrogant, in black armour, behind them stand,
    Disdaining the reins, with fluttering whips, the charioteers.

They cry unto the night their battle-name;
    I moan in sleep when I hear afar their whirling laughter;

138

They cleave the gloom of dreams, a blinding flame,
  Clanging, clanging upon the heart as upon an anvil.

They come shaking in triumph their long green hair;
  They come out of the sea and run shouting by the shore:
My heart, have you no wisdom thus to despair?
  My love, my love, my love, why have you left me alone?

In both these poems we have a strength and a fibrousness of sound which almost prohibits the thought of their being "set to music" or to any music but that which is in them when spoken; but we notice a similarity of the technique with the earlier poems, in so far as the beauty of movement is produced by a very skilful, or perhaps we should say a deeply intuitive, interruption of metric mechanical regularity. It is the irregularity which has shown always in the best periods.

The book is an excellent antidote for whose who find Mr. Joyce's prose "disagreeable" and who at once fly (*à la* Mr. Wells, for example) to conclusions about Mr. Joyce's "cloacal obsessions," &c. I have yet to find in Joyce's published works a violent or malodorous phrase which does not justify itself not only by its verity, but by its heightening of some opposite effect, by the poignancy which it imparts to some emotion or to some thwarted desire for beauty. Disgust with the sordid is but another expression of a sensitiveness to the finer thing. There is no perception of beauty without a corresponding disgust. If the price for such artists as James Joyce is exceeding heavy, it is the artist himself who pays.

If Armageddon has taught us anything it should have taught us to abominate the half-truth, and the tellers of the half-truth, in literature.

ULYSSES

Incomplete as I write this. His profoundest work, most significant— 'Exiles' was a side-step, necessary katharsis, clearance of mind from continental contemporary thought—*Ulysses*, obscure, even obscene, as life itself is obscene in places, but an impassioned meditation on life.

He has done what Flaubert set out to do in *Bouvard and Pécuchet*, done it better, more succinct. An epitome.

Bloom answers the query that people made after *The Portrait*. Joyce has created his second character; he has moved from auto-

139

biography to the creation of the complementary figure. Bloom on life, death, resurrection, immortality. Bloom and the Venus de Milo.

Bloom brings life into the book. All Bloom is vital. Talk of the other characters, cryptic, perhaps too particular, incomprehensible save to people who know Dublin, at least by hearsay, and who have university education plus medievalism. But unavoidable or almost unavoidable, given the subject and the place of the subject.

NOTE: I am tired of rewriting the arguments for the realist novel; besides there is nothing to add. The Brothers de Goncourt said the thing once and for all, but despite the lapse of time their work is still insufficiently known to the American reader. The program in the preface to *Germinie Lacerteux* states the case and the whole case for realism; one can not improve the statement. I therefore give it entire, ad majoram Dei gloriam.

PRÉFACE
DE LA PREMIÈRE ÉDITION

Il nous faut demander pardon au public de lui donner ce livre, et l'avertir de ce qu'il y trouvera.

Le public aime les romans faux: ce roman est un roman vrai.

Il aime les livres qui font semblant d'aller dans le monde: ce livre vient de la rue.

Il aime les petites oeuvres polissonnes, les mémoires de filles, les confessions d'alcôves, les saletés érotiques, le scandale qui se retrousse dans une image aux devantures des libraires, ce qu'il va lire est sévère et pur. Qu'il ne s'attende point à la photographie décolletée du plaisir: l'étude qui suit est la clinique de l'Amour.

Le public aime encore les lectures anodines et consolantes, les aventures qui finissent bien, les imaginations qui ne dérangent ni sa digestion ni sa sérénité: ce livre, avec sa triste et violente distraction, est fait pour contrarier ses habitudes et nuire à son hygiène.

Pourquoi donc l'avons-nous écrit? Est-ce simplement pour choquer le public et scandaliser ses goûts?

Non.

Vivant au dix-neuvième siècle, dans un temps de suffrage universel, de démocratie, de libéralisme, nous nous sommes demandés si ce qu'on appelle 'les basses classes' n'avait pas droit au roman; si ce monde sous un monde, le peuple, devait rester sous le coup de l'interdit littéraire et des dédains d'auteurs qui ont fait jusqu'ici le silence sur l'âme et le coeur qu'il peut avoir. Nous nous sommes demandé s'il y avait encore, pour l'écrivain et pour le lecteur, en ces années d'égalité où nous sommes, des classes indignes, des malheurs trop bas, des drames trop mal embouchés, des catastrophes d'une terreur trop peu noble. Il nous est venu la curiosité de savoir si cette forme conventionnelle d'une littérature oubliée et d'une société disparue, la Tragédie, était définitivement morte; si, dans un pays sans caste et sans aristocratie légale, les misères des petits et des pauvres parleraient à l'intérêt, à l'émotion, à la pitié aussi haut que les misères des grands et des riches; si, en un mot, les larmes qu'on pleure en bas pourraient faire pleurer comme celles qu'on pleure en haut.

Ces pensées nous avaient fait oser l'humble roman de 'Soeur Philomène', en 1861; elles nous font publier aujourd'hui 'Germinie Lacerteux'.

Maintenant, que ce livre soit calomnié: peu lui importe. Aujourd'hui que le Roman s'élargit et grandit, qu'il commence à être la grande forme sérieuse, passionnée, vivante, de l'étude littéraire et de l'enquête sociale, qu'il devient, par l'analyse et par la recherche psychologique, l'Histoire morale contemporaine, aujourd'hui que le Roman s'est imposé les études et les devoirs de la science, il peut en revendiquer les libertés et les franchises. Et qu'il cherche l'Art et la Vérité; qu'il montre des misères bonnes à ne pas laisser oublier aux heureux de Paris; qu'il fasse voir aux gens du monde ce que les dames de charité ont le courage de voir, ce que les reines d'autrefois faisaient toucher de l'oeil à leurs enfants dans les hospices: la souffrance humaine, présente et toute vive, qui apprend la charité; que le Roman ait cette religion que le siècle passé appelait de ce large et vaste nom: *Humanité;* il lui suffit de cette conscience: son droit est là.

E. et J. de G.'

A SERIOUS PLAY.[7]

"Exiles," by James Joyce (Grant Richards, 3s. 6d.), is a play perhaps unstageable, but infinitely more worth staging than the inanities which the once active Stage Society now indulges in. We find the most brilliant of our novelists here trying the inferior form. He has not, to my mind, a sufficient sense either of the public dulness or of the limitations of the play-house.

A novel, to be practicable, implies only 500 to 1,000 readers. It is

[7] *The Future,* II, 11 (November 1918), page 287.

just barely possible to print for a public of that size. But a play, to be commercially possible on the stage, implies at least twenty-one separate audiences of 1,500 each, and demands that they assemble on twenty-one consecutive nights. As there are not 30,000 people interested in either serious literature or serious drama, it is hopeless sighing to imagine that there is going to be an interesting "theatre" in our time.

As chamber drama, Mr. Joyce writes with all the talent he had as a novelist. He adds a sense of possible stage comedy in a scene furnished with a perfume sprayer.

One is troubled by the feeling that the main "point" would not come over the footlights, and even a play that one reads must give one the feeling (even though it be incorrect) that it would "go" on the stage. The book could not be turned into a novel because of its construction.

Joyce is so important an author that a certain interest attaches to anything he chooses to publish. His pictures of Irish life are, or should be, of value to bewildered administrators, and to Britons who are concerned with that disthressful chounthry of Erin.

At hazard one would say that Joyce had been deflected rather from the main course of his work (as shown in "Dubliners," "The Portrait of the Artist" and "Ulysses") by a continental post-Ibsen influence.

Pound wrote few letters between June and December 1918; only one is printed in his *Letters*, to Quinn in November. It was an active and important year. He was preparing for *The Little Review* his studies "Henry James" (August 1918) and "Remy De Gourmont" (January-February 1919), which he later called his "General summary of state of human consciousness in decades immediately before my own, the H. James and De Gourmont compendium"; these probably stimulated his expanded insights into *A Portrait* in his 1918 essay on Joyce and helped focus his view of *Ulysses*. He had completed a Provençal song-book, *Homage à la Langue D'Oc*, and an ironic modern counterpart, *Moeurs Contemporaines*, a Jamesian family album or "prose kinema," at the end of 1917, and in 1918 he completed his Gourmontian *Homage to Sextus Propertius*. But during the year he became more and more harried, occupied not only with his editing but also with writing extensively for *The Little Review*, *The New Age*, *The Egoist*, and *The Future*. Overwork became aggravated by illness, and these produced a new stridency and

142

cantankerousness in his tone. This tone was exacerbated by objections from America that *The Little Review* was becoming "Ezraized"; stung, Pound began to publish more frequent and sharper barbs, mostly anonymous, against American provinciality. Furthermore, Harriet Monroe had rejected *Langue D'Oc* and *Moeurs Contemporaines* (he had hoped that as juxtaposed series they would relieve him of the charge of passéism) and accepted only part of *Propertius*. *Propertius*, which Pound thought his best work to date and his culminating major persona, was of course at once grossly misunderstood to be merely an inaccurate translation. Against this background the essay in *The Future* and the three letters to Joyce stand out strikingly for their spontaneous enthusiasm. The next letter is his response to the "Proteus" episode, in which Stephen, on the strand, watches a dog enter and inspect another dog's drowned corpse. The play on "W. C." refers notably to Pound's own reservations but also recalls H. G. Wells's discovery in *A Portrait* of a "cloacal obsession."

[*letterhead*]

THE LITTLE REVIEW

7 June 1918   *London Office:—5, Holland Place Chambers, W.8.*

Dear Joyce: Your third section is bloody inspirin' fine. Want to let off a little steam over it. Much easier to see it in print . . . . even with the damn'd printer's errors.

(My own verses have suffered extinction in the May number. Windeler died in the April pages.[8] AND his typescript and mine were both clearer than yours ever is.

BUT damn it, Chap. three does come up.

It is too full of meat to read all at once. Ought to be a division mark of some sort, possibly before the dog comes in.

Mere matter of convenience But even my titanic intellect wants a pause somewhere in the 14 pages.

Gawd damn it, it is Writing, with a large W. and no C.

I hear someone HAS actually seen a copy of "Exiles" published by G. Richards.

Am writing to him, to see what he has to say for himself.

[8] Pound's *Langue D'Oc and Moeurs Contemporaines,* and *Elimus* by C. B. Windeler. For what is probably Pound's explosion against the typesetting of *The Little Review's* Serbo-Croatian printer, see Margaret Anderson, *My Thirty Years' War, an autobiography,* New York: Covici, Friede, 1930, page 162.

Am trying to send you extra March, April and May numbers via chief censor.

Hope your eyes are better.

Yours ever
Ezra Pound

17 July 1918   *5, Holland Place Chambers, London W.8.*
                                    [longhand]

Dear Joyce: Am flat on my back with some crotchety variant of the chill-cum-flu-cum-spew. Faint animation reviving=Not enough to get you [*insert:* Fred] Manning's indecent lines on Clongowes which he asked me to send you.[9]

I suppose I may announce you as a contributor—or one concerned in the new quarterly I still hope to start=on lines of L. R. with rubbish left out & more serious matter inserted. Hope it will last long enough to print something you do after you finish the glorious & wily "Ulysses" of blessed memory

forgive letters & queries unanswered=

Heard from a friend of yrs called Wadsworth alias (? ?) forget. sent him some L.R. with Ulysses & recd. disjecta membra, groping in yr. vestiges.

Hope you are in better health—seem few chances of getting South into sun.

Hope you will like my Propertius=I have as much Trouble as you do in getting printed—tho' I am much milder & far less indecent =au moins=je suis peut être un peu plus phallique, mais mi interessent moins les excremens et les feces humains et des bestiaux; et les puces paraissent peu etc—even so the publisher's—reading public seem to be horripiled by the most unforseeable turns of language=any reference to any racial habit—even to the habits most necessary for the preservation of the species

—enough of this dribble forgive the maunderings of a convalescent.

Yrs ever
E Pound

[9] Clongowes Wood School, the school attended by Joyce and by Stephen Dedalus in *A Portrait.*

22 November 1918   *5, Holland Place Chambers, Kensington. W.*

Dear Joyce: Bloom is a great man, and you have almightily answered the critics who asked me whether having made Stephen, more or less autobiography, you could ever go on and create a second character. "Second character is the test" etc. etc., jab jab jobberjabble.

I think you would like Wells. I lunched with him about a month ago, first time I had seen him for six years. His remarks on Q. Victorias monument before Buckingham palace I shall reserve for some future prose work of my own.[1]

I looked back over Bouvard and Pecuchet last week. Bloom certainly does all Flaubert set out to do and does it in one tenth the space, and moreover there is the sense all the time that something might happen, in fact that anything might happen at any moment, while in Bouvard they are anchored in the mud and even when some thing does happen you keep on feeling that nothing can.

Lewis is a little annoyed with my note on Tarr.[2] W. B. Y. seems to have come off in his "Round Tower".[3] The females have maliciously ruined DeBosscheres drawings by saving 2d. on bunf [4]

Rodker has done an appreciation of Exiles, to appear Little Review, I suppose January.[5]

Must devise some mechanism for cash purposes as the L.R. wont magnetize the american pocket much longer. Your balance is secure, but after April I dont see much more coming in. Why in Christ's name we arent all millionaires I dont know. It is a bloody and grimy bore.

I hope my Propertian ravings will amuse you IF I ever find anyone to print 'em. Thank gawd the war is at least partly over. We will now have the competition of all the returning troops to contend with. Must say the effect on Aldington is excellent. He went to the fields of glory full of doctrinaire bosh contracted from a returned

[1] *Canto* XLII, lines 3–5.

[2] Probably "Books Current," *The Future*, September 1918. Pound conflated several notices of *Tarr* for *Instigations,* 1920.

[3] "Under the Round Tower," *The Little Review,* October 1918.

[4] "bunf" seems to be a slip for "bumf," defined by Eric Partridge as "A schoolboys' and soldiers' abbreviation of *bum-fodder,* toilet paper . . . Hence, from ca. 1870, paper" (*A Dictionary of Slang and Unconventional English,* page 107). Pound doubtless refers to the paper used for De Bosschère's drawings, which were printed with his poems in *The Little Review,* October 1918.

[5] " 'Exiles,' A Discussion of James Joyce's Plays [*sic*]," *The Little Review,* January 1919.

English hun, but has come back purged, and with a surface of modesty.

Has "Ulysses" 24 Odyssean books? I don't want to ask silly questions, and I hope it continues forever, but people are continually asking ME about it and about. Fortunately my ignorance of Bloom's future is complete.

Still, let me know, if you know yourself. I will fork up the remaining £20 of the fifty promised, as soon as I get it from America.

If there are going to be chapters after April, I will try to bone a few quid more out of someone. BUTTTTT Khrrisst knows how or where. I've got to "promote" some new venture to keep my own roof on

The world is too fucking with us. One of my secondary phases has blossomed as much appreciated critic of what music London provides; for [*sic:?* so] far the blossom fruits very little.⁶ The owner of the Manchester guardian admits the stuff is "brilliantly written" but shows no disposition to have it in his own better paid cols. et bloody coetera.

I want to see the Lago di Garda sometime . . . ma che, I dont know when one will be able to travel.

yrs.

ye complete journaliste and pantechnicon patent attachment.

E. P.

As his letters on *Ulysses* show, Pound came more and more to think that Joyce's imagination, either by temperament or because of his subject, was essentially analytical and satiric and tended toward the excremental. His own imagination, by contrast, was essentially phallic in its motive of desire. "Phallic" and "excremental" appeared to Pound to be an essential difference between poetry and prose. Poetry asserts positive emotional values and works toward emotional synthesis. Prose arises from an instinct of negation, proceeds by intellectual analysis, and presents something one wants to eliminate.⁷ Yet as Pound keeps saying in his essays on Joyce, a

---

⁶ Pound wrote "Art Notes. By B. H. Dias" for *The New Age* from November 1917 to April 1920, and "Music. By William Atheling" from December 1917 to January 1921. He had written to his father on January 24, 1918: "Am doing art and music critiques under pseudonyms, paying the rent. Rather entertaining work. *NOT to be mentioned*. It may be I have at last found a moderately easy way to earn my daily. Bloody queer what a man will do for money. MUSIC!!!!" (at Yale).

⁷ "Henry James," *The Little Review*, V, 4 (August 1918); *Literary Essays*, page 324.

146

sense of beauty lies behind any intense presentation of "external shabbiness, squalor, and sordidness," and "there is no perception of beauty without a corresponding disgust." If prose must have beauty as its background to be "realist," poetry must have ugliness; the motive of both is beauty, and each according to its own laws must hold ugliness and beauty (or as Yeats put it and Pound agreed, "reality and justice") in a single thought. The close of the next letter, "But for the cloacal labour you might have camped on line of plagiat," indicates how Pound thought of his work and Joyce's as complementary treatments of the same subject, the modern mind. Pound was trying to move from the ironic sketches of *Lustra* and *Moeurs Contemporaines* to satire of epic magnitude; his "need of bottling London" in "some more ample modus" foreshadows the "hell cantos" (*Cantos* XIV and XV), which were probably drafted in 1919. The main critical texts for Pound's effort to define the place of poetry in relation to the realistic and naturalistic novels are "The Serious Artist" (1913), his essays on James and Gourmont, his essays on Joyce in 1918 and 1922, and "On Criticism in General" (*The Criterion*, January 1923). The main poetic texts which apply these principles are *Propertius*, an expression of desire, *Moeurs Contemporaines*, an expression of negation, *Hugh Selwyn Mauberley*, a "study in form" intended to conflate the poetic and prose motives by condensing a James novel, and *Canto* VII.

12 December 1918   *London (no address)*

Dear Joyce: Many thanks for the receipt; only it's not the least what I meant. The money is sure to arrive; bar some calamity to Quinn; only I don't know when it will arrive. I will send on the balance when it does. £50 is a beggarly enough sum for Ulysses, but . . . . . can't be helped.

I don't want to hurry you; and the slowness of making permanent literature is incomprehensible to all save the few of us who have tried.

The only thing is that these women in New York may go bust, and be unable to print the end of the novel. In which case no lasting harm is done, as presumably Huebsch will print the bound volume in 1930 or 40.

The Signore Sterlina has rash moments of believing the gift of immortality lies within his reach, but Giorgio and Lucia had much better trust to their connection con il loro illustrissimo padre. The

Signore Sterlina is perhaps better at digging up corpses of let us say Li Po, or more lately Sextus Propertius, than in preserving this bitched mess of modernity.

"Bitched mess of modernity" is no reflection on the innocents Giorgio and Lucia, who may be pictured as floating somewhere on the top of this none too alluring liquid.

The Little Review will have to paddle mostly on its own after April. I can't raise any more cash (after the second year's lot runs out.) and can't give my time to it without that meagre allowance for self and contributors.

I am trying, with I think some chance, to start a Quarterly here. What good that will do you, I don't know. As it won't be able to serialize novels. (Anyhow Egoist has Ulysses). But I want to put you down among prospective contributors, and will pay what I can for any short work you may do. (up to let us say 10,000 words of story or essay. 10,000 not an absolute limit, but a general estimate.)

I have some of the money promised.

/ / /

As to Hamlet,[8] or whatever, Dorothy is among your constant readers, and so far as ascertainable from close scrutiny, has never jibbed any [sic:? at] any remarks by Telemachus Daedalus or other protagonists. She has a growing affection for Bloom.

/ / /

Wells has taken both our names in [longhand: vain] amity in his last botch of a sociolo-educatorial romanto-sermon. [longhand: "Joan & Peter"] I am on a book-shelf with several despicable writers (who would have been there, while I shouldn't), and you are recorded in one of the authors little excursions as having preserved "one of these types" (Catholic educated) for the "amazement of posterity". [longhand: in The Portrait of Artist.] [9] It is amiably intended advertisement. I trust he has by now read the remarks on the Cloacal Romans.[1]

---

[8] *Ulysses,* the "Scylla and Charybdis" episode.

[9] H. G. Wells, *Joan and Peter, the story of an education,* New York: The Macmillan Company, 1918. The passages referred to are "such moderns as Compton MacKenzie, Masefield, Gilbert Cannan and Ezra Pound," who "appealed in those days to animated youth" (page 285), and "Mr. James Joyce in his *Portrait of the Artist as a Young Man,* has bottled a specimen of that Catholic atmosphere for the astonishment of posterity" (page 290).

[1] Professor McHugh orates in *Ulysses,* "Aeolus": "The Roman, like the Englishman who follows in his footsteps, brought to every new shore on which he set his foot (on our shore he never set it) only his cloacal obsession. He gazed about him

Must say, in discussion with ex-co-editress of Yellow Book [2] yesterday I felt need of bottling London, some more ample modus than permitted in free-verse scherzos, and thumb-nail sketches of Marie Corelli,[3] H. James etc. (in Moeurs Contemporaines)

But for the cloacal labour you might have camped on line of plagiat.

vale et me ama

Ezra Pound

in his toga and he said: *It is meet to be here. Let us construct a watercloset"* (New York: Random House, The Modern Library, New Edition, Corrected and Reset, 1961, page 131.)

[2] Probably Ella D'Arcy (d. 1939), story-writer and novelist who assisted editor Henry Harland informally after Aubrey Beardsley left *The Yellow Book* in 1895 (Katherine Mix, *A Study in Yellow,* Lawrence: University of Kansas Press, 1960, page 190).

[3] Pseudonym of Mary Mackay (1855-1924), writer of melodramatic historical romances, chiefly on moral and religious subjects.

1919-1920

Pound continued to be afflicted by uncertainties about his future and his work. In part it was a letdown after his arduous World War I years. He was winding up his affairs with *The Little Review* and soon would be without a connection or financial resources. In London, the vorticists had returned and all sorts of activity seemed about to begin. But things had changed. There were new faces and new voices. Pound seemed to be out of it. Indeed, his job had been done; one phase of *avant-garde* magazines was over, for the new artists were established and the war had altered things in a way that was not yet clear. One ear was cocked to the Continent; he wrote to William Carlos Williams in January 1919: "All sorts of 'projects' artoliteresque in the peaceconferentialbolshevikair. Switzerland bursting into Dadaique Manifestoes re the nothingness of the All." In 1920 he embraced these currents, but now he remained aloof, "rejoicing in vacancy," skeptical, and unattached.

Many signs suggest that Pound was no longer able to identify himself with London. In *Homage to Sextus Propertius* he had taken an ironic attitude toward the British imperialistic culture, but had nevertheless assumed a place within it. The misgivings he had expressed to Joyce about "digging up corpses" reflected not only his sense of *Propertius*'s passéism but also his awareness that it had not adequately represented his attitude toward "this bitched mess of modernity." His desire to "bottle" London expresses the mood of *Mauberley*, a peculiar combination of bitterness and nostalgia toward London as well as bitterness against the war and against the civilization that produced it. The new conditions and this mood were bringing to the surface a more urgent awareness of the precarious place of the artist and were impressing Pound deeply with a sense that the war had been caused by a failure of intelligence. Intelligence was society's best resource and artists were "the antennae of the race." Not to use them was to court disaster. The split between the arts and modern society was a symptom of ignorance or paralysis; or, worse, of willful management by private interests. Since 1917 he had begun more and more to explore the conditions of

"Contemporary Mentality" and the apparent lack of social and political direction; he had begun to refer to "the economic reality": "Here," he said, "is the future struggle." Sometime late in 1918 he met Major C. H. Douglas, the founder of Social Credit, in Orage's office. Pound's 1919 articles in *The New Age*, his "school" of social and political thought since 1911, signal a major expansion and a change in direction: his effort to incorporate the entire scope of society and history into his thought and his poetry, and his "break" with the prevailing tendencies in western civilization.

Joyce continued on in Zurich. For some time his life had been going smoothly. But he was always able to turn a mild ripple into a storm. This time he became embroiled with the British Empire, whose vindictiveness (Joyce was certain) had been awakened by a lawsuit that had developed out of his joint partnership in the English Players of Zurich.[1] In the spring of 1918 a young employee at the British Consulate, Henry Carr (Private Carr of "Circe"), who had acted the part of Algernon Moncrieff in a performance of Wilde's *The Importance of Being Earnest*, became dissatisfied with a token payment. A comedy of errors and counterlungings ensued. Carr wanted to be paid for the trousers he had bought for the part, but was not. On May 1, 1918, when Joyce went to the Consulate to collect some money for tickets which had been sold, Carr allegedly called him "a cad and a swindler" and then threatened "to wring his bloody neck and chuck him down the stairs." Joyce, an Irishman, took righteous offense at the use of such language in a British Empire office. He wrote a registered letter to the British Acting Consul-General in Zurich, Andrew Percy Bennett, demanding an apology. Receiving no answer, he engaged a solicitor and sued Carr for threats of violence and for the price of three unpaid-for tickets. Carr countered with a suit for the price of the trousers and other garments.

According to Joyce the Consulate then withdrew support from the English Players (indeed sabotaged these friendly efforts). Worse, "as I lay dangerously ill and in danger of blindness" (Joyce wrote), Consul Bennett invited him to betray his vow to the Austrian government that he would remain neutral: that is, to perjure himself by volunteering for service in the British army. If he did not, the alleged threat implied, he would be "penalised." In October Joyce

[1] Gorman, *James Joyce*, pages 250–263 and Ellmann, *James Joyce*, pages 435–472 passim. Joyce's account of the affair and other letters are in *Letters of James Joyce*, II, pages 437–441 and passim.

won £1 plus 5 per cent interest for the tickets and £2/10/0 for damages, while Carr's claim was disallowed. But Joyce persisted. He wrote a complaint to Sir Horace Rumbold, the British minister in Berne, and pressed his suit against Carr for the threats of violence, with the result that, when two consular witnesses failed to support his version of the encounter, Joyce was ordered to pay court costs of 150 Swiss francs (about £4/6/0). He refused, and nearly had his possessions taken away. Joyce got no satisfaction from Rumbold, whom he later made the butt of numerous satiric verses and whom he immortalized in "Cyclops" and "Circe" as the hangman hired to gibbet the Irish nation. Pound, always ready to support artists' causes against indifferent and hostile authorities, also wrote to Rumbold. He reflected (with some exaggeration) the challenge to western society which he was brewing. Rumbold did not reply.

11 April 1919 [2]   *The Little Review, London Office,*
                                               5 Holland Place Chambers, W. 8

Dear Sir, If it be not already too late, I should like to caution you that you can find no surer means of making a few converts to Bolshevism or to the more violent revolutionary factions than by continuing or permitting to continue the persecution of James Joyce by the Zurich officials within the sphere of your influence.

I don't want to write "scare heads" to you, and I don't imagine the converts would be numerous, but they would probably be extremely vocal and active; a number of young men are not far from the borderline of these opinions; and a case like Joyce's would considerably enflame their imaginations. I would therefore request that if possible some ambassadorial courtesy might be extended to this, without exception, the most distinguished of the younger English prose authors. After all, literature was once considered an honourable calling. There are very few living writers who can carry on the process of writing permanent books; Mr. Joyce is one of these; I should very much regret having to undertake a publicity campaign on his behalf, and I should certainly take all possible measures to get statements from the Zürich consulate, etc. as to the circumstances from which the present difficulties seem to have risen.

If his present work is interrupted, i.e., his novel "Ulysses" which we are using as a serial, some brief explanation will have to be given

[2] *Letters of James Joyce,* II, pages 437–438.

to our readers. I am not a[n] excitable critic but I believe that he is doing in this work what Flaubert attempted but did not quite bring off in "Bouvard and Pecuchet". If Joyce chooses to make a statement of his position and relations with Messrs. Bennett and Carr, I can scarcely deny him as much space as he chooses for the purpose, but I would much prefer to keep our pages for literature. Respectfully yours,

Ezra Pound

Since Pound had severed his connection with *The Little Review*, it is not exactly clear what "space" he threatened to give Joyce's statement. The statement, dated April 28, was one of Joyce's several open appeals to public opinion and to fellow artists at large. When Pound received it he may have felt that the documents Joyce sent made his "case" sound "a little like Gilbert and Sullivan." Pound sought aid from Augustine Birrell, H. G. Wells, and Richard Aldington. Birrell, lawyer and literary essayist, had been chief secretary for Ireland from 1907 until 1916, when he resigned after the Easter rebellion; Pound had consulted him in 1916 in the argument with Elkin Mathews about *Lustra*. Pound also suggested that Joyce write to his old supporter Gosse and to Charles Frederick Gurney Masterman, wartime director of Wellington House, the propaganda department, whom Pound had approached in 1916 seeking a commission or transfer for Wyndham Lewis. Wells's answer to Pound has apparently been lost. Birrell's, which he enclosed to Joyce, is an example of the kind of response Pound or Joyce could always elicit. When Birrell received Joyce's statement he warmly endorsed his position, calling the Foreign Office's behavior "outrageous." (Both of Birrell's letters are at Cornell.)

[c.1] May 1919   *London* (*no address*)

Dear Joyce: I enclose missive from Mr Birrell (Rt. Hon. Augustine) and Mrs H. G. Wells.

IF I didn't enclose your letter to me in my note to Mr Birrell, hell knows where it is.

I suggest that you write a clear statement of MAIN facts to both Wells and A. B.

FER Chrrisst's sake realize that you have given me no "case" to present.

I have your statement. I have a lot of documents proving that a company of players put on a Chesterton play (for which they ought all to be poisoned until dead of gangrene).

I have also a letter from embassy to you giving you a flat dementi, calling you in fairly clear terms an infernal liar.

The official mind here is just as likely to believe that official denial (especially as it is more convenient and less disturbing for them to suppose you in the wrong.) as [*crossout:* it is for them] they are to believe you.

In the present state of international affairs NO man of any influence has leisure to read one tenth of such a dossier as you have sent me.

Aldington is to come here tomorrow and see what he can do about it, and I shall leave things in his charge.

His address is
> Hotel Littoral, 15 Moor St. W. 1
(not sure I didn't send you the wrong number).

The main facts are ? ? ?

Bailiffs on you.

? ? Do you or do you not want to pay the fine ? ? ? or raise shindy by refusing and claiming inability ? ? ? or ? ? ? ? ?

Would money if sent by post be sequestered? ? ?

Advise you to write to Gosse
> 17 Hanover Terrace. W. 1
Rt. Hon. C. F. G. Masterman
> 46 Gillingham St. S.W. 1.

BUT for God's sake be as clear and as BRIEF as possible. [*longhand:* facts only, no comment.]

Same if you write to Quinn. If you write to Quinn, you can say that there is £20 due you from Little Review and that if not inconvenient to him I should be very glad if he would pay it straight to you. He can take his time about the rest of L. R. subsidy which wd. mostly go to Yeats and myself.

Yours ever

Ezra Pound

Enclosure

Sunday, [c. April] 1919   *70, Elm Park Road, Chelsea, S.W.*

Dear Mr. Pound: You failed to enclose Joyce's letter. I assure you—despite your description of yourself as 'an aggressive and incommodious' person—I would be *most* willing to do what I can to oblige you, and to assist a fellow-countryman in a hole. But, a man of my inferior build cannot curse *at large*—he must *know* either the *persons* concerned, or the *facts* of the case. I *know neither*. It is horrible to be so handicapped in life, but in my 70th year I cannot demand a fresh start.

Yours sincerely,

Augustine Birrell

In May 1919 Pound and his wife left London for a vacation. They returned to southern France, the country of Pound's forerunners the troubadours, where they had spent their honeymoon in 1914. Wyndham Lewis wrote to Quinn that Pound had "vanished into France and is in a mist of recuperation and romance." [3] From Toulouse he sent to *The New Age* his series of articles "The Regional." There he not only covered everything he had been thinking for ten years, but also probed further into "the economic reality" and began to include political as well as literary and intellectual history in his consideration of the past. It is notable that "The Regional" and *Propertius* were serialized in *The New Age* simultaneously with Douglas's *Economic Democracy*. In Toulouse he was receiving proofs of *Quia Pauper Amavi*, a collection of his new poetry of 1917–1918: *Homage à la Langue D'Oc, Moeurs Contemporaines*, the early versions of *Cantos I–III*, and *Propertius*. A retrospect of his prose of 1917–1918, *Instigations*, to be published in America, had been refused by Knopf but was about to be accepted by Boni & Liveright. He was probably also working on *Mauberley* and *Cantos V, VI*, and *VII*, having just published *Canto IV*.

[3] September 3, 1919, *Letters of Wyndham Lewis,* edited by W. K. Rose, Norfolk, Conn.: New Directions, 1963, page 80.

While Pound and his wife were eking their way in southern France, Joyce received news that £5000 in war loan securities, which paid 5 per cent, had been bestowed by his still unknown benefactress. Joyce sent "Sirens" to Pound in Toulouse; Joyce's method, and once again his physiological realism, aroused strong reactions.

30 May 1919   *13 rue St Ursule, Toulouse*
                          [longhand]

Dear Joyce: I enclose my wife's cheque for £15. I am not living on her illicit earnings, nor are you about to profit from the softness of the feminine heart (vide "Dubliners" p. 1 ? ?)—Simply, the L. R. funds have arrived here.—where it will take me some days to get them mobilized.—And I think you may save a few days & possibly the adv. of English exchange. by this method of payment.—Fr. exchange being downish. if *cf*. with English.—

The other £5 will be sent you by my belle mere, in my name from London.—This is necessary as my wife's balance is only £15, 6s. 1d. and a cheque for the full £20 wd. therefore be of less value than the enclosed.

—Re. yr. letter. I too wd. have preferred the Lago di Garda, via your paisable demeure. but the trouble of passing *one* frontier is quite enough—

Besides living is comparatively cheap here. Cheaper than at the bouche du Rhone –even; let alone the Nice section. Have been over to Nimes & Arles to renew my retina with certain outlines, & Avignon. but 10 days of it run to as much "sec ou liquide" as a month of stasis here.

Month of complete stasis or constipation in my affairs, also; tho' things seem now catharcized some what. At least proofs of "Quia Pauper Amavi" begin to arrive.

And Knopf's perfidy re "Instigations" is said to be about to be remedied by one "Liverlight", "mousing about for"—

La Depeche, anent this, announces the arrival of Mr Bloom at Versailles—so I suppose the peace will be concluded—unless by chance it is another & less worthy blossom.

                          Yrs ever—with regards to your wife & branches.
                                                        Ezra Pound

10 June 1919   *13 rue St Ursule, Toulouse*
                [*longhand*]

O gloire et decor de la langue Irso-Anglais :

The peri-o-perip-o-periodico-parapatetico-periodopathetico—I dont-off-the markgetical structure of yr. first or peremier para-petitec graph—will cause all but your most pig-o-peripatec-headed readers to think you have gone marteau-dingo-maboule— [4]

Even I cd. do with indication of whose jag—possibly Blooms (?) it is.

—A red headed jew Chicago reporter long since assured me that Ulysses had bitched the American market which had begun to take "Portrait" seriously.

In the interest of literature, I refrained from boring you with his unskilled & philistine tip.

—In face of *mss* just arrived, I think however I may adjoin personal op. that you have once again gone "down where the asparagus grows" and gone down as far as the lector most bloody benevolens can be expected to respire.

I dont arsk you to erase—But express opinion that a few sign posts. perhaps twenty words coherent in bunches of 3 to 5 *wd.* [*crossout:* do] not only clarify but even improve the 1st. page.

I am sending *mss* today to Egoist & L. R. & if you have any relentings, please communic. direct to said offices.

Hope you have recd. recently £20. in £15 & £5 lots.

Also even the assing girouette of a postfuturo Gertrudo Steino protetopublic dont demand a new style per chapter. If a classic author "shows steady & uniform progress" from one oeuvre to ensanguined next, may be considered ample proof of non-stagnation of cerebral Rodano—flaming Farinatas included— [5]

[4] For this paragraph the reader may, as Pound has done, turn loose his linguistic imagination. On reading the opening pages of "Sirens" Pound doubtless thought of μαργίτες, madman, hero of Μαργίτεια, a mock-epic poem ascribed to Homer (Aristotle, *Poetics*). The last phrase means something like "got knocked on the head or bit by a wild dog and gone dotty."

[5] Allusions to Dante's *Inferno,* IX–X, passim, where the hellscape reflects the addled brains of the heretics.

Indeed simple Maupassant wd. given excellent contents content the avid eye (and be quite as difficult to write)

"E 'bengh'! ça traine. (I mean your chap. recd.

In brief: subject good enough to hold attention without being so allbloodily friccaseed!

For which license of speech you will probably recommend me to a course of Boylen hell—however!!

Yours ever

E. P.

Later

Caro mio: Are you sending this chapter *because* you feel bound to send in copy on time?

Let the regularity of appearance be damned. If you want more time take it.

I shall send off mss. to Egoist & L. R. tomorrow. But you will have plenty of time to hold up publication if you want to, and to revise if you want to.

1. you have got some new effects.

2. It is too long

3. One *can* fahrt with less pomp & circumstance

[3a. gallic preference for Phallus—purely personal—know mittel europa humour runs to other orifice.—But don't think you will strengthen your impact by that particular.

Mass effect of any work depends on conviction of author's sanity=

Abnormal keenness of insight O.K. But *obsessions* arseore-ial, cloacal, deist, aesthetic as opposed to arsethetic, any obsession or tic shd. be very carefully considered before being turned loose.=

Besides. Bloom has been disproportionately on

? ? ?

or hasn't he. Where in hell is Stephen Tellemachus?

all the bloody makintosh while.

4. fahrt yes, but not as climax of chapter=not really the final resolution of fugue.[6]

[6] Joyce wrote to Miss Weaver on August 6 that "Sirens" was constructed as "all the eight regular parts of a *fuga per canonem*" (*Letters,* I, page 129). Whether Pound had been informed of this principle or perceived it from his reading, he habitually applies musical analogies to poetry, especially to the "fugal" form *of The Cantos.*

Classic detachment wd. suggest Racinian off stage, suppression of
last two lines, & simple constation [no p. for second t.] [7]

$$\overline{\overline{}} \qquad \overline{\overline{}}$$

   "Mr B. felt relieved."

Rest lightly upon this editor
For he rested lightly upon thee.

?Leave it. & use two lines to begin next installment

over

P.S. *And* you may be right—
Anyhow send on this record of uncertainty.

Since his recovery from his eye operation of August 1917 Joyce
had had calmer sailing. He had been working steadily on his book, it
was being printed regularly, and both Pound and the editresses of
The Little Review had offered encouragement beyond what he might
have hoped. It did not matter, as Margaret Anderson has recorded,
that the response from "the world's intellectuals" was minimal, that
the New York literary world was indifferent or hostile, that many
readers wrote in to express outrage, and that several issues were
burned.[8] Indeed Joyce, preoccupied with his writing, may not even
have known about these reactions. What was important was that he
could count on being read and even on being paid a small amount,
and that he once more had the useful discipline of an editor's dead-
line. He was receiving the 1000 francs monthly stipend that Edith
Rockefeller McCormick had granted in March 1918, and despite the
altercation with Carr the English Players had been a success.

But a series of disappointments and difficulties was brewing. The
first was Pound's reaction to "Sirens," which was seconded by Miss
Weaver. On June 19 he remarked to Frank Budgen of Pound's letter,
amused:

Pound writes disapprovingly of the *Sirens*, then modifying his
disapproval and protesting against the close and against "obsession" and wanting to know whether Bloom (prolonged
cheers from all parts of the house) could not be relegated to
the background and Stephen Telemachus brought forward.[9]

But on July 2 he wrote to Miss Weaver that *Ulysses* would not be
finished for a year or so, and that even if it were finished he did not

[7] I.e., "consta[ta]tion," not "constipation." The last two lines of "Sirens" are
"Pprrpffrrppfff./ Done," *Ulysses*, page 291.
[8] Anderson, *My Thirty Years' War*, pages 175–176.
[9] *Letters of James Joyce*, I, page 126.

think anyone in the United Kingdom would publish it or even find printers to set it. Personal worries were also retarding its progress—"to the relief of the few readers who honour it with their attention"; the book might eventually be printed—"possibly, in Africa." Finally, his customary self-pity prompted him to conclude of Pound, defying all previous evidence, "I fear he does not like the book." [1] To add to these woes, Miss Weaver replied that his worries must have to some extent affected his writing (Joyce was also under treatment for nervous strain), for "Sirens" did not seem to her to reach his usual pitch of intensity. (On June 4 Pound had written to Miss Weaver of "Sirens," "Not so good as usual": at Yale.) In answering her on July 20 Joyce revealed how dependent he could be on his friends' opinions of his work, yet retained a frosty and ironic determination:

You write that the last episode sent seems to you to show a weakening or diffusion of some sort. Since the receipt of your letter I have read this chapter again several times. It took me five months to write it and always when I have finished an episode my mind lapses into a state of blank apathy out of which it seems that neither I nor the wretched book will ever more emerge. Mr Pound wrote to me rather hastily in disapproval but I think that his disapproval is based on grounds which are not legitimate and is due chiefly to the varied interests of his admirable and energetic artistic life.... If the *Sirens* have been found so unsatisfactory I have little hope that the *Cyclops* or later the *Circe* episode will be approved of: and, moreover, it is impossible for me to write these episodes quickly. The elements needed will only fuse after a prolonged existence together. I confess that it is an extremely tiresome book but it is the only book which I am able to write at present.[2]

Nevertheless, Pound quickly demonstrated what Joyce might have seen had he allowed himself to: that Pound's "*And* you may be right—Anyhow send on this record of uncertainty" was indeed the statement of a benevolent, open-minded reader. Later, upon reading "*Cyclops*," Pound wrote to Joyce "enthusing" on it. Unfortunately Pound's letter has not survived, but he wrote to Quinn (October 25):

[1] *Letters of James Joyce,* I, page 127.
[2] *Letters of James Joyce,* I, page 128.

Last ms. chapter of Joyce perhaps the best thing he has done. . . . Parody of styles, a trick borrowed from Rabelais, but never done better, even in Rab.

Our James is a grrreat man. I hope to God there is a foundation of truth in the yarn he wrote me about a windfall. Feel he may have done it just to take himself off my mind.

Pound's enthusiasm increased when he received "Circe" and when he read in its final form the at last completed book.

But that was in the future; Joyce was soon hit by other adversities. *The Little Review* had been seized because of the "Laestrygonians" and "Scylla and Charybdis" episodes. *Exiles* was finally produced in August, in German and in Munich, but was not well received. In October he lost Mrs. McCormick's subsidy; he tried to appease her by sending her manuscripts of *Ulysses,* but he was unsuccessful. At the same time he was negotiating with Quinn to sell manuscripts of *Ulysses* to him. A series of cables, marked by the usual misunderstandings, passed between Joyce and Quinn between June 1919 and February 1920; not until then did Joyce finally recover the manuscript and complete the sale. In November 1919 Joyce returned to Trieste disoriented and uncertain. He did not write to Pound but to Frank Budgen, cryptically: "Give no information about me to anyone. . . . As for *Ulysses*—it is like me—on the rocks." He could not find a flat in Trieste, he was forced to return to giving lessons, and for six weeks after his arrival, he wrote Budgen, he neither read nor wrote nor spoke; he had started "Nausikaa" in Zurich, but he found it difficult to continue.[3] Pound's enclosure in the next letter, a note from Leon Fleischman, Paris agent of Boni & Liveright, might have given a glimmer of encouragement, but it did not overcome Joyce's bouts of gloom.

24 November 1919   *5, Holland Place Chambers, Kensington. W.*
                              [*longhand*: Boni Liveright Inc.
                                      105 W. 40th St.
                                      N. Y.]

Dear Joyce: Pinker answers my phone call to the effect that he has answered your letter by express letter.

A note from Quinn this a.m. says he has recd. your cable. He adds

---

[3] *Letters of James Joyce,* I, pages 130–132.

"Don't write to him [*insert*: i.e. you] about it. I shall have to write to him direct."

So I shant. write to you "about" it, further than this.

As "them females" dont send me the little Review any longer I cant forward it to you. I will ask Rodker to do so, and suggest that a note from you to N. Y. office might help.

The enclosed from my N. Y. publishers may interest you. Unless Pinker has already collected from Huebsch. I think Liveright wd. give you 15%. At least thats what he is giving me. You might get an advance above that.

Also his sentence re/unexpurgation is valuable.

yrs
E Pound

Enclosure [4]

10 November 1919   *Boni, Liveright Inc.,*
105 W. 40th St., New York

We would be delighted to hear from you or Joyce further in regard to "Ulysses." I have read a great deal of this in The Little Review, and I think it's amazing work.

Your typewriter seems to have slipped a little. You say "for it's just possible considering" and there's a blank "that you would have to print an unexpurgated edition." What do you refer to? We are not at all afraid of unexpurgated editions.

You have been awfully kind, dear Mr. Pound, and I assure you we appreciate highly the suggestions you have made and the interest you have displayed.

Sincerely yours,
L. F.

Pound returned to London in September. He had difficulty finding a means of supporting himself, for London, trying to return to normal after the war, remembered his thorny presence. He took up again his work with *The New Age*. "The Regional" had concluded

---

[4] Page two only; in the possession of Gordon N. Ray.

"Universal peace will never be maintained unless it be by a conspiracy of intelligent men." "The Revolt of Intelligence," which appeared in *The New Age* in ten installments (November 13, 1919, to March 18, 1920), is a manifesto of his disaffiliation from the prevailing direction of western society. But that kind of journalism could neither support nor satisfy him. Through the efforts of Eliot and Quinn he finally became attached to *The Dial* as a European correspondent. At the same time he was taken on by John Middleton Murry's *Athenaeum*, for which he wrote drama criticism during the spring of 1920. On the strength of these associations he could afford to travel to Paris and Italy. In May he again left London, partly for another vacation, partly to seek out material for *The Dial*, and partly to meet Joyce. By the time he left he had prepared *Mauberley* for publication, had ready versions of *Cantos* V, VI, and VII, probably completed from drafts written in 1915, and may also have drafted the cloacal "hell cantos" (XIV and XV). But in a letter to his father in December 1919 he had written, "done cantos 5, 6, 7, each is more incomprehensible than the one preceding it; I don't know what's to be done about it" (at Yale). There, unexpectedly, but probably because the first versions of *Cantos* I–III lack a firm conception of method and form, work on the poem stopped. *Canto* VII expresses a nostalgia for the old epic subjects and forms. His next canto, old *Canto* VIII, written after a long hiatus and published in *The Dial*, May 1922, opened with a lament for the passing of the Homeric epic of adventurous deeds and proceeded with the metamorphosis which now constitutes *Canto* II. This nostalgia and uncertainty persisted until Pound brought his ideas into focus in 1922.

Joyce was still suffering in Trieste. He wrote to Frank Budgen in January 1920 that he felt lost in "damnable boredom. Not a soul to talk to about Bloom. . . . O shite and onions! When is this bloody state of affairs going to end?" [5] Near despair, he recounted to Miss Weaver several days later how, in a fit of rage on account of the trouble over *Dubliners*, he had torn up the " 'original' original" manuscript of *A Portrait*. He also recalled obliquely his disappointment at her and Pound's criticism of "Sirens," telling her that he found it consoling that she at least still considered him a writer, since "every time I sit down with a pen in my hand I have to persuade myself (and others) of the fact." [6] Despite these baths in self-

[5] *Letters of James Joyce*, I, page 134.
[6] *Letters of James Joyce*, I, page 136.

pity, however, he had managed to finish "Nausikaa" early in
February and "The Oxen of the Sun" in May, and had sent both to
Pound in London. But he felt that he could not go on and was seeking
new surroundings where he could finish his book. The stage was set
for the meeting at Sirmione.

3 May 1920 [postcard]   *Present address Albergo Pilsen-Manin, Venice.*
                                           [longhand]

Must stay here till 30th of May. Will then descend upon Trieste—
unless you come here in the interim. Are there any lights of Italian
Literature now in Venice. ?

Yrs
E. Pound

8 May 1920   *Pilsen-Manin, Venice.*
                          [longhand]

Dear Joyce: Thanks for your card. The Venetian air has been too
much for my spouse and she's neither in condition to be left here
alone, nor to be carried to Trieste; am ignominiously retreating to
Lago di Garda at earliest possible date.

I will write you again from Sirmione, where I shall stop for a
month if anything save the damn de luxe hotel is open.

I wish I had come straight through to Trieste while I was on the
through express; but as Venice is to me a place of repose I didn't
calculate on its affecting quasi-complete disintegration—

If you are doing anything save "Ulysses", I shd. be glad if you
wd. send it to The Dial with one of the enclosed slips. I am trying
without much hope to mode a new Cititatem Dei, shall have stodge in
lieu of lunacy (as on L. R.) to contend with.

Dial gives me to understand that (being an old established relatively expensive periodical) they can't on any account risk suppression by p.o. authorities.

They cdn't on any account print "Ulysses" but "wd. like something of yours" etc. same old story. "in the magazine."

It wont be as much fun as the L. R.; but it can afford more *lire* per
page, & pays in American.

For which sordid reasons; and because the Mercure de France is
really too gaga to be left the sole arbiter of weldtlitteratur! ! !

Are there any Italians who can write. I still hope to see Linati [7] in Milano. Wish I felt there were some chance of seeing you at Sirmione or in Verona.

The Dial thinks it wants "continental contributors".

Shall ask Linati for some brief notes on the absence of modern Italian literature. / /

Yours
Ezra Pound

13 May 1920   *Hotel Eden, Sirmione, Lago di Garda*
          [longhand]

Dear Joyce: Qui sono in casa mia.

I dont know what your bonds in Trieste may be or whether you are in health enough for the trip, but I wish you would spend a week here with me ("on me", as my guest, or whatever the phrase is.).

The place repays the train trip.—you have Catullus & the subsigned for surety.

Am writing to urge Eliot to take his holiday here, but hope you wont wait that extremely doubtful conjunction, though your being here wd. be an added [*crossout:* urge] instigation to him to come if one cd. get word to him (T. S. Eliot, 18 Crawford Mansions, Crawford St. London. W. 1) in time.

God alone knows when the posts leave this peninsula. Desenzano is 23 minutes by boat & on the direct Milan-Venice line. Perhaps you cd. drop him a line if you are coming, it might save a week=that however is a parenthesis.

The general state of air, lake, olive trees, food here makes me less diffident in inviting you than I cd. have been otherwise—certainly neither Venice nor Verona wd. in their present states have made me feel that an invitation to either of them was wholly amiable.

Here I honestly think the locus wd. induce you [to] forgive the horrible modus.

Yours ever,
Ezra Pound

Say when, but dont trust the post, come without waiting for me to say I have recd. yours of the nth saying you arrive on the mth.

E P

Shall be here, really this time till June 12th–20th.

---

[7] Carlo Linati, Italian writer and friend of Joyce, who translated into Italian *Exiles* (1920) and a section of *Ulysses* (1926).

19 May 1920 *Hotel Eden, Sirmione, Lago di Garda*

[*longhand*]

Dear Joyce: I am extremely glad you are willing to come. I don't think the trip is really murderous for uomo solo carrying a pair of pyjamas and tooth brush. It is worse with three months luggage male & female.

A train starts from Trieste 17.35 and is alleged to arrive at Desenzano at 2.46, which means you wd. probably catch the 5.30 boat & be here at 6.00. I take it you wd. prefer to come in the cool of the night.

I think a week on the lake here is probably worth the journey. That train has 1st. & 2nd. only, but you ought to come 2nd. in any case=

I have done Venice-Paris 3d. often enough in the past—but one's youth doesn't last in full fury.

I dont want to miss you on a mere technicality—if your phrase "try to come" implies fiscal uncertainty, it can be obviated at this end. I have just about enough Italian money to see me to Milan, but cd. probably reimburse you with some form of sec ou liquide negotiable in Trieste.

Will the week of June 1st.–8 suit you—or wd. you rather leave Trieste on a Friday night,—I dont know what you may be wasting time on for practical reasons.—I hope—nothing.=

I am writing Eliot to say your coming isn't impossible—

—I suppose I shall leave between the 15th & 19th of June, and Eliot wd. want a fortnight here—with Mantua, Verona etc. to repay him for trip.—

We might lure over Linati with offer of dinner & night's lodging—if you want, for any reason, to see him. It is only 3 hrs. to Milan, boat and all.

Better bring your "Oxen" with you by hand, unless they are already typed.

=The Dial will never print "Ulysses". The Dial will never be any real fun.=

Will you however ask Benco [8] to send them something (review of Tarr recd.—am forwarding it to W. L.)

[8] Silvio Benco, editor of *Il Piccolo della Sera*, Trieste, for which Joyce wrote several articles.

D[orothy]. has considerably recovered. I enclose her endeavours to convey the colour scheme from the end of the peninsula.=

There *ain't no* real views. The card shows the Roca dei Scaligeri =Also olive trees, lizards (ordinary & larger, 2 emerald green ones of prestigious size   Flora as per enclosure.=

   re/ sketch=all I can say is that the water is quite as blue at times as the bluest part of the paint.=I have never found anything quite up to it save in the Capri grotto, where the entrance acts as a lens & throws the light under the water.=

You ought to stop a night in Venice on your way back to Trieste. (trains fit better that way).

S. Marco is worth looking at.

With regards to your family & to the egregious brother whom I shall regret not seeing.

Yr Ezra Pound

During the first days of June Joyce tried at least once and probably twice to leave Trieste for Sirmione—unsuccessfully. The following letters reflect the confusion of trying to make arrangements by mail during the disorders that were breaking out in postwar Italy. But they reflect even more Joyce's famous propensity for decision and revision and his concern for omens. Richard Ellmann dates the next letter June 5. But May 31 seems more likely; at least the letter contains much that must have been in another letter of about May 31. The wreck Joyce mentions seems to be one that occurred at 1:35 A.M., May 31, at Monfalcone; the strike of wagons-lits personnel, in progress on May 31, ended June 1 (the cuttings Joyce sent were probably from *Il Piccolo della Sera* of May 31; *Il Piccolo*, the morning newspaper, printed the story on June 1, page 1). At any rate, Joyce's letter is dated here May 31 because it clarifies Pound's letters that follow.

[31 May 1920] [9]   *via Sanità, 2^III, Trieste*

Dear Pound: I went to the station this morning to start at 7.30. On my arrival there I was told that a passenger train which had left some hours before had collided with another, result as per enclosed cutting. Luckily I was not on it. I was also told that the 7.30 express Trieste Paris is now off owing to strike. There are two trains between T and Desenzano, viz: one at 11:30 A. M. reaching there about the witching hour of midnight. The other at 5, travel-

---

[9] Ellmann, *James Joyce*, pages 491–493, and *Letters of James Joyce*, II, pages 467–469.

167

ling (or crawling) all night and reaching there about 6 next morning. This train is impossible for me.

Now it is my intention to travel over that line en route for England and Ireland as soon as possible but I think it is unprofitable to go now. I suppose after 12 June you will go on to London. In that case we shall meet then, I hope. My only reason for accepting your kind invitation to Sirmione was to meet you. But still it would be a big expense for you. And also for me if I travelled secondclass. You may judge of the state of the railway here by second cutting.

My reasons for travelling north are these. I am in need of a long holiday (by this I don't mean abandonment of *Ulysses* but quiet in which to finish it) away from here. Without saying anything about this city (*De mortuis nil nisi bonum*) my own position for the past seven months has been very unpleasant. I live in a flat with eleven other people and have had great difficulty in securing time and peace enough to write those two chapters. The second reason is: clothes. I have none and can't buy any. The other members of the family are still provided with decent clothes bought in Switzerland. I wear my son's boots (which are two sizes too large) and his castoff suit which is too narrow in the shoulders, other articles belong or belonged to my brother and to my brother-in-law. I shall not be able to buy anything here. A suit of clothes, they tell me, costs 600–800 francs. A shirt costs 35 francs. I can just live with what I have but no more. Since I came here I suppose I have not exchanged 100 words with anybody. I spend the greater part of my time sprawled across two beds surrounded by mountains of notes. I leave the house at 12.22 and walk the same distance along the same streets buy the Daily Mail which my brother and wife read and return. Idem in the evening. I was once inveigled into a theatre. I was once invited to a public dinner, as professor of the Scuola Superiore here, and next day received from there a request to subscribe 20,000 or 10,000 or even 5000 lire of Italian war loan. I must buy clothes so I think I ought to go to Dublin to buy them.

Thirdly, my two children have not slept in a bed since we came. They repose on hard sofas and the climate here is very trying in July–September.

Fourthly, the rate of exchange is readjusting itself. While the pound (I mean the other pound, the English not the American one) stood at 100 or 90 I could fight the prices here because my money was in English currency. Today the pound is at 62 and my brother-in-law (who is cashier of a bank here) says it is gravitating towards a lower price owing to certain trade manoeuvres or nobody could buy at such high figures. If it reaches 50 I cannot swim any more but disappear under the surface. If I went to Switzerland I could not keep myself or family there: besides I dislike returning to places. Prices here are from 8 to 10 times what they were in 1914.

I could give lessons here (most people expected it of me) but I will not. I have a position in that school which the government has now raised to the rank of a university. My pay is about 3/- an hour for 6 hours a week. This I shall resign as it wastes my time and my nerves.

I cannot find a flat here. To find one you must hold in the right hand a check for 20,000 or 30,000 lire as keymoney.

So I propose to pass three months in Ireland in order to write *Circe* and the close of the book. I should return here with my family in October (if anyone finds a flat for us in the meantime) or, if not, without them in order to write the end of it.

Financially my position is that I shall receive on 25 June (£62-10-0) and if my New York publisher advances (£25). I presume that by the time this £87 is finished I shall [be] within measurable distance of 25 September when I get another £62-10-0. My wife and children could stay in Galway. I too there or in Dublin. The disturbed state of Ireland is of course a reason for not going. There may be other reasons. But I could not go to an English seaside town as it would be too dear. If I manage to do this and if you are in London at the end of June there are, I suppose, several things I could do such as seeing my agent. What do you think of this plan? I must finish my book in quiet even if I sell off the furniture I have here.

I hope you received safely *The Oxen of the Sun* and have sent it off to London and New York. I was bringing down another copy this morning. The worst of it is I fear that Linati may come down on you. I wrote him yesterday express that I should be in Sirmione tonight and mentioned your suggestion of our meeting!

Have you seen *Poesia* or shall I send it?

I hope Mrs. Pound is still well. It is a pity that I cannot see my way to go now but perhaps it is better so if I can manage the other and in that case we can meet more comfortably.

Let me know as soon as possible about the safe arrival of chapter.

With many regrets and regards

Sincerely yours
James Joyce

P.S. This is a very poetical epistle. Do not imagine that it is a subtly worded request for secondhand clothing. It should be read in the evening when the lakewater is lapping and very rhythmically.

2 June 1920 *Hotel Eden, Sirmione, Lago di Garda*
[*longhand*]

Dear Joyce: You may have recd. my telegram acknowledging receipt of Ulysses. We waited dinner till 8:00 and I had prepared such a nice opening speech offering you either food or an invitation to meet my friend the *lavatrice* from up the road.

That evening & all night the tempest raged, at 4:25 such peals of thunder burst on Desenzano, as I thought cd. portend only the arrival of Vulcano Daedalus, attended befittingly with pomps & trumpets.

DAMN

(upon which exclamation the door open'd and the maid brought in a pale envelope.—contents presumably from Linati to Eg. Sig. J. J. am forwarding same.)

Christ. what can I advise you to do.

This hotel is not the cheapest place here, they offer pensione for 4 persons. 2 rooms, 70 lire. and might go lower.

Or you might get cheaper accommodation at the Splendido or Catullo.

Is it any use my saying I will give you l[ire]. 1000 on arrival here. Take this stage of your journey now, and proceed to Ireland later.

I don't quite see how I [can] manage a full invitation to the full family from now till June 25.—

But if it is any use my putting the invitation in the cruder form, for heavens sake waive formality.

By paying up bill at end of 10 days you wd. establish credit & be able to stay here till arrival of your £62—which you cd. have transferred and get at Brescia.

I (contrary to my telegram) can wait till the [*crossout:* 12th or] 14th. =

At any rate you wd. be more comfortable here than in Trieste, and cd. decide when we meet, whether you wd. come on to Paris & Ireland or stay here for quiet.

I must rush this to post.

France was the cheapest place last year.

You could make a living in London. Athenaeum wd. be glad of you.[1]

[1] Joyce composed a limerick on the back of this sheet, see page 179.

[longhand]

Dear Joyce: To continue and (as J. Q. wd. say confirm) epistle just by dint of 100 yd dash to p. o. & down rain-washed pier delivered to piroscafo Angelo Emo.

The best plan I can think of if you are going to Ireland (or even if you are going to try vacation nearer your present "seat".

Is that you shd. come here with family—regarding it as 1st. stage of journey to Ireland.

I shall be glad to contribute lire 1000 [*insert:* (one thousand)] to campaign fund, but cant wrestle with further details. Still that shd. serve to establish yr. credit on the peninsula until arrival of your £62.

upon which you cd. decide whether you wd. go on to Ireland or take Italian villiagiatura.

I dont see how I can stay here after the 14th

Aldington used to stay in Sirmione comfortably at less than the rates of this hotel.—at any rate the l. 1000 wd. break the back of a fortnights expenses here and we cd. then discuss matters, relative cheapness of France & Isles Britanique I can report on from Paris.

You cd. have yr. £62 sent on to Brescia, if it cant be postal ordered here.

Dont know what you make by being a Professore.

With your reputation you shd. be able to live—oh christ, I don't know how anyone lives.

I live but haven't offspring, & dont in the least know how to calculate to a family of four.

Still shd. think the Athenaeum & Dial cd. provide you food & shelter with less waste of energy than is implied in your Trieste job.—[*insert:* cant judge your tastes or what gets on your nerves—cant recommend a course to you till we meet.]

Clothing emphatically <u>not</u> needed in Sirmione.

I cant offer you full expenses between arrival & June 25 as I shd like to; I've got a bloody draft on Genoa & christ knows how & how long it will take to get it cashed.

171

I can risk a delay in Milan, but not to be there without car fare to get to Paris.

Besides your food in Trieste *wd.* cost you something between now & the arrival of £62.

I wont make further alternative suggestions until I hear from you.

You might telegraph if this suggestion is utterly unacceptable for reasons unknown to me and I will then animadvert upon the rest of your letter.—

At any rate a stop here wd. ease the trip to London considerably.

I shd. see you during your transit of Paris if you go to Ireland.

But much better have a week's peace together here if possible.

Later

N. B. Have just found 2 rooms at Albergo de la Pace. looks clean, kitchen smells good. proprietor friend of my old friend Menegatti. Offers pensione @ 14 lire. i.e. 56 lire per day for the four of you. Am wondering if I wont try the place myself if I come here again.

I think that price with the appearance of place. ought to make feasible the fiscal side.

Caffe latte., mezzo giorno. suppa & paste, piatto carne con legume, frutta & formaggio.—

evening same. Rooms larger than ours here, & view on lake & with garden.

tutto compreso, no dieci percento servizio in su.

Only come as soon as you can. I want to see something of you before I go north.

Wire and I'll reserve the rooms at Pace; though I dont think there is likelihood of their being *all* full. better get the best ones.

I think you can get clothes in Verona at better terms than in London. I bought a coat there once & it wore like iron—however I will leave those details in hope we can soon talk.

Yrs
Ezra Pound

air here wd. be good for the children where there will be someone capable of taking care of same.

_____

Re. your *mss.* I don't make out whether a section has gone astray.

I recd. in London & forwarded Nausika (?) Bloom by the sea waves & the lady of delectable shins.

Also communicated with you re/same; I being in the wrong, but not in position to know it until adumbrations of chapter recd. here.

Feast in House of Horne,[2] of which I have forwarded one copy to Little Review. I think it better to carry other copy to Paris for safety's sake, as The Egoist isn't printing it, and 3 or 4 days don't matter.

My mother-in-law does not appear to have recd. any other packet from you since my departure.—

As there are no numbers or headings to the typescript of yr. chapters it is not always easy to keep an exact tab.

My last ten days in London were such that ANYTHING may have happened; I may have recd. a mss. & forwarded it during the last 24 hrs.

But this seems extremely unlikely.

[*crossout:* I never have done] That sort of thing [*insert:* not exactly my habit] but one grows increasingly gaga with time's attrition.

_____

Paris shd. certainly be convenient. If by any chance the Elysée shd. be full (very unlikely) I wd. get rooms near by.

We cd. meet again in London, but I don't think the accommodations wd. be as easily found. Though will of course find them for you, if you give me specifications.

However you have to go via Paris & will certainly be ready for a couple of nights' rest when you get there.

I am glad you have got your voice, or part of it back. I have the organ of a tree toad, fortunately, for if I had been able ever to sing "My Countree tiz of Theeee," without going off the key four times in each bar, I shd. have warbled & done no bloomin' thing else—che peccato

[2] The lying-in hospital, "Oxen of the Sun."

173

& wot a loss to litterchure. It wd. however be an exaggeration to say that

> In vainest of exasperation
> Mr. P. passed his vacation
>   the cause of his visit
>   To the Eyetaliann cities
> Was blocked, by a wreck, at the station.

I hope you like the yidd in the short ones.

As a matter of fact, I have damaged my vacation by trying to write 12 articles for the New Age [3]—I have scribbled something or other on 96 sheets of paper, and may the gods rest my soul.

I was going give you the advance sheets of my last cameos,[4] but will reserve same until you get to Paris or London, & you will already have bloody enough printed matter about you in Triest.

Heard from edtr. of Convegno yesterday. Shall see him, I presume in Milan, and tell him to translate Portrait.

Have sent rev. of Lewis to Eliot; W. L. will get it in due time.

Greeting to your spouse and offshoots. Will hope to inspect & possibly to equal Giorgio's appetite in some of the lower caravansaries of the French Babylon.

─────────

Your "having nothing to offer Dial & Ath" is not really the point. Wot t'ell do I offer the Ath. save a general dislike of the modern English theatre?

However it is a question of how much this sort of work wd. bore you, & how much it wd. put you off your real work.

I cling to the rock of Gautier, deluding myself perhaps with the idea that he did journalism for years without becoming an absolute shit.

A bientot, speriamo.

yrs
E. P.

[3] "Indiscretions, or Une revue de deux mondes," twelve installments, *The New Age, May–August* 1920. These articles about his family and American social history reflect Pound's search for a fuller perspective on himself as an American in Europe.
[4] Probably *Hugh Selwyn Mauberley,* London: The Ovid Press, 1920.

At this point negotiations become confusing. Pound, scribbling, breaking off, running to hotels to make arrangements as though he were Catullus's one-man chamber of commerce, and then sending off a second letter before the ink on the first was dry, reflects the multiple cross-purposes. At the same time Joyce reflected an indecision opposite to Pound's determination in a card, postmarked Thursday, June 3, which he sent to Nora from Portogruaro, a station halfway between Trieste and Venice: "Take the two tickets for *Friday* night and go whether I am back or not. If I arrive on Friday." Then, however, he added, "*No*, better wait till I write again" (at Cornell).[5] Apparently he had started out after the track had been cleared and the strike ended, but with no very certain idea when he might get to Sirmione, how long he might stay—or, for that matter, whether he would go at all, even though he had traveled part way. Presumably (perhaps agitated by his "dread of thunderstorms and detestation of travelling"—"Very boring day with storm threatening," the card concludes) he turned back. Having regained Trieste, he apparently wrote Pound another letter in which, also responding to Pound's of June 2, he reiterated that he wanted nothing to interfere with *Ulysses* and that it would be impossible for him to write articles for living expenses; he also must have repeated his suggestion that Pound come to Trieste, for, as the next letter indicates, Pound very nearly did. The fitting end to this glorious mix-up was a further change of Joyce's mind. As he wrote to Miss Weaver on July 12:

> Mr Pound wrote to me so urgently from Sirmione (lake of Garda) that in spite of my dread of thunderstorms and detestation of travelling I went there bringing my son with me to act as a lightning conductor.[6]

While Pound was writing the following letter, Joyce was on his way.

7–8 June 1920   *Sirmio*
                      [*longhand*]

Dear Joyce:
                    I. Point of agreement:
Nothing is to be done to impede finishing of Ulysses, or with any aim than to facilitate said wk. & subsequent TelemaX, Atreidae or other.

[5] *Letters of James Joyce,* II, page 467.
[6] *Letters of James Joyce,* I, page 142.

Having cast spare parts into ruck-sack, ex. u-shrt. etc. I followed St. Augustine's council: In coitu sapientia, in balneo consolatio.[7]

After 40 minutes in hot sulphur (40° cent.)—10 minutes longer that Dr. of Regie Therme prescribes. It struck me that I shd. be an ass to come to Trieste this p. m., especially as one Woodward had just written that he wd. try to effect junction in Milan on the 10th and that I haven't seen him for ten yrs. or am likely to unless I go to U.S.A.

I shd. be in Paris from June 15th until at least the middle of July. I suggest that, as you have to go to Ireland via Paris (Brussels route not working) you let me put you up for a couple of days in Paris.

Presuming that you will arrive early in July (? ?) I expect to be at

Hotel de l'Elysée

3 rue de Beaune.

at any rate that is my next postal address unless you have something Expresso, care Linati, whom I shall try to see on Thursday. (10th)

I shall have to be in Milan long enough to get a Genoa draft put through, probably till Tuesday. (14th)

I think, with Dial business in flow, I shall be seeing people in Paris who shd, or might be useful to you, & that it is worth while trying to make this junction.

The Portrait ought to be translated into french. God knows who has the wits, but! ! !

Might get Dubliners started. Ulysses is impossible save in original, or tr. by some one more intelligent than is now in Paris.

Probably more important or more solidly sensible that we shd. be together in Paris, than that we shd. meet here.

Only I had fixed idea; and my suggestion that you shd. bring family here was more an offshoot of it, than manifestation [of] thought, or of real consideration for your comfort.

The curse of me & my nation is that we always think things can be bettered by immediate action of some sort, any sort rather than no sort.

God forbid that I shd. urge you to live where you don't want to; I thought from yours before last, that you found Trieste had gone bad.

[7] "In coitus wisdom, in the bath consolation" (a take-off? Pound's adaptation of the first phrase, "in coitu inluminatio," is prominent in *The Cantos*).

If your teaching is literally 6 hrs. $\times$ 3 shillings⚯=£50 per annum. If your free income is £250 & if you can live on ? ? ? £300; I don't think it is necessary for you to go on teaching unless you want to.

I think that small sum of difference cd. easily be found among a half dozen people who like your work & who wd. prefer you continue it without petty hindrance.

I know that people have in times past suggested that I shd. make money by writing stories, and that it may be just as impossible for you to write "articles."

Also that any by-product might waste more of your energy than does teaching.

That is the sort of thing that can only be settled in talk.

All I want to indicate is that I don't think you need regard yourself as tied to Trieste by your job, IF you are fed up with the place & want to pull out of it.

Its effect, or lack of effect, on your work has certainly been satisfactory.

The important thing is that you shd. do what you like, or what at any rate you dislike least of possible alternatives, and that there shd. be minimum possible interference with your writing.

Other Points.

Certainly send books in my care to London, not to the flat where there is but a witless female porter, but to

  12 Brunswick Gdns. W.8.

[letter breaks off]

And then, unexpectedly, Joyce arrived. The very form of Pound's letter reflects the scene. One would like to think that Joyce unexpectedly walked in while Pound was writing. But it is only *almost* so melodramatic. More likely, Pound suddenly received a telegram from Nora that announced that Joyce was on his way and gave his time of arrival. Pound went to Desenzano to meet him.

So, after nearly seven years of correspondence, the two writers

177

met at last, largely because of Pound's irrepressible insistence. Pound asked about the source of the first anonymous grant Joyce had received in Zurich. "A minute after I had made his acquaintance in Desenzano, as we drove across the country by night, he asked me, 'Was it John Quinn then?' My high tenor shout of 'Who?' must have been heard in Milan," Joyce wrote to Harriet Weaver later.[8] They discussed *The Dial* and European contributors; Pound wrote to Linati explaining what *The Dial* wanted for an article on Italian writing, and Joyce appended a note (at Yale).[9] Joyce thought Pound "a large bundle of unpredictable electricity," "a miracle of ebulliency, gusto, and help," but suspected that "Pound had been disappointed in him at their first meeting and considered him pretty much of a hopeless bourgeois."[1] Pound later took exactly this view of Joyce, but now he wrote to Quinn from Paris, June 19:

Joyce finally got to Sirmione; don't yet know whether he has got back to Trieste. Strike started half an hour after I got to Milan, and many trains stopped where they were at the stroke of 12.

Joyce—pleasing; after the first shell of cantankerous Irishman, I got the impression that the real man is the author of *Chamber Music*, the sensitive. The rest is the genius; the registration of realities on the temperament, the delicate temperament of the early poems. A concentration and absorption passing Yeats'—Yeats has never taken on anything requiring the condensation of *Ulysses*.

Also great exhaustion, but more constitution than I had expected, and apparently good recovery from eye operation.

He is coming up here later; long reasons, but justified in taking a rest from Trieste.

He is, of course, stubborn as a mule or an Irishman, but I failed to find him at all *unreasonable*. Thank God, he has been stubborn enough to know his job and stick to it.

Re his personal arrangements, etc., all seems clear in light of conversation.

He is also dead right in refusing to interrupt his stuff by writing stray articles for cash. Better in the end, even from practical point of view. Also justified in sticking it out in

[8] February 1, 1927, Ellmann, *James Joyce,* page 602.
[9] *Letters of James Joyce,* II, pages 469–471.
[1] Gorman, *James Joyce,* page 272.

Trieste, at least for the present. Both climate and other considerations.

In the stories of his early eccentricities in Dublin, I have always thought people neglected the poignant feature, i. e., that his "outrageous" remarks were usually *so*.

His next work will go to the *Dial*, but he should rest after *Ulysses*.

Joyce remained for two days; after he had explained his circumstances and purposes fully, it was decided that he would follow Pound to Paris. Joyce commemorated the meeting by writing on the back of Pound's first letter of June 2 an answer to the limerick Pound had enclosed in his second letter:

> A bard once in lakelapped Sermione
> Lived in peace, eating locusts and honey,
> > Till a son of a bitch
> > Left him dry on the beach
> Without clothes, boots, time, quiet or money [2]

Joyce returned to Trieste to gather his family. The Joyce caravan departed for Paris on about July 4, 1920.

---

[2] Joyce composed his limerick carefully to achieve both precise realism and classic form:
    A [*crossout:* hermit] bard once [*insert:* in lakelapped] Sermione
    [*crossout:* On locusts pure air & wild honey]
    Lived in peace, [*crossout:* fed on] eating locusts and honey,
    [*crossout:* But] Till a son of a bitch
    [*crossout:* But] Left him dry on the beach
    Without [*crossout:* time], clothes, boots, [*insert:* time] quiet [*crossout:* and] or money

1920-1924

When the Joyce family arrived in Paris on July 9 Pound was there to help them settle. Joyce's most pressing needs were money, a place to live, and freedom to complete the book he had begun in 1914. Perhaps even more he needed acquaintances in the Paris literary world—acquaintances who could bring recognition to his work and perhaps at last make it a real means of support. Pound, who was considering a move to Paris, but was about to return to London for a last try there, set Joyce up in a flat near his own lodgings. He then took him in tow and they began to make the rounds. Pound placed copies of *A Portrait* in influential hands as harbingers of Joyce's own appearance with his enigmatic demeanor and his fertilizing flood of press notices. Jenny Serruys was chosen to translate *A Portrait*, but she decided she could not undertake so difficult a task. Joyce must be helped, Pound insisted:

Chère et Delicieuse, Yes, I know he is a great author; in fact the best prose author we have, since James (Henry) and Hardy.

But still, and for Christ's sake, get him a bed for his too large son to sleep on and some (if possible) bedding.

This prayer after a day's hell hunting visas—and I also a respectable author whose soul—such as it is—vale et me ama—should not be dragged down to a question of sheets and truckle-beds for the errors J.J.'s his misspent premalthusian youth Benedictions,

E.P.[1]

Miss Serruys was at least able to rustle up a portable bed for the lanky Giorgio and to persuade A.F. Lugné-Poë, who had been successfully staging experimental plays, to consider producing a translated version of *Exiles* at the Théâtre de l'Oeuvre. As for *A Portrait*, Pound persuaded Mme. Ludmilla Bloch-Savitsky to put aside another work that she was about to translate: "You must translate Joyce's book, and right away. There's nothing in the literature of the world today, and not much in the literature of the past, that is

[1] *Letters of James Joyce*, III, page 9.

up to it" [2] (*A Portrait* appeared in 1924 as *Dedalus*). Mme. Bloch-Savitsky also lent her flat to the Joyce family from mid-July until the end of August. Pound introduced his protégé to various other persons who could put him in touch with editors and publishers. The most important contact occurred on July 11, when Pound took the Joyces to a soirée at André Spire's. There Joyce first met Sylvia Beach, soon to become the publisher of *Ulysses*.

While he was in Paris and after he had returned to London, Pound put at Joyce's disposal whatever money he could lay his hands on, and as he had done in the past took up Joyce's cause with practical action and extravagant schemes. Joyce wrote jokingly to Stanislaus on July 25: "Pound wanted to get the Duchess of Marlborough to apply for the position vacated by Mrs. M[cCormick]. but her bloody old father W K Vanderbilt died here in the next street to us the day before yesterday, very inconsiderately, I think" (at Cornell).[3] Pound sent Joyce to visit one of Pound's admirers, the Belgian art critic Fritz Vanderpyl; Joyce obtained a loan. When Pound returned to London to try to arrange his own affairs, he stirred up Joyce's agents, seeking payment of royalties. After Pound had interviewed "Messrs Box and Cox" and extracted a royalty check, which Pinker sent on, Joyce proposed to Pound in a letter of July 31 that a series of press notices appear in England and America: "Joyce gets Large Haul. Prompt Pinker Saves Desperate Dedalus. Glut of Greenbacks for Poet in Poverty." [4] Joyce assumed that $200 sent by John Quinn for manuscripts of *Ulysses* and a third benefaction by Miss Weaver were due to Pound's efforts, though there is no evidence that Pound was behind either.

Pound was also involved in the complicated negotiations for an edition of *Ulysses*. Miss Weaver and Huebsch were considering publication but were having difficulties because of printers' refusals and fear of suppression. Quinn suggested a private edition, to be published either by Huebsch or by Boni & Liveright, whom Pound had interested in the book. John Rodker proposed that, to bypass recalcitrant printers, the book be published in France under the *Egoist* imprint and imported across the channel. Urged by Pound, the Rodkers visited Joyce to discuss arrangements, at the same time sustaining the hungry family by inviting them all to a much-needed

[2] Ludmilla Savitsky, "Dedalus in France," in Joyce, *Dedalus,* Paris, 1943, page 7 (Ellmann, *James Joyce,* page 500).

[3] *Letters of James Joyce,* III, page 10.

[4] *Letters of James Joyce,* III, page 12. "Box and Cox" (Pinker is meant) alludes to an operetta of that name by F. Burnand and Sir Arthur Sullivan, 1867.

dinner. Pound also sent T. S. Eliot and Wyndham Lewis, of whom Pound had been speaking for years but whom Joyce had never met. Eliot and Lewis transported across the Channel a big package carefully wrapped in brown paper and painstakingly tied with innumerable knots. When Joyce opened the expected treasure in their awed presences it was discovered to contain some second-hand clothes and a used but serviceable pair of old brown shoes.[5] (Pound had not forgotten the inventory of complaints Joyce had sent him at Sirmione). All in all, Pound was Joyce's sponsor and provider during the difficult days when Joyce was new in Paris and had not yet established his position there. As Joyce commented to Miss Weaver on July 12, "I hope that all this will lead to something practical. It is all due to Mr Pound's energy." [6]

In London, Pound tried to pick up again his connection as a drama critic with John Middleton Murry's *Athenaeum*; he had not yet decided to give up London, but when the *Athenaeum* job fell through he began to think of leaving the "brass-bound clay-hummock" for good. He leaned toward Paris but was entertaining the idea of a return to the United States. His first note from London recalls his asides to the censor about his enclosures and his apparently cryptic remarks, and Joyce's cautions that he should avoid crossouts; it illustrates in another way the problem posed by the gap between "normal" writing and modern literature. Pound encountered similar suspicions in 1945 when he was trying to send manuscripts of *The Pisan Cantos* from the U. S. Army Disciplinary Training Center at Pisa; he wrote a letter to the camp censor explaining that the poetry contained "nothing in the nature of cypher or intended obscurity," but alluded to previous cantos and prison camp life.[7]

[?July] 1920 *London*

Dear James: News item or rather phrase of conversation from ex-govt. official: "The censorship was very much troubled by it (*Ulysses*) during the war. Thought it was all code."

Joyce, still nursing a grudge against his old enemies, the British consular officials in Switzerland, replied to Pound's note:

[5] Wyndham Lewis, *Blasting and Bombardiering,* London: Eyre and Spottiswoode, 1937, pages 273–275.

[6] *Letters of James Joyce,* I, page 143.

[7] *Paris Review,* Paris and New York, 28 (Summer-Fall 1962), page 17.

As regards the information concerning the intelligent government official (who would go with Pinker as secretary to the Nith office when Rumbold is made king of Neland) I believe the instigation came direct from the consul in Zurich, Mr Percy Bennett, at present in Panama. As no one has taken any steps to remind him that he is a public servant he can sleep peacefully. The typescript could not have seemed suspicious except *Sirens* which was published long after the armistice. And as for said government official if he has no money to give let me never hear of him again in this life or the next.[8]

2 August 1920   *London*

My dear Joyce: You are probably cursing me for not taking more direct action. I enclose both Huebsch and another epistle, i.e. from *Athenaeum* to myself, re what shd. have been my chief local asset, and which was (fu) my chief cash reason for return to this brass-bound clay-hummock.

Kindly return same. Modest mensuality amounting roughly to £120 per annum. Of course I shall welcome the leisure.

Equally of course I never had the faintest belief in Huebsch paying £ £ £ advance on mss. he hadn't seen; what*ever* he or anyone else might have written about it.

Re your letter before last. I shall take it as an extremely unfriendly act if you instruct your damn solicitors to do anything of the sort; which wd. be pure imbecility on the one hand, you being sure to need the cash three weeks later; and damn'd unpleasant of you on the other, as I should like to make at least that small contribution to the running expenses of *Ulysses*.

If you find your circle kantankerrrrous, you might also reflect upon the fact that Murry wrote me two letters while I was in Paris, and might conceivably have included in one of them the news so amiably conferred in his of 27th ult., as it wd. only 'ave clouded the last Parisian hours.

I don't on the hole despair of hitting another couple of *small* bunches between now an' Sept. 25.

Rodker was delighted to see you, but his wife is in an interestin' condition and I suppose they are savin' for the layette. However, he offers to give an imprint to *Ulysses* if the *Egoist* will provide the £ for the actual printing somewhere else, which may possibly be a

[8] *Letters of James Joyce*, III, page 13.

183

solution, though I think American printing is the most economical way out of the difficulty. By printing near the sea-board the work can be legally exported.

Eliot leaves for France, via Paris, on about Aug. 15.

1 September 1920   *London*

Dear Joyce: (You can forward this note to Dr. Ferrieri.[9]) I strongly recommend that Rodker be asked to do the article on English literature. There are only a very few decent critics with "tendenze moderne." Neither Hueffer nor Eliot are to be had free, and both are very busy. I have recently said my say in *Instigations* besides doing articles on state of literature in England for French and Spanish magazines. Rodker will take more trouble, and be more interested in writing the article than any of the rest of us.

Dr. Ferrieri's article has been translated I think quite well, I will know when it comes back from the typist, as I can't be expected to read handwriting, life is too short. Am sending the article to New York as soon as it comes in from typist.

Regards to Sig. Ferrieri and Linati.

Hope your news is all good.

[c. October] 1920 [1]   *London*

Dear Joyce: I enclose a letter from Quinn, which you need not of necessity read. Point is that "Nausikaa" has been pinched by the PO-lice. Only way to get *Ulysses* printed in book form, will be to agree not to print any more of it in the *L.R.*

I had already made this suggestion on other ground, namely that the expensive private edition planned by Quinn wd. have wider sale if it contained final chapters which had not already appeared in *L.R.*

Also in Paris I did, I think, explain to you that M. A. and j. h. had not spent any money on you. I got the original trifle that was sent you, and the printing deficits were paid by J. Q., and in general the editrices have merely messed and muddled, NEVER to their own loss.

The best thing to do, now that things have come to present pass is

[9] Dr. Enzo Ferrieri, editor of *Il Convegno*, Milan, which had just printed Linati's translation of *Exiles* (April–May–June 1920). The article Pound refers to is one or both of Ferrieri's "Italian Letters," *The Dial*, January and February 1921.

[1] Erroneously dated 1919 in *Letters*, page 150.

to turn the whole matter over to Quinn. He is on the spot and both will and can deal with local conditions better than we can from here.

The excuse for parts of *Ulysses* is the WHOLE of *Ulysses*; the case for publication of bits of it serially is weak; the editrices having sent copy to someone who hadn't asked for it further weakens case.

ANYHOW, the only thing to be done now is to give Quinn an absolutely free hand. His cable address is QUINLEX, New York; and you will have to cable your full authorization to him at once if it is to arrive in time.

QUINLEX

New York

As you have said—"No country outside of Africa" wd. permit it.[2]

Issues of *The Little Review* for January and May 1919 and January 1920 had been banned by the U.S. Post Office because of "Laestrygonians," "Scylla and Charybdis," and "Cyclops," but *The Little Review* had continued to print *Ulysses* anyway. The July–August issue was not only seized but also prosecuted by the New York Society for the Prevention of Vice. Quinn defended *The Little Review* but in February 1921 the case was lost. The suppression of "Nausikaa" brought serial publication of *Ulysses* to an end. When Huebsch and then Boni and Liveright, who had been considering publication in New York, decided not to print it, all hopes for either an English or an American edition were ended.

Joyce meanwhile had been caught up in the whirlwind of Paris. He felt himself to be a part of an Odyssean movement. In his July 25, 1920, letter to Stanislaus he wrote: "Odyssey very much in the air here. Anatole France is writing *Le Cyclope*, G. Fauré, the musician an opera *Pénélope*. Giraudoux has written *Elpenor* (Paddy Dignam). Guillaume Apollinaire *Les Mamelles de Tirésias*. . . . Madame Circe advances regally towards her completion after which I hope to join a tennis club." [3] He discussed Gide and read some Proust. From editors who were supposedly prepared to print his works he sought definite commitments. But he was annoyed because his books had been delayed in arriving from Trieste; moves from flat

---

[2] Ellmann quotes Joyce, "No country outside of Africa will print it," *James Joyce,* page 512.
[3] *Letters of James Joyce,* III, pages 10–11.

to flat and househunting fatigued him; his eye troubles recurred; gradually it became apparent that his works would not be translated and published in France as early as expected. Various schemes for publishing *Ulysses* in America, or even for continuing *The Little Review* in the face of pending prosecution, made Joyce vacillate between hope and skepticism. His Christmas card to Pound in 1920 expresses his darkly humorous fatalism. (His verses refer to Richard Wallace, an American book illustrator connected with the advertising business who was trying to help revive *The Little Review*.)

Bis Dat Qui Cito Dat [4]

Yanks who hae wi' Wallace read,
Yanks whom Joyce has often bled,
Welcome to the hard plank bed,
    And bolshevistic flea.
Who for Bloom and Inisfail
Longs to pine in Sing Sing jail,
Picking oakum without bail,
    Let him publish me.

Nevertheless he was able to tell Pound that he had finished "Circe" and would send it on when it had been revised and typed.

At the end of 1920, Pound, having failed to establish a connection in London, finally confirmed the attitude implicit in *Mauberley* and decided to leave, perhaps for a year, perhaps for good. Further thought about contemporary history and further study of Douglas's critique of economic practices had confirmed what he had stated in "The Revolt of Intelligence." He had begun to write essays on Douglas and economic history for *The New Age, The Little Review*, and other periodicals. He seemed headed for Paris, which promised some vitality and a new setting for artistic heroism. During his hurried visit in 1920 he had sought among the ornamental sphinxes which dot Paris "the triple extract of literature for export purposes, . . . a poetic serum to save English letters from postmature and American letters from premature suicide and decomposition." [5] He had been intrigued by Julien Benda's desire for "lack of organization," which he defined later as Paris's "greatly

[4] "He gives quickly who gives twice," Latin proverb. *Letters of James Joyce,* III, page 34.
[5] "The Island of Paris: A Letter," *The Dial,* LXIX, 4 (October 1920), page 406.

blessed indiscipline": "Indiscipline is perhaps in this aspect [an "instinct against the vested interests"] the only basis of culture." [6] He had sensed common interests and a stir of life in such young French writers as André Breton, Louis Aragon, and others who were close to the dadaists and cubists. In 1918 they had begun to publish from Zurich papers which "satirized the holy church of our century (journalism)" and "the sanctimonious attitude toward 'the arts.'" They had begun to talk about "'metallurgie' and the international financiers," and had no capital invested in the erection of themselves into literary monuments. "They have given up the pretense of impartiality. They have expressed a desire to live and to die, preferring death to a sort of moribund permanence." [7] Pound's decision was based on a conviction that the moribundity of western civilization made a voluntarist "break" and a "rappel à l' ordre" the only viable action. His personal "break" was no less than a decision to identify his personal life with what he took to be the direction of history.

At the same time he had been preparing for a new direction in his own life and in his work. "Indiscretions" is a symptom of the former; the latter is evident in *Umbra* (1920), a new collection of his poetry before *Lustra*, and in *Poems 1918–21*, which collects *Propertius, Langue D'Oc-Moeurs Contemporaines*, and *Mauberley* as "Three Portraits," and *Cantos* IV–VII. These reassessments of his past and regroupings of his work appear in retrospect as necessary steps toward his once more taking up work on *The Cantos* in 1922. Pound announced his departure from London and implied this new direction in "Axiomata," his "intellectual will and testament," *The New Age*, January 13, 1921. "Axiomata" is a metaphysical counterpart of his poetic farewell in *Mauberley* and of the Odyssean departure from Circe's house in *Canto* I. In a series of maxims he asserted the existence of transcendental states of mind accessible to the free imagination and attacked the tyranny over mind and personality which he felt in London. The theme: "Belief is a cramp, a paralysis, an atrophy of the mind in certain positions." His motive is almost precisely that of Stephen Dedalus in *A Portrait;* "Axiomata" recalls Stephen's last diary entries before he left for Paris two decades earlier.

When Joyce finished revising "Circe" he thought it the best part of

[6] "Paris Letter," *The Dial,* LXXI, 4 (October 1921), page 463.

[7] "The Island of Paris: A Letter," *The Dial,* LXIX, 4 (October 1920), pages 407–408.

his book. He wrote to Miss Weaver on February 4, 1921, that he wanted to send it off to Pound as usual, though it seemed doubtful that "the reading of such a Walpurgisnacht will do his or anybody else's health much good." [8] Such self-deprecation seems almost to have conjured up difficulties in getting "Circe" and "Eumaeus" typed. Even the arrival of the typed copies failed to console him. On April 3 he wrote to Miss Weaver that 1921 $(1 + 9 + 2 + 1 = 13)$ would be a year of incessant trouble, adding dejectedly "They (the copies) are so irritating that I wish I knew where to throw them. It is risky to send them to Mr Pound at a possible address and he does not appear to be interested in receiving the embarrassing parcel and Mr Rodker or the *Little Review* or Mr Quinn or Mr Huebsch may not want them either." [9] What was going on in the mind of the "non-conformist parson from Aberdeen" (as Pound had called him) is not clear; in all likelihood, however, he felt that his foremost trumpet-blaster's reservations about "Sirens" had turned into disinterest.

But Joyce had already found other champions. Sylvia Beach and Adrienne Monnier, proprietors of the Shakespeare and Company and La Maison des Amis des Livres bookshops, had brought the French writer and critic Valery Larbaud to meet Joyce at a party on Christmas Eve 1920, and Joyce had lent Larbaud the copies of *The Little Review*. In February, after two months of silence, Larbaud had suddenly burst forth with the kind of enthusiasm Pound had displayed about *A Portrait* and the early chapters of *Ulysses*. Joyce wrote to Budgen in February 1921, portentously juxtaposing Pound and Larbaud: "No word or syllable of a word from Pound. I had a letter from Mr Valery Larbaud (French translator of S. Butler and novelist) says he has read *Ulysses* and is raving mad over it, that Bloom is as immortal as Falstaff (except that he has a few more years to live—Editor) and that the book is as great as Rabelais (Merde du bon Dieu et foutre de nom de nom —comment of Monsieur François))." [1] Larbaud decided to translate some pages to go with an article in the *Nouvelle Revue Française*, and Misses Beach and Monnier persuaded Larbaud to introduce *Ulysses* to France at a public meeting of Les Amis des Livres at Miss Monnier's bookshop later in the year. Finally, Miss Beach proposed early in April that Shakespeare and Company print *Ulysses*. Joyce, close to despair after Huebsch and Boni & Liveright had

[8] *Letters of James Joyce,* I, page 157.
[9] *Letters of James Joyce,* I, page 161.
[1] *Letters of James Joyce,* I, page 159.

declined the book because of the decision against *The Little Review*, accepted. A contract was signed and *Ulysses* was to appear at last—as soon as it was finished.

Just at this point—Joyce had lost track of him for several months—Pound suddenly reappeared. Instead of settling in Paris at once he had headed for his adopted regions in Provence, as he had done in 1919 (indeed, he had still been considering a return to America). Surprised at receiving a card from Pound, Joyce met him on April 16 and gave him "Circe" and "Eumaeus" to read. All of Pound's enthusiasm flooded back. He wrote of "Circe": "Joyce next chapter great stuff"; "Joyce 'Circe' chapter here in transcript. Magnificent, a new Inferno in full sail"; "Joyce's new chapter is enormous—megaloscrumptious-mastodonic." [2] With that flurry and fanfare Pound threw himself into the international life in Paris.

The first enterprise was an attempt to reconstitute *The Little Review* as a quarterly, beginning with material from Parisian writers and from the sculptor Constantin Brancusi; Pound wrote to Marianne Moore in April that it was also to be "a protest against the imbecile suppression of Joyce's *Ulysses*." He was translating Remy de Gourmont's *Physique de l'amour; essai sur l'instinct sexuel* to keep the pantechnicon going and was working on what was to become his opera *Villon*. In August *Cantos* V, VI, and VII, completed before the end of 1919, appeared in *The Dial* and then in his *Poems 1918–21*. He also threw himself into the promotion of the long-awaited *Ulysses*, becoming involved in a long controversy by letter with George Bernard Shaw, who had refused to subscribe. In October 1921 his "Paris Letter" became a regular feature in *The Dial*. Parisian civilization, he began to report, was superior to that in England and America. He urged resignation from any modern "hyperunity," be it political (the capitalist state), intellectual (coercive ideologies), religious (monotheism), or syntactical (the "rocking cradle" of the English sentence). In *The Dial* and elsewhere he continued to emphasize "the economic factor" and Major Douglas's theories. In the special issue of *The Little Review* (Autumn 1921), in "Historical Survey," an up-to-date version of his "Meditatio" of 1916, probably written as before with Joyce in mind, he extended his old antagonism against the idea that an artist "ought" to govern his work by a desire "to get or *keep* an audience, or to conform to some standard of culture, or to avoid a 'vulgarity,'

[2] Letters to Isabel Pound, April 24, and Homer Pound, April 20, 1921, at Yale; to Agnes Bedford, *Letters,* April 1921.

or to please a cult (ethical, religious, arty)." "A work of art, one almost ought to call it an 'act of art,' is enjoyable in proportion as the maker has made it to please himself." That was the test of the real, the alive. Art seemed to be less concerned with shaping society than with "the question of survival of personality," a question Pound now called "metaphysical rather than ethical."

After assurances and reassurances offered in the contract with Sylvia Beach and by Larbaud's enthusiasm, Joyce's life returned to the tenor he had predicted for 1921. He was oppressed by the rush to finish his book, and fatigue and chronic difficulties with his eyes continued to afflict him. Proofs began to come in, demanding immediate correction, and although publication and critical support had been assured they had not yet materialized. By summer the discouragements had piled up. He complained to Miss Weaver on June 24 about the slow process of getting *Dubliners* and *A Portrait* translated and about the time-consuming weekly reunions at which he had to listen to literary gossip and to "enthusiastic expressions about my (unread) masterpiece"; moreover, Lugné-Poë had rejected *Exiles* (the pessimistic Joyce won a box of apricots from Pound, who had bet that Lugné-Poë would accept it). Joyce closed the list of his complaints by remarking, "The only person who knows anything worth mentioning about the book [*Ulysses*] is Mr Valery Larbaud. He is now in England." [3]

Joyce had been explaining to Larbaud the Odyssean parallels. Thus at his séance on *Ulysses*, which took place on December 7, 1921, with great success, Larbaud developed Joyce's "line," emphasizing the Homeric key and the elaborate symbolisms. Piqued by charges that his work was formless and chaotic, Joyce had lent the famous "summary-key-skeleton-scheme (for your personal use only)" to Carlo Linati [4] and to Larbaud, and had urged Eliot to follow up Larbaud's line in replying to Richard Aldington's criticism that *Ulysses* represented chaos chaotically. [5] Whether Joyce explained the key to Pound or not, Pound was conspicuously absent from Larbaud's séance. Richard Ellmann attributes to Pound the motive that he was "annoyed to have his discovery rediscovered." [6]

[3] *Letters of James Joyce,* I, pages 165–167.

[4] *Letters of James Joyce,* I, page 146.

[5] Richard Aldington, "The Influence of Mr. James Joyce," *English Review,* London, April 1921. Eliot discussed Aldington's article with Joyce in 1921 (*Letters of James Joyce,* I, page 157, and III, page 42), but his well-known "'Ulysses,' Order and Myth" did not appear until November 1923, in *The Dial.*

[6] Ellmann, *James Joyce,* page 535.

However that may be, Pound took his own line; Joyce confided more and more in Larbaud and others.

The fact is that Joyce proportioned his esteem to the interest in, enthusiasm for, and support of what he was doing; his willingness to confide depended upon the number of these attitudes another person held and the intensity with which he held one or more at a particular moment. Accordingly, Pound recalled in 1955:

... to best of my recollection he never alluded to any of his eng/ & am/ contemporaries as writers. Discrete silence re everything save Mauberley and one discrete sentence re/ that. W. L. "a draughtsman," "I am going to write it. You are going to paint it." (an indirect ref/to colour, but unique).[7]

About 1922 Joyce had a dream in which Pound appeared as a journalist rather than as a poet. Herbert Gorman recounts:

Joyce once described to me a dream that led up to the writing of this parody [of "Molly Brannigan"]. He saw Molly Bloom on a hillock under a sky full of moonlit clouds rushing overhead. She had just picked up from the grass a child's black coffin and flung it after the figure of a man passing down a side road by the field she was in. It struck his shoulders, and she said, "I've done with you." The man was Bloom seen from behind. There was a shout of laughter from some American journalists in the road opposite, led by Ezra Pound. Joyce was very indignant and vaulted over a gate into the field and strode up to her and delivered the one speech of his life. It was very long, eloquent and full of passion, explaining all the last episode of *Ulysses* to her. She wore a black opera cloak, or *sortie de bal*, had become slightly grey and looked like *la* Duse. She smiled when Joyce ended on an astronomical climax, and then, bending, picked up a tiny snuffbox, in the form of a little black coffin, and tossed it towards him, saying, "And I have done with you, too, Mr. Joyce." [8]

The dream suggests how Joyce tended to exaggerate what were candid criticisms, delivered in good faith and with a willingness to be

[7] Letter to Professor Thomas E. Connolly, University of the State of New York, Buffalo, September 5, 1955.

[8] Gorman, *James Joyce,* page 283; Ellmann, *James Joyce,* pages 560–561.

shown, into opposition and even ridicule. Joyce once asked Robert McAlmon: " 'Do you think Eliot or Pound has any real importance?' McAlmon replied, 'Now, Joyce, is that a question for you to ask, who can doubt anything, even yourself?' Joyce laughed but looked disgruntled." [9]

It is clear that Joyce had begun to think of Pound not as a poet and a critic but as the impresario who had been putting him over. Joyce wrote to Miss Weaver on April 10, 1922, that Larbaud's article in the *Nouvelle Revue Française* had caused a great deal of stir; there would be another, he added, by Pound in the *Mercure de France*. He remarked Pound's impresarioship by alluding to Pound's "long and wordy war" with George Bernard Shaw about Shaw's refusal to subscribe for *Ulysses*, noting Shaw's last word, "I take care of the pence because the pounds won't take care of themselves." [1] In November 1922, after Joyce had received a copy of an attack on *Ulysses* by Alfred Noyes, he asked Miss Weaver to send copies of it to Larbaud, to Edmond Jaloux, and to Pound. Doubtless Joyce was still thinking of Pound as his defender against the philistines, while Larbaud was his "official critic" and Jaloux a critic who, Joyce had been told, "considered *Ulysses* 'au-dessus de tout éloge.' " [2] A sidelight that illustrates Joyce's mystical sense of coincidence may be taken as one authority. Joyce had remarked to Miss Weaver on November 1, 1921, that *Ulysses* had been begun in 1914 on Frank Budgen's birthday (March 1) and finished in 1921 on Pound's (October 30). [3] These coincidences reflect the fact that Budgen had been intimately related to the actual writing of the book, while Pound had been its impresario. From Pound's point of view the memorial might have implied some authority over interpretation as well as publication. Indeed, Pound concocted a calendar which announced the end of the Christian Era on his own birthday in 1921, proclaiming a new pagan era, "YEAR 1 p. s. U." (notably, the "Pound Era" preceded the Era Fascista). [4] In doing so he all but absorbed, into his own figure of Pound-as-Odysseus, Joyce the novelist and Bloom the advertising canvasser and forerunner of the messiah. But Joyce then asked Miss Weaver on whose birthday *Ulysses* would appear. Answer? His own, February 2, 1922. He insisted,

[9] Ellmann, *James Joyce,* page 528.
[1] *Letters of James Joyce,* I, page 184.
[2] *Letters of James Joyce,* I, pages 187, 192.
[3] *Letters of James Joyce,* III, page 52.
[4] "The Little Review Calendar," *The Little Review,* VIII, 2 (Spring 1922), pages 2, 40.

and amid flurries it did. Astrologically speaking, Joyce made sure that his own authority was supreme.

Joyce knew his purpose and his method; Larbaud, as a critic, expressed it. Pound was a socially conscious, working poet interested in how the book mirrored the modern world and in what he could learn about ways of expressing modern life. When Pound read *Ulysses* early in 1922, all of his thoughts and critical perceptions about Joyce, and all of the work of the London years, came to a focus. By chance it was also the centenary of Flaubert's birth. In several essays Pound drew together his previous critical thought about Flaubert, the Goncourts, Remy De Gourmont, and Henry James as the chief delineators and creators of the modern consciousness, and viewed Joyce's work as the culmination of the whole previous era. The "Paris Letter" of May 1922 and "James Joyce et Pécuchet" are the critique of *Ulysses* Pound announced every writer had to make "afin d'avoir une idée nette du point d'arrivée de notre art, dans notre métier d'écrivain." Joyce had found a way to conflate the older tradition of the epic poem and what the epic poem had become in the nineteenth century (the novel), and to integrate them in a single, new, modern form. With new insights and a new burst of energy, the source of which is these essays, Pound completed sketching out the cantos for his first volume during the summer of 1922. For the January 1923 issue of *The Criterion* he composed his "De Vulgari Eloquio," a delineation of "the better tradition" which stretches from Homer to Joyce and which constitutes the literary background for *The Cantos.* By the summer of 1923 he had completely revised the beginning of his poem.[5] It no longer followed Browning and "the builder's whim." Homer became Pound's guide and Odysseus his central figure; instead of being merely random evocations of the dead, the poem was now motivated by the fictional pattern of a voyage of discovery and by a traditional epic idea, the *nostos* or return home, which Pound made the symbol of an entire theory of history. Pound's essays are studies in modern epic form; in them he is exploring the methods which enabled him to transform his own personal experience of the "break"

[5] Most of the evidence for the chronology of Pound's composition of the early cantos, especially that at Yale, is in Myles Slatin, "A History of Pound's *Cantos* I–XVI, 1915–1925," *American Literature,* Durham, N.C., XXXV (May 1963), pages 183–195. I have described how the form of *A Draft of XVI Cantos* emerged from Pound's development in "Pound, Joyce, and Flaubert: the Odysseans," to be published in a collection of essays on Pound edited by Eva Hesse. This essay is the basis for a study of Pound and *The Cantos* in the epic tradition.

in modern history into an Odyssean *nostos*, a life and travels whose aim was to rebuild a new city out of fragments of the old.

PARIS LETTER [6]

May, 1922

Πολλῶν δ' ἀνθρώπων ἴδεν ἄστεα, καὶ νόον ἔγνω.[7] All men should "Unite to give praise to Ulysses"; those who will not, may content themselves with a place in the lower intellectual orders; I do not mean that they should all praise it from the same viewpoint; but all serious men of letters, whether they write out a critique or not, will certainly have to make one for their own use. To begin with matters lying outside dispute I should say that Joyce has taken up the art of writing where Flaubert left it. In Dubliners and The Portrait he had not exceeded the Trois Contes or L'Education; in Ulysses he has carried on a process begun in Bouvard et Pécuchet; he has brought it to a degree of greater efficiency, of greater compactness; he has swallowed the Tentation de St Antoine whole, it serves as comparison for a single episode in Ulysses. Ulysses has more form than any novel of Flaubert's. Cervantes had parodied his predecessors and might be taken as basis of comparison for another of Joyce's modes of concision, but where Cervantes satirized one manner of folly and one sort of highfalutin' expression, Joyce satirizes at least seventy, and includes a whole history of English prose, by implication.

Messrs Bouvard and Pécuchet are the basis of democracy; Bloom also is the basis of democracy; he is the man in the street, the next man, the public, not our public, but Mr Wells' public; for Mr Wells he is Hocking's public, he is *l'homme moyen sensuel;* he is also Shakespeare, Ulysses, The Wandering Jew, the Daily Mail reader, the man who believes what he sees in the papers, Everyman, and "the goat" . . . πολλὰ . . . πάθεν . . . κατὰ θυμόν.[8]

Flaubert having recorded provincial customs in Bovary and city habits in L'Education, set out to complete his record of nineteenth century life by presenting all sorts of things that the average man of the period would have had in his head; Joyce has found a more

[6] *The Dial,* LXXII, 6 (June 1922), pages 623–629. Reprinted in *Literary Essays,* 1954, pages 403–409.
[7] "He saw the cities of many men, and knew their minds," *Odyssey,* I, 3.
[8] "He suffered all things . . . in his heart," *Odyssey,* I, 4.

expeditious method of summary and analysis. After Bouvard and his friend had retired to the country Flaubert's incompleted narrative drags; in Ulysses anything may occur at any moment; Bloom suffers *kata thumon;* "every fellow mousing round for his liver and his lights": he is *polumetis*[9] and a receiver of all things.

Joyce's characters not only speak their own language, but they think their own language. Thus Master Dignam stood looking at the poster: "two pluckers stripped to their pelts and putting up their props. . . .

"Gob that'd be a good pucking match to see, Myler Keogh, that's the chap sparring out to him with the green sash. Two bob entrance, soldiers half price. I could easy do a bunk on ma. When is it? May the twenty second. Sure, the blooming thing is all over."

But Father Conmee was wonderfully well indeed: "And her boys, were they getting on well at Belvedere? Was that so? Father Conmee was very glad to hear that. And Mr Sheehy himself? Still in London. The House was still sitting, to be sure it was. Beautiful weather it was, delightful indeed. Yes, it was very probable that Father Bernard Vaughn would come again to preach. O, yes, a very great success. A wonderful man really."

Father Conmee later "reflected on the providence of the Creator who had made turf to be in bogs where men might dig it out and bring it to town and hamlet to make fires in the houses of poor people."

The dialects are not all local, on page 406 we hear that:

"Elijah is coming. Washed in the Blood of the Lamb. Come on, you winefizzling, ginsizzling, booseguzzling existences! Come on, you doggone, bullnecked, beetlebrowed, hogjowled, peanutbrained, weaseleyed fourflushers, false alarms and excess baggage! Come on, you triple extract of infamy! Alexander J. Christ Dowie, that's yanked to glory most half this planet from 'Frisco Beach to Vladivostok. The Deity ain't no nickel dime bumshow. I put it to you that he's on the square and a corking fine business proposition. He's the grandest thing yet, and don't you forget it. Shout salvation in King Jesus. You'll need to rise precious early, you sinner there, if you want to diddle Almighty God. . . . Not half. He's got a cough-

[9] "Many-minded," or "of many contrivings," the primary epithet of Odysseus, which Pound had applied to himself in London.

195

mixture with a punch in it for you, my friend, in his backpocket. Just you try it on."

This varigation of dialects allows Joyce to present his matter, his tones of mind, very rapidly; it is no more succinct than Flaubert's exhaustion of the relation of Emma and her mother-in-law; or of Père Rouault's character, as epitomized in his last letter to Emma; but it is more rapid than the record of "received ideas" in Bouvard et Pécuchet.

Ulysses is, presumably, as unrepeatable as Tristram Shandy; I mean you cannot duplicate it; you can't take it as a "model," as you could Bovary; but it does complete something begun in Bouvard; and it does add definitely to the international store of literary technique.

Stock novels, even excellent stock novels, seem infinitely long, and infinitely encumbered, after one has watched Joyce squeeze the last drop out of a situation, a science, a state of mind, in half a page, in a catechismic question and answer, in a tirade *à la Rabelais*.

Rabelais himself rests, he remains, he is too solid to be diminished by any pursuer; he was a rock against the follies of his age; against ecclesiastic theology, and more remarkably, against the blind idolatry of the classics just coming into fashion. He refused the lot, lock, stock, and barrel, with a greater heave than Joyce has yet exhibited; but I can think of no other prose author whose proportional status in pan-literature is not modified by the advent of Ulysses.

James (H.) speaks with his own so beautiful voice, even sometimes when his creations should be using *their* own; Joyce speaks if not with the tongue of men and angels, at least with a many-tongued and multiple language, of small boys, street preachers, of genteel and ungenteel, of bowsers and undertakers, of Gertie McDowell and Mr Deasey.

One reads Proust and thinks him very accomplished; one reads H. J. and knows that he is very accomplished; one begins Ulysses and thinks, perhaps rightly, that Joyce is less so; that he is at any rate less gracile; and one considers how excellently both James and Proust "convey their atmosphere"; yet the atmosphere of the Gerty-Nausika episode with its echoes of vesper service is certainly "conveyed," and conveyed with a certitude and efficiency that neither James nor Proust have excelled.

And on the home stretch, when our present author is feeling more or less relieved that the weight of the book is off his shoulders, we find if not gracile accomplishments, at any rate such acrobatics, such sheer whoops and hoop-las and trapeze turns of technique that it would seem rash to dogmatize concerning his limitations. The whole of him, on the other hand, lock, stock, and gunny-sacks is wholly outside H. J.'s compass and orbit, outside Proust's circuit and orbit.

If it be charged that he shows "that provincialism which must be forever dragging in allusions to some book or local custom," it must also be admitted that no author is more lucid or more explicit in presenting things in such a way that the imaginary Chinaman or denizen of the forty-first century could without works of reference gain a very good idea of the scene and habits portrayed.

Poynton with its spoils forms a less vivid image than Bloom's desired two story dwelling house and appurtenances. The recollections of In Old Madrid are not at any rate highbrow; the "low back car" is I think local. But in the main, I doubt if the local allusions interfere with a *general* comprehension. Local details exist everywhere; one understands them *mutatis mutandis*, and any picture would be perhaps faulty without them. One must balance obscurity against brevity. Concision itself is an obscurity for the dullard.

In this super-novel our author has also poached on the epic, and has, for the first time since 1321, resurrected the infernal figures; his furies are not stage figures; he has, by simple reversal, caught back the furies, his flagellant Castle ladies. Telemachus, Circe, the rest of the Odyssean company, the noisy cave of Aeolus gradually place themselves in the mind of the reader, rapidly or less rapidly according as he is familiar or unfamiliar with Homer. These correspondences are part of Joyce's mediaevalism and are chiefly his own affair, a scaffold, a means of construction, justified by the result, and justifiable by it only. The result is a triumph in form, in balance, a main schema, with continuous inweaving and arabesque.

The best criticism of any work, to my mind the only criticism of any work of art that is of any permanent or even moderately durable value, comes from the creative writer or artist who does the next job; and *not*, not ever from the young gentlemen who make generalities about the creator. Laforgue's Salomé is the real criticism of Salammbô; Joyce and perhaps Henry James are critics of Flaubert. To me, as poet, the Tentation is *jettatura*, it is the effect of Flaubert's time on Flaubert; I mean he was interested in certain questions now dead as mutton, because he lived in a certain period; fortunately he managed to bundle these matters into one or two books and keep them out of his work on contemporary subjects; I set it aside as one sets aside Dante's treatise De Aqua et Terra, as something which matters now only as archaeology. Joyce, working in the same medium as Flaubert, makes the intelligent criticism: "We might believe in it if Flaubert had first shown us St Antoine in Alexandria looking at women and jewellers' windows."

Ulysses contains 732 double sized pages, that is to say it is about the size of four ordinary novels, and even a list of its various points of interest would probably exceed my alloted space; in the Cyclops episode we have a measuring of the difference between reality, and reality as represented in various lofty forms of expression; the satire on the various dead manners of language culminates in the execution scene, blood and sugar stewed into clichés and rhetoric; just what the public deserves, and just what the public gets every morning with its porridge, in the Daily Mail and in sentimento-rhetorical journalism; it is perhaps the most savage bit of satire we have had since Swift suggested a cure for famine in Ireland. Henry James complained of Baudelaire, "Le Mal, you do yourself too much honour . . . our impatience is of the same order as . . . if for the 'Flowers of Good' one should present us with a rhapsody on plumcake and eau de cologne." Joyce has set out to do an inferno, and he has done an inferno.

He has presented Ireland under British domination, a picture so veridic that a ninth rate coward like Shaw (Geo. B.) dare not even look it in the face. By extension he has presented the whole occident under the domination of capital. The details of the street map are local but Leopold Bloom (*né Virag*) is ubiquitous. His spouse Gea-Tellus the earth symbol is the soil from which the intelligence strives to leap, and to which it subsides *in saeculum saeculorum*. As Molly she is a coarse-grained bitch, not a whore, an adultress, *il y en a*. Her ultimate mediations are uncensored (bow to psychoanalysis required at this point). The "censor" in the Freudian sense is removed, Molly's night-thoughts differing from those versified in Mr Young's once ubiquitous poem are unfolded, she says ultimately that her body is a flower; her last word is affirmative. The manners of the genteel society she inhabits have failed to get under her crust, she exists presumably in Patagonia as she exists in Jersey City or Camden.

And the book is banned in America, where every child of seven has ample opportunity to drink in the details of the Arbuckle case, or two hundred other equodorous affairs from the 270,000,000 copies of the 300,000 daily papers which enlighten us. One returns to the

Goncourt's question, "Ought the people to remain under a literary edict? Are there classes unworthy, misfortunes too low, dramas too ill set, catastrophies, horrors too devoid of nobility? Now that the novel is augmented, now that it is the great literary form ... the social inquest, for psychological research and analysis, demanding the studies and imposing on its creator the duties of science ... seeking the facts ... whether or no the novelist is to write with the accuracy, and thence with the freedom of the savant, the historian, the physician?"

Whether the only class in America that tries to think is to be hindered by a few cranks, who cannot, and dare not interfere with the leg shows on Broadway? Is any one, for the sake of two or three words which every small boy has seen written on the walls of a privy, going to wade through two hundred pages on consubstantiation or the biographic bearing of Hamlet? And ought an epoch-making report on the state of the human mind in the twentieth century (first of the new era) be falsified by the omission of these half dozen words, or by a pretended ignorance of extremely simple acts. Bloom's day is uncensored, very well. The foecal analysis, in the hospital around the corner, is uncensored. No one but a Presbyterian would contest the utility of the latter exactitude. *A great literary masterwork is made for minds quite as serious as those engaged in the science of medicine.* The anthropologist and sociologist have a right to equally accurate documents, to equally succinct reports and generalizations, which they seldom get, considering the complexity of the matter in hand, and the idiocy of current superstitions.

A Fabian milk report is of less use to a legislator than the knowledge contained in L'Education Sentimentale, or in Bovary. The legislator is supposed to manage human affairs, to arrange for comity of human agglomerations. *Le beau monde gouverne*—or did once—because it had access to condensed knowledge, the middle ages were ruled by those who could read, an aristocracy received Machiavelli's treatise before the serfs. A very limited plutocracy now gets the news, of which a fraction (not likely to throw too much light upon proximate markets) is later printed in newspapers. Jefferson was perhaps the last American official to have any general sense of civilization. Molly Bloom judges Griffith derisively by "the sincerity of his trousers," and the Paris edition of the Tribune tells us that the tailors' congress has declared Pres. Harding to be our best dressed Chief Magistrate.

Be it far from me to depreciate the advantages of having a president who can meet on equal trouserial terms such sartorial paragons as Mr Balfour and Lord (late Mr) Lee of Fareham (and Checquers) but be it equidistant also from me to disparage the public utility of accurate language which can be attained only from literature, and which the succinct J. Caesar, or the lucid Machiavelli, or the author of the Code Napoléon, or Thos. Jefferson, to cite a local example, would have in no ways despised. Of course it is too soon to know whether our present ruler takes an interest in these matters; we know only that the late pseudo-intellectual Wilson did not, and that the late bombastic Teddy did not, and Taft, McKinley, Cleveland, did not, and that, as far back as memory serves us no American president has ever uttered one solitary word implying the slightest interest in, or consciousness of, the need for an intellectual or literary vitality in America. A sense of style could have saved America and Europe from Wilson; it would have been useful to our diplomats. The *mot juste* is of public utility. I can't help it. I am not offering this fact as a sop to aesthetes who want all authors to be fundamentally useless. We are governed by words, the laws are graven words, and literature is the sole means of keeping these words living and accurate. The specimen of fungus given in my February letter shows what happens to language when it gets into the hands of illiterate specialists.[1]

Ulysses furnishes matter for a symposium rather than for a single letter, essay, or review.

Pound wrote "James Joyce et Pécuchet" in French. Though Larbaud's lecture had been printed in April, he called it in "Date Line," *Make It New*, 1934, "the first serious French criticism of Mr Joyce (that is to say it was in 'French' of a sort, but at any rate comprehensible)." "James Joyce et Pécuchet" is an expansion of the May "Paris Letter," though it is not certain which was written first. Pound extended his discussion of Flaubert in his "Paris Letter" of August; he had also written on Flaubert in his March letter.

JAMES JOYCE ET PÉCUCHET [2]

James Joyce, né à Dublin vers 1882, reçut une éducation catholique, étudia à l'université de Dublin, passa des années ou des

---

[1] Pound's letter, dated March 1922, ridicules John Middleton Murry's "Gustave Flaubert," *The Dial*, December 1921, as a typical piece of British critical fatuity.

[2] *Mercure de France*, Paris, CLVI, 575 (June 1, 1922), pages 307–320; reprinted *Polite Essays*, 1937. An English translation by Fred Bornhauser appeared in *Shenandoah*, Lexington, Va., III, 3 (Autumn 1952), pages 9–20.

semaines à Paris et à Padoue, se fit, à Dublin, une réputation d'«excentrique», débuta en 1908, avec *Chamber Music*, une trentaine de pages de vers conventionnels et délicats, qui montrent l'âme et la vraie personnalité de cet auteur aujourd'hui si redouté.

Ce premier livre ne dissipa point le silence; son deuxième livre, une série de contes intitulée *Dubliners*, fut brûlé par une main mystérieuse et sa ville natale ne cessa de se montrer insensible aux mérites de l'auteur. A Londres, *The Egoist*, revue de cénacle, protesta et entreprit la publication de son roman: *Portrait of the Artist as a Young Man*, maintenant traduit en suédois, en espagnol et en français (le volume va paraître sous le titre *Daedalus*).

Son drame *Exiles* fut joué à Munich, et la traduction italienne parut dans *Convegno*. L'accueil de Joyce par ses compatriotes tardait encore à se faire.

§

L'année du centenaire de Flaubert, première d'une ère nouvelle, voit aussi l'édition d'un nouveau volume de Joyce, *Ulysses*, qui, à certains points de vue, peut être considéré comme le premier qui, en héritant de Flaubert, continue le développement de l'art flaubertien, tel qu'il l'a laissé dans son dernier livre inachevé.

Bien que *Bouvard et Pécuchet* ne passe pas pour la «meilleure chose» du maître, on peut soutenir que *Bovary* et l'*Education* ne sont que l'apogée d'une forme antérieure; et que les *Trois Contes* donnent une espèce de sommaire de tout ce que Flaubert avait acquis en écrivant ses autres romans, *Salammbô*, *Bovary*, l'*Education* et les premières versions de *Saint Antoine*. Les trois tableaux, païen, moyenâgeux, moderne font un tout qui se balance sur la phrase: «Et l'idée lui vint d'employer son existence au service des autres», qui se trouve au milieu de *Saint Julien*, le premier des trois contes qu'il écrivit.

Bouvard et Pécuchet continue la pensée et l'art flaubertien, mais ne continue pas cette tradition du roman ou du conte. On peut regarder «l'Encyclopédie en farce» qui porte en sous-titre: «Défaut de méthode dans les sciences», comme l'inauguration d'une forme nouvelle, une forme qui n'avait pas son précédent. Ni *Gargantua*, ni *Don Quijote*, ni le *Tristram Shandy* de Sterne n'en avaient donné l'archetype.

Si l'on considère les grandes lignes de la littérature universelle depuis 1880, on peut dire que les meilleurs écrivains ont exploité Flaubert plutôt que développé son art. La règle absolue d'un succès instantané, c'est qu'il ne faut jamais donner à une lectrice un instant, un demi-instant de travail cérébral. Maupassant a fait du

Flaubert plus léger; les autres l'ont suivi. Anatole France se sert de Flaubert comme d'une espèce de paravent, et se retire dans son XVIIIᵉ siècle. Galdos, en Espagne, fait du bon Flaubert; Hueffer, en Angleterre, écrit une prose lucide; Joyce, lui-même, dans *Dubliners* et dans *The Portrait of the Artist as a Young Man*, fait du Flaubert, mais ne dépasse pas les *Trois Contes* ni l'*Education*. Dans l'héritage de Flaubert il y a de bonnes œuvres et une espèce de décadence, les meilleurs disciples emploient les mêmes procédés, les mêmes découvertes techniques pour représenter des scènes différentes; pour décrire les Indes Kipling fait du Maupassant inférieur. En France, Flaubert détient le «record»: personne ne développe son art.

Le développement de Henry James et de Marcel Proust vient plutôt des Goncourt, pas même de leurs romans, mais d'une préface:

Le jour où l'analyse cruelle que mon ami Zola, et peut-être moi-même avons apportée dans la peinture du bas de la société sera reprise par un écrivain de talent, et employée a la reproduction des hommes et des femmes du monde, dans les milieux d'éducation et de distinction, ce jour-là seulement le classicisme et sa queue seront tués.

Le Réalisme n'a pas en effet l'unique mission de décrire ce qui est bas, ce qui est répugnant... Nous avons commencé, nous, par la canaille, parce que la femme et l'homme du peuple, plus rapprochés de la nature et de la sauvagerie, sont des créatures simples et peu compliquées, tandis que le Parisien et la Parisienne de la société, ces civilisés excessifs, dont l'originalité tranchée est faite toute de nuances, toute de demi-teintes, tout de ces riens insaisissables, pareils aux riens coquets et neutres avec lesquels se façonne le caractère d'une toilette distinguée de femme, demandent des années pour qu'on les perce, pour qu'on les sache, pour qu'on les *attrape*, et le romancier du plus grand génie, croyez-le bien, ne les devinera jamais, ces gens de salon, avec les *racontars* d'amis qui vont pour lui à la découverte dans le monde...

Dans cette voie Henry James a créé la meilleure part de son œuvre, très exacte, très réaliste; et, à la remorque de James, Marcel Proust a clarifié ses intentions, c'est-à-dire qu'il avait commencé par la lecture de Balzac, Dostoïevsky, H. James, ou des œuvres de tendance analogue. Il voyait que l'intérêt «sexe» dominait et appauvrissait les romans français contemporains. Il comprit qu'il y avait un coin vide dans la littérature française. Il y courut, et sur son pastiche enduisit un vernis de nacre symboliste. Plus tard il épurait son style, et, dans le diner Guermantien, il ne lui en reste que l'élément qui ressemble à James. En effet, James n'a rien fait de mieux.

Mais ces tableaux de la haute société sont une spécialisation, une arabesque, charmante, intéressante, tant que vous voudrez, plutôt qu'un progrès radical de méthode. Et tout cela correspond dans l'œuvre de Flaubert à *Bovary*, à l'*Education*, et au *Cœur Simple*.

Quant aux romans historiques, ils n'ont jamais ressuscité depuis que Laforgue leur lançait ce coup dans l'épigastre : *Salomé*.

Les vrais critiques ne sont pas les juges stériles, les faiseurs de phrases. Le critique efficace est l'artiste qui vient après, pour tuer, ou pour hériter ; pour dépasser, pour augmenter, ou pour diminuer et enterrer une forme. Depuis les exactitudes du télescope de Salomé on ne s'attaque plus aux détails historiques.

«Il y a même, écrit Remy de Gourmont, à la mi-carême, le costume historique.»

A côté de tout cela il y a la Russie, la profondeur un peu alcoolique, ou épileptique, et informe de Dostoïevsky, ses disciples et ses inférieurs ; il y a le Strindbergisme et le subjectivisme qui n'offre peut-être rien de plus réussi qu'*Adolphe*.

Mais qu'est-ce que *Bouvard et Pécuchet?* Heureusement le livre de votre plus solide flaubertien, René Descharmes, et les paroles de Flaubert lui-même m'évitent une définition trop «amateur», trop «étranger» : «Encyclopédie mise en farce.» (Flaubert soutient, ou a soutenu pour cinq minutes une autre mienne irrévérence ; il appelle *La Tentation* une «ancienne toquade», mais passons.)

Autour de Bouvard et Pécuchet [3] est charmant comme toute œuvre définitive qui ose être «trop» méticuleuse afin de trancher la question une fois pour toutes, de mettre fin à des blagues, à de vagues pérambulations. Les arguments de M. Descharmes sont tellement solides, les faits qu'il apporte si incontestables que j'ai presque peur de proposer quelques divergences de vue. Mais de temps en temps il emploie des phrases qui, sorties de leur contexte, peuvent devenir tendancieuses ou occasionner des malentendus. Je trouve :

[3] *Autour de Bouvard et Pécuchet,* Etudes Documentaires et Critiques par René Descharmes, Paris : Librarie de France, 1921.

Page 44 . . . des traits de la passion de Frédéric ne revêtent toute leur importance psychologique que si on les rapporte à la passion éprouvée par Flaubert pour Mme Schlesinger.

Plus tard je me demande ce qu'il entend par «l'intelligence complète d'une œuvre».

Il a, peut-être, employé les termes justes. Mais on doit souligner que si on ne comprend pas une œuvre seulement par la lecture de cette œuvre et rien que de cette œuvre, on ne la comprendra jamais ; même avec toute la masse de documents, de citations, de détails biologiques ou biographiques que vous voudrez. Tout ce qui n'est pas l'œuvre appartient à la biographie de l'auteur ; ce qui est un autre sujet, sujet d'un autre livre réaliste, mais qui n'appartient nullement à «l'intelligence de l'œuvre» complète ou autre. (J'exagère.)

Il y avait un fait-divers Delamarre ; il y avait mille autres faits aussi divers. Flaubert en avait choisi un. Il y avait un vitrail à Reims, à Rouen, une peinture de Breughel à Gênes ; tout cela est fort intéressant quand on s'intéresse énormément à cet être intéressant entre tous qu'était Gustave Flaubert ; mais le lecteur de *Saint Julien* et de *Bovary* peut s'en ficher de bon cœur. M. Descharmes est presque de mon avis, mais il confine à cet imbécile de Sainte-Beuve,* et on a envie alors de crier «gare !»

Descharmes démontre que l'action de *Bouvard et Pécuchet* est impossible dans le temps donné. Il pose la question de savoir si Flaubert avait l'intention de se passer de son réalisme habituel et de se présenter ses deux bonshommes comme une espèce de prodige doué d'une avant-vieillesse éternelle. C'est un détail qu'une dernière revision aurait pu facilement arranger ; un détail, je crois, de l'espèce de ceux qu'on laisse au dernier remaniement.

Descharmes nous présente des recherches fort amusantes sur la mnémotechnie de Feinaigle, et sur la gymnastique d'Amoros. Il fait là une œuvre nouvelle et réaliste. Et il prouve que Flaubert n'a rien exagéré.

Pour *Bouvard et Pécuchet* il ne trouve aucun fait-divers ; mais il

* Sainte-Beuve : Je demande pardon de traiter ainsi un Monsieur qui a son monument au Jardin du Luxembourg avec ceux de Clémence Isaure, Scheurer-Kestner (1833–1899), Fifine de Médicis, Adam, Ève, Rûcher Ecole, et tant d'autres gloires de la race françoise ; avec celui de Flaubert lui-même, mais ses arrière-petits-bâtards, c'est-à-dire les arrière-petits-fils de Sainte-Beuve ont tellement empesté le monde Anglo-Saxon, où chaque pignouf, qui n'a aucune aptitude à comprendre une œuvre se met à faire de la critique "littéraire" en vomissant des paperasses sur les factures de la blanchisseuse de Whitman, la correspondence de Géo. Eliot et sa couturière, etc., etc. . . que . . . que Bossuet reste l'Aigle de Meaux [E.P.].

me semble qu'il y avait à Croisset deux hommes dont l'un au moins avait une curiosité sans borne. Si Flaubert, qui satirise tout, n'a pas satirisé un certain M. Laporte et un certain M. Flaubert bien connus et peu considérés des Rouennois, il est certain qu'il passait sa vie toujours avec «un autre»; avec Le Poittevin, avec l'erreur Du Camp, avec Bouilhet; rien de plus naturel que cette conception de deux hommes qui font des recherches. Les recherches de Flaubert hors de la littérature n'auraient jamais pu le satisfaire; de là sa sympathie pour ses bonshommes; la vanité de sa propre lutte contre l'imbécillité générale donne de l'énergie au portrait de ces autres victimes des circonstances. La supposition vaut bien les autres qu'on fait dans les analyses chimiques et cliniques des œuvres d'art. Descharmes l'effleure, page 236.

Mais c'est surtout dans le chapitre sur les «idées reçues» qu'il nous intéresse, et c'est par là qu'on voit un rapport entre Flaubert et Joyce. Entre 1880 et l'année où fut commencé *Ulysses* personne n'a eu le courage de faire le sottisier gigantesque, ni la patience de rechercher l'homme-type, la généralisation la plus générale.

Descharmes établit la différence entre le «dictionnaire» et l'Album qui «seul était destiné à faire la deuxième partie de *Bouvard et Pécuchet*». Il indique de quelle façon le dictionnaire était déjà entré dans les livres de Flaubert. Mais c'est d'un seul trait qu'il se prouve le profond flaubertien, et se distingue de tous les philologues secs. Il montre sa compréhension profonde de son héros, quand il déclare:

...depuis le jour où petit enfant il notait déjà les bêtises d'une vieille dame qui venait en visite chez sa mère.

Comme critique cela vaut bien tous les arguments élaborés.

§

Qu'est-ce que l'*Ulysses* * de James Joyce? Ce roman appartient à la grande classe de romans en forme de sonate, c'est-à-dire, dans la forme: thème, contre-thème, rencontre, développement, finale. Et à la subdivision: roman père-et-fils. Il suit la grande ligne de l'*Odyssée*, et présente force correspondances plus ou moins exactes avec les incidents du poème d'Homère. Nous y trouvons Télémaque, son père, les sirènes, le Cyclope, sous des travestissements inattendus, baroques, argotiques, véridiques et gigantesques.

* Shakespeare et Cie, éditeur, 12, rue de l'Odéon, Paris [E. P.].

Les romanciers n'aiment dépenser que trois mois, six mois pour un roman. Joyce y a mis quinze ans. Et *Ulysses* est plus condensé (732 grandes feuilles) que n'importe quelle œuvre entière de Flaubert; on y découvre plus d'architecture.

Il y a des pages incomparables dans *Bovary*, des paragraphes incomparablement condensés dans *Bouvard* (voir celui où on achète les sacrés-cœurs, images pieuses, etc.). Il y a des pages de Flaubert qui exposent leur matière aussi rapidement que les pages de Joyce, mais Joyce a complété le grand sottisier. Dans un seul chapitre il décharge tous les clichés de la langue anglaise, comme un fleuve ininterrompu. Dans un autre chapitre il enferme toute l'histoire de l'expression verbale anglaise, depuis les premiers vers allitérés (c'est le chapitre dans l'hôpital où on attend la parturition de Mrs Purefoy). Dans un autre on a les «en-tête» du *Freeman's Journal* depuis 1760, c'est-à-dire l'histoire du journalisme; et il fait cela sans interrompre le courant de son livre.

Il s'exprime différemment dans les différentes parties de son livre (comme le permet même Aristote), mais ce n'est pas, comme le dit le distingué Larbaud, qu'il abandonne l'unité de style. Chaque personnage, non seulement parle à sa propre guise, mais il pense à sa propre guise, ce n'est pas plus abandonner l'unité de style que quand les divers personnages d'un roman dit de style uni parlent de manières diverses: on omet les guillemets, voilà tout.

Bloom, commis de publicité, l'Ulysse du roman, l'homme moyen sensuel, la base, comme le sont Bouvard et Pécuchet, de la démocratie, l'homme qui croit ce qu'il lit dans les journaux, souffre κατὰ φυμόν. Il s'intéresse à tout, veut expliquer tout pour impressionner tout le monde. Non seulement il est un «moyen» littéraire beaucoup plus rapide, beaucoup plus apte à ramasser ce qu'on dit et pense partout, ce que les gens quelconques disent et ramâchent cent fois par semaine, mais les autres personnages sont choisis pour l'aider, pour ramasser les vanités des milieux autres que le sien.

Bouvard et Pécuchet sont séparés du monde, dans une sorte d'eau dormante. Bloom, au contraire, s'agite dans un milieu beaucoup plus contagieux.

Joyce emploie un échafaudage pris à Homère, et les restes d'une culture moyenâgeuse allégorique; peu importe, c'est une affaire de cuisine, qui ne restreint pas l'action, qui ne l'incommode pas, qui ne nuit pas à son réalisme, ni à la contemporanéité de son action. C'est un moyen de régler la forme. Le livre a plus forme que n'en ont les livres de Flaubert.

Télémaque, Stephen, fils spirituel de Bloom, commence par réfléchir sur une vanité moyenâgeuse, ramassée dans une école catholique; il prolonge une vanité universitaire, le rapport entre Hamlet et Shakespeare. Toujours réaliste dans le plus stricte sens flaubertien, toujours documenté, documenté sur la vie même, Joyce ne dépasse jamais le moyen. Le réalisme cherche une généralisation qui agit non seulement sur le nombre, sur la multiplicité, mais dans la permanence. Joyce combine le moyen âge, les ères classiques, même l'antiquité juive, dans une action actuelle; Flaubert échelonne les époques.

Dans son élimination acharnée des guillemets, Joyce présente l'épisode du Cyclope avec les paroles ordinaires, mais à côté il pose la grandiloquence, parodie et mesure de la différence entre le réalisme et un romantisme de fanfaron. J'ai dit que la critique vraie vient des auteurs; ainsi Joyce à propos de Saint Antoine: «On peut le croire s'il (Flaubert) nous avait présenté Antoine à Alexandrie gobant les femmes et les objets de luxe.»

Un seul chapitre de *Ulysses* (157 pages) correspond à la *Tentation de saint Antoine*. Stephen, Bloom et Lynch se trouvent ivres dans un bordel; tout le grotesque de leur pensée est mis à nu; pour la première fois, depuis Dante, on trouve les harpies, les furies, vivantes, les symboles pris dans le réel, dans l'actuel; rien ne dépend de la mythologie, ni de la foi dogmatique. Les proportions se réaffirment.

Le défaut de *Bouvard et Pécuchet*, défaut que signale même M. Descharmes, est que les incidents ne se suivent pas avec une nécessité assez impérieuse; le plan ne manque pas de logique, mais un autre aurait suffi. On peut avancer une thèse plus élogieuse pour Flaubert, mais si bref, si clair, et si condensé que soit *Bouvard et Pécuchet*, l'ensemble manque un peu d'entrain.

Joyce a remédié à cela; à chaque instant le lecteur est tenu prêt à tout, à chaque instant l'imprévu arrive; jusqu'aux tirades les plus longues et les plus cataloguées, on se tient aux aguets.

L'action se passe en un jour (732 pages), dans un seul endroit, Dublin. Télémaque erre παρὰ θῖνα πολυφλοίσβοιο θαλάσσης;[4] il voit les sages-femmes avec leur sac professionnel. Ulysse déjeune, circule: messe, funérailles, maison de bains, tuyaux des courses; les autres personnages circulent; le savon circule; il cherche la publicité, l' «ad» de la maison Keyes, il visite la bibliothèque nationale

[4] To adapt Pound's translation (cf. *Mauberley,* 1920, III), "along the shores of the shingle-surging sea," *Odyssey,* XIII, 220.

pour vérifier un détail anatomique de la mythologie, il vient à l'île d'Aeolus (bureau d'un journal), tous les bruits éclatent, tramways, camions, wagons des postes, etc.; Nausikaa se montre, on dîne à l'hôpital: rencontre d'Ulysse et de Télémaque, bordel, combat, retour chez Bloom, et puis l'auteur présente Pénélope, symbole de la terre, dont les pensées de nuit terminent le récit, balançant les ingéniosités mâles.

Cervantes ne parodiait qu'une seule folie littéraire, la folie chevaleresque. Seuls Rabelais et Flaubert attaquent tout un siècle, s'opposent à toute une encyclopédie imbécile,—sous la forme de fiction. On ne discute pas ici les Dictionnaires de Voltaire et de Bayle. Entrer dans la classe Rabelais-Flaubert n'est pas peu de chose.

Comme pages les plus acharnées on peut citer la scène du bourreau, satire plus mordante qu'aucune autre depuis que Swift proposa un remède à la disette en Irlande: manger les enfants. Partout dans les litanies; dans la généalogie de Bloom, dans les paraphrases d'eloquence, l'œuvre est soignée, pas une ligne, une demi-ligne qui ne reçoive une intensité intellectuelle incomparable dans un livre de si longue haleine; ou qu'on ne sait comparer qu'aux pages de Flaubert et des Goncourt.

Cela peut donner une idée du travail énorme de ces quinze ans troublés de pauvreté, de mauvaise santé, de guerre: toute la première édition de son livre «Dubliners» brûlée, la fuite de Trieste, une opération à l'œil, autant de faits qui n'expliquent rien du roman, dont toute l'action se passe le 16 juin 1904 à Dublin. On peut trouver des personnages disséqués d'une page, comme dans *Bovary* (voir Father Conmee, le gosse Dignam, etc.). On peut examiner les descriptions encyclopédiques, la maison rêvée de Bloom, avec texte de bail imaginaire; toute la bouillabaisse pseudo-intellectuelle des prolétaires se présente, toute équilibrée par Pénélope, la femme, qui ne respecte nullement cet amas de nomenclatures, vagin, symbole de la terre, mer morte dans laquelle l'intelligence mâle retombe.

C'est un roman réaliste par excellence, chaque caractère parle à sa guise, et correspond à une réalité extérieure. On présente l'Irlande sous le joug britannique, le monde sous le joug de l'usure démesurée. Descharmes demande (page 267):

Qui donc a réussi dans cette tentative quasi surhumaine de montrer, sous forme de roman et d'œuvre d'art, le pignoufisme universel?

208

J'offre la réponse: si ce n'est pas James Joyce, c'est un auteur qu'il faut encore attendre; mais la réponse de cet Irlandais mérite un examen approfondi. *Ulysses* n'est pas un livre que tout le monde va admirer, pas plus que tout le monde n'admire *Bouvard et Pécuchet*, mais c'est un livre que tout écrivain sérieux a besoin de lire, qu'il sera contraint de lire afin d'avoir une idée nette du point d'arrivée de notre art, dans notre métier d'écrivain.

Rien d'étonnant si les livres de Joyce ne furent pas accueillis en Irlande en 1908; le public rustre et les provinciaux de Dublin étaient alors en train de manifester contre les drames de Synge, les trouvant un attentat à la dignité nationale. Les mêmes drames viennent d'être représentés cette année à Paris comme propagande et comme preuve de la culture de la race irlandaise. Ibsen, si je me rappelle, n'habitait pas la Norvège: Galdos, dans *Doña Perfecta*, nous montre les dangers de posséder une culture, pas même internationale, mais seulement madrilène, dans une ville de province, que l'on devine être Saragosse. Quant aux «aînés» romantiques en Irlande, je les crois simplement incapables de comprendre ce que c'est que le réalisme. Pour George Moore et Shaw, il est de la nature humaine de ne pas vouloir se voir éclipsé par un écrivain de plus grande importance qu'eux-mêmes. On sait qu'à Dublin on lit Joyce en cachette. Ce manque de cordialité n'a rien d'étonnant. Mais la loi américaine, sous laquelle fut supprimée quatre fois la *Little Review* pour les fragments d'*Ulysses*, est une curiosité tellement curieuse, une telle démonstration de la mentalité des légistes incultes, des spécialistes illettrés, qu'il mérite bien l'attention des psychologues européens, ou plutôt des spécialistes en méningites. Non, mes chers amis, la démocratie (qu'il faut tant sauvegarder, selon notre feu calamité Wilson) n'a rien de commun avec la liberté personnelle, ni avec la déférence fraternelle de Koung-fu-Tseu.

Section 211, du code pénal des-Etats-Unis d'Amérique, (je traduis mot à mot, dans l'ordre du texte):

Chaque obscène, impudique, lascif, et chaque sale livre, pamphlet, tableau, papier, lettre, écriture, cliché, ou autre publication de caractère indécent et chaque article ou objet désigné, adapté ou fait dans l'intention d'empêcher la conception ou pour provoquer l'avortement ou pour tout usage indécent ou immoral et chaque article, instrument, substance, drogue, médecine ou objet auquel on donne la publicité, ou qu'on décrit d'une façon à pousser une autre personne à l'em-

ployer, ou à l'appliquer pour empêcher la conception ou
pour obtenir l'avortement ou pour tout but indécent ou
immoral, et chaque écrit, ou imprimé, carte-lettre, feuillet,
livre, pamphlet, avertissement, ou notice de toute espèce qui
donne information, directement ou indirectement de comment,
ou du quel, ou par quel moyen desdits articles ou choses, peut
être obtenu ou fait, ou d'où, ou par lequel, tout acte d'opération
de toute espèce pour obtenir ou produire l'avortement, sera
fait ou exécuté, ou comment ou par lesquels moyens la conception peut être empêchée ou l'avortement produit, ou cacheté
ou non cacheté, et chaque lettre, paquet, colis ou autres objets
postaux qui contiennent aucun sale, vil, indécent objet, artifice,
ou substance, chaque et tout papier, écriture ou avis qu'aucun
article, instrument, substance, drogue, médecine ou objet puisse
ou peut être employé ou appliqué pour l'empêchement de la conception ou pour la production de l'avortement, pour aucun but
indécent ou immoral, et chaque description destinée à induire ou à
inciter personne à employer ainsi ou appliquer tel article, instrument, substance, drogue, médecine, ou objet est par ceci déclaré
être matière non recevable à la poste, et ne doit pas être porté à la
poste, ni distribué par aucun bureau des postes, par aucun fac-
teur des postes. Quiconque déposera, à son escient, ou fera dé-
poser pour être transporté un objet déclaré par cette section non
recevable à la poste, ou à son escient, prendra, ou fera prendre
par la poste afin de la faire circuler ou contribuer, ou d'aider à la
dite circulation et distribution, subira une amende de 5000 (cinq
mille) dollars au maximum ou un emprisonnement de cinq ans,
au maximum, ou les deux peines à la fois.

C'est le vingtième siècle: paganisme, christianisme, muflisme, pignoufisme; si aucun doute réside dans le cerveau du lecteur, on peut
l'éclairer par la décision d'un juge américain, débitée à l'occasion
de la troisième suppression de la *Little Review*. Le grand avocat,
collectionneur d'art moderne, chevalier de votre Légion d'honneur,
John Quinn fit le plaidoyer pour la littérature: les classiques
même, dit-il, ne peuvent échapper à de telles imbécillités.

La voix de la Thémis états-unisienne lui répond (citation du Juge
Hand):

Je ne doute guère que beaucoup d'œuvres vraiment grandes qui
entreraient dans cette prescription, si on les soumettait aux

épreuves couramment et souvent employées, échappent de temps
à autre seulement parce qu'elles entrent dans la catégorie des
«classiques»; il est entendu pour la mise en acte de cette loi
qu'elles ont ordinairement l'immunité d'intervention parce
qu'elles ont la sanction de l'antiquité et de la renommée, et font
appel, ordinairement, à un nombre relativement restreint de
lecteurs.

N'est-ce pas que nous avons ici deux joyaux que le grand Flaubert aurait saisis pour son Album, et que ces citations auraient
même dépassé son espérance?

Quant aux deux dernières pages de Descharmes, je les regrette un
peu; je me réserve le privilège de croire que Spinoza avait la tête
plus solide que M. Paul Bourget.[5] Et si la pensée en soi est un mal
nuisible à l'humanité, je remercie, tout de même, M. Descharmes
pour s'en être tant donné.

Paris during 1921–1924 was the world center of literary activity. Almost everyone who was there during those exciting years has
recorded his or her recollections, and both Pound and Joyce figure
prominently in almost as many ways as there were observers.
Pound's studio was a gathering place and a point of interest; he
pursued there the arts of poetry, sculpture, music, boxing, and fenc-
ing, as well as innumerable minor artistries. Pound knew many
French writers and editors from his visits to Paris before and during the war. Wyndham Lewis, T. S. Eliot, and William Carlos Williams visited him. He met Gertrude Stein, E. E. Cummings, and Ernest
Hemingway. His former editresses, Harriet Monroe and Margaret
Anderson, called. He championed the experimental American com-
poser George Antheil and became one of the outspoken supporters
of *avant-garde* music. These colorful years have been recounted
fully elsewhere, especially, for Joyce, by Richard Ellmann. Nonethe-
less it is worth remarking that for Pound the years in Paris
apparently made much less of an impression than did his earlier
years in America and London, or his later years in Italy. While Joyce
settled in, Pound seems to have felt himself to be a sojourner or part
of a special coterie, one of the "Heimatlos," for his memories of the
Paris years figure only briefly and fragmentarily in *The Pisan
Cantos*.

In July 1922 Pound once more summoned his Odyssean inventive-

[5] Paul Bourget, French critic, poet, and psychological novelist.

ness to prescribe for Joyce's physical ailments: his failing eyes, his arthritic back, and his bad teeth. In 1917 Pound's prescriptions had been based on a hypothetical relation between eyestrain and genius; in 1921, in his "Postscript" to his translation of Gourmont's *Physique de l'amour,* he had speculated on a relation between creative genius and what might be called the spermatozoic imagination. Now it was genius and glands. In March 1922 Pound had reviewed enthusiastically in *The New Age* Dr. Louis Berman's *Glands Regulating Personality.* "The new therapy," as Pound called it, seemed especially suitable for Joyce's ailments. Since Dr. Berman was visiting in Paris, Pound persuaded Joyce to submit himself to an examination. Dr. Berman proposed endocrine treatment for Joyce's arthritic back and, after one look at his teeth, insisted that they be X-rayed immediately.[6] The teeth proved to be in such bad condition that he advised complete extraction. Joyce accepted the endocrine treatment, but although Dr. Berman must have gained his confidence by comparing Joyce's glaucoma to Homer's (which, however, had made Homer blind), Joyce put off the extraction until he had consulted another ophthalmologist, Dr. Louis Borsch, who was to become his long-standing ministrant. Dr. Borsch confirmed Joyce's hopes that extraction of his teeth and operations on his eyes might be put off, and although they continued to plague him he managed to postpone the operations until April 1923.

During the rest of 1922 Pound not only continued his work on *The Cantos* but also took on various jobs as translator and anthologist. In August he agreed to edit for William Bird's Three Mountains Press a series of short books which he later said indicated "the state of prose after *Ulysses,* or the possibility of a return to normal writing"; the writers in this "Inquest series," which included his own "Indiscretions" and volumes by Ford, Williams, and Hemingway, had "set out . . . to tell the truth about *moeurs contemporaines* without fake, melodrama, conventional ending."[7] But by the end of 1922 Pound had become restless. Paris, he felt, was typified by "the indisputable enervation of Proust"; he was drawn by the energies of emerging Italy. Recalling his distinctions between prose and poetry he contrasted Proust to D'Annunzio, whom he had set against Woodrow Wilson in 1919 as his first exemplar (though an imperfect one) of "the revolt of intelligence." D'Annunzio "lies with a bandaged eye in a bombarded Venice, foam-

<hr>

[6] Ellmann, *James Joyce,* pages 550–552, 556.
[7] *Pavannes and Divagations,* Norfolk, Conn.: New Directions, 1958, pages 50–51.

ing with his own sensations, memories, speculations as to what Dante might or might not have done had he been acquainted with Aeschylus." Pound felt the need to exert "some sort of vigour, some sort of assertion, some sort of courage, or at least ebullience that throws a certain amount of remembered beauty into an unconquered consciousness." [8]

In May 1923, for reasons which are not entirely clear, his association with *The Dial* ended. He put little stock in requests from *Vanity Fair* and Eliot's *Criterion*, shrugged his shoulders, and for the moment contented himself with the fact that "imperfect Paris is still breathing, still respiring." In May too William Bird agreed to publish the famous de luxe edition of *A Draft of XVI Cantos*. At this point Pound's first career as editor, critic, evangelist, and literary arbiter, which had dominated his life since 1912, came to an end. He now concentrated almost all of his energies on *The Cantos*, contributing very little to periodicals until 1927, when he inaugurated a second public career from Rapallo.

Joyce meanwhile, having recovered from the ordeal of *Ulysses*, had projected another work. In August 1922, while visiting London, he replied to Miss Weaver when asked what he would write next, "I think I will write a history of the world." [9] But his eyes had become worse and advice that they be operated on (given by the English doctors Henry and James) sent him flying back to Paris. Once more he put off operations and attempted to winter in Nice, but there too his eyes became aggravated and he was forced again to return to Paris. In spring 1923, however, he began to take notes, probably inspired by the Book of Kells, which was to be one of his models for a history of the world based upon Irish mythology and the Irish race. On March 11, 1923, he wrote to Miss Weaver that he had written two pages, the first since the final "Yes" of *Ulysses*.[1] But in April he submitted to extraction of his teeth and an eye operation, then went to England to recuperate. Whether Pound knew what Joyce was working on is doubtful, for when Joyce returned from England to Paris in August 1923, Pound wrote to his father: "The Joyce family back in Paris. And J. J. launched on another work. Calculated to take the hide off a few more sons of bitches" (at Yale). Clearly, Pound had in mind the Rabelaisian-Swiftian aspects of *Ulysses* and thought Joyce was continuing on the same tack in

[8] "Paris Letter," *The Dial*, LXXIII, 5 (November 1922), pages 553–554.
[9] Ellmann, *James Joyce*, page 551.
[1] *Letters of James Joyce*, I, page 202.

what was to become first *Work in Progress* and finally *Finnegans Wake*.

Late in 1923, when he was arranging for the start of a new review, Pound brought together Quinn (the backer), Ford (the editor), Joyce, and himself; the magazine was the short-lived *Transatlantic Review*, for which Pound wrote the music columns during 1924. Joyce gave Pound the four-old-men section ("Mamalujo"), including the Tristan and Isolde passages, to read. Ford then asked Joyce for something for the magazine and Pound told Joyce that the front pages of the first issue were to be reserved for him "with a trumpet blast." Actually Joyce had already declined to let Eliot have these pages for *The Criterion*, for he did not consider them ready. But when Ford reminded Joyce of support given him in the past (probably Pound's and Quinn's), Joyce gave in, though he thought the review "very shabby." The piece was printed in the review's second issue, April 1924.

Pound's only existing letter to Joyce of the Paris years, his verses on Buck Mulligan, reflects his increasing emphasis on the humor of *Ulysses*. Joyce himself had declared to Djuna Barnes in an interview:

> The pity is the public will demand and find a moral in my book, or worse they may take it in some serious way, and on the honor of a gentleman, there is not one single serious line in it. . . . They are all there, the great talkers, they and the things they forgot. In *Ulysses* I have recorded, simultaneously, what a man says, sees, thinks, and what such seeing, thinking, saying does, to what you Freudians call the subconscious—but as for psychoanalysis, it's neither more nor less than blackmail.[2]

Pound was following the same track by himself trying in *The Cantos* to turn the great doers and civilizers into great talkers; like Joyce he was interested less in psychoanalysis or interior decoration than in what "seeing, thinking, saying" did, does, and can do to the mind that chooses values and makes civilizations. For both, humor was one of the conditions for being able to be serious. Pound would have agreed with Joyce's rejoinder when his cousin Kathleen told him that his Aunt Josephine thought *Ulysses* unfit to read: "If *Ulysses* isn't fit to read, life isn't worth living."[3]

[2] *Vanity Fair*, XVIII (April 1922), page 65 (Ellmann, *James Joyce*, page 538).
[3] Hutchins, *James Joyce's World*, page 139.

Pound's verses, composed in the spirit of *Ulysses*, commemorate a dramatic escapade of Joyce's old friend and antagonist, Dr. Oliver St. John Gogarty, the original for Buck Mulligan. On the night of January 12, 1923, Irish rebels kidnapped Gogarty, a senator of the new Irish Free State, while he was in his bathtub. They took him to a deserted house on the banks of the Liffey and seemed about to assassinate him. The ebullient, athletic Gogarty feigned a bowel seizure. When his captors took him outside he threw his greatcoat over their heads, leapt into the Liffey, and escaped by swimming across the turbid, icy river. He later kept his vow to offer the Liffey two swans if she bore him to safety, and entitled his first book of poems *An Offering of Swans*.[4] The meeting with the girl is Pound's invention.

16 January 1923   *Rapallo*

Ballade of the most gallant Mulligan, Senator in ordinary
              and the frivolous milkwench of Hogan
                                          afftl. dedicated to
                                              S. Daedalus
                                                  Tenor
                                            by his friend
                                            Simm McNulty

              Ohe, ohe, Jock Hielandman,
              The strong and brawny Mulligan
              Took off his overcoat and ran
                    Unto the river Liffey,

              Peeled off his breeches and jumped in,
              Humecting thus his hairy skin;
              All heedless of pursuers' din
                    He struck out like a porpoise.

              "Who goes there, where the waters pour
              "Across the mill-dam, say, koind sir?"
              "I am a celtic senator,"
                    To her replied Buck Mulligan.

[4] Gogarty, *It Isn't This Time of Year at All!, An Unpremeditated Autobiography*, Garden City, N.Y.: Doubleday and Company, Inc., 1954, pages 208–215.

215

"Put on your breeches, sir, again,"
To him replied the milk-maiden,
"before you land by our hog-pen,
    on this side of the Liffey."

"Ach, darlint, do but lend me yours,
"Oi left moine wid them rebel boors
"whom you see fearin' wather-cures
    on t'other side the Liffey."

"Oi will, sir," says she, as cute a cheeze,
"To shield you from the gaelic breeze,
"Bedad, oi think they'll reach your knees,
    "Kind, kindly kind, sir senator,

"And I but one condition make
"Before I doff now for your sake
"—think—Jaysus! think what oi've at stake,
    "O kindly kind, sir senator,

"If you will wear them and go down
"To the senate hall in Dublin Town
"In that attire,—do not frown,
"Promise me, dear; or, damn you, drown."

In early 1924 Pound brought his ten-year struggle for Joyce to a climax by arguing that on the strength of *Ulysses* Joyce should receive the Nobel Prize for literature—if not as an Irish writer, then as a member of "the republic of letters, or of the Heimatlos" (the exiles). The occasion was the outcry in London over the award of the 1923 prize to Yeats. In his essay Pound mentions previous Nobel awards to the Belgian-French dramatist and poet Maurice Maeterlinck (1911), to the Bengali poet Rabindranath Tagore (1913), to the Swiss poet Carl Spitteler (1919), and to Anatole France (1921).

LE PRIX NOBEL [5]

THE spectacle of impoverished England howling over the loss of the only thing literary England can understand namely a sum of moneys, to wit le Prix Nobel, sterling 7500, is so touching that the

[5] *Der Querschnitt*, Berlin, IV, 1 (Spring 1924), pages 41–44.

springs of thought are thereby set working. One is moved to speculate upon causes.

And it seems quite possible that the apeeved British committee has been for years so silly and petulant and overbearing, that they have, like swine, cut their fat throats with the little sharp hooves of their forefeet.

In any case if the award had not gone to Mr Yeats it should have been given to his most distinguished compatriot, the author of "ULYSSES"; who is younger and who has approved the Nobel Award, and who was very probably not recommended by the Irish committee.

The more tempered english yowl to the effect that Thomas Hardy deserves the award does not apply to the year 1923 in any way which has not been applicable for the last twenty years, or since the founding of the Prix Nobel.

It is incontestable that Hardy is an author in the Nobel Prize class; and that an award made to him, at any time during the Nobel period would have been widely applauded, but there is no special reason for it's having happened this year and we are open to speculate upon earlier awards, from data gained by twelve years residence in his island.

In the first place it seems likely that british literary politics has been so tangled and murky that the English committee has tried to put over all sorts of deals on the Swedish academy, and that that body has very properly rebelled, or even gone into a chronic state of rebellion against insular dictates.

This prize has been going on for some time, they the Britannics, are perfectly capable of having recommended their Laureate, or Mr Gosse, or Mr Dobson, or even the late Dr Nicoll.[6] If they haven't howled about the non-acceptance of Hardy in the past, we must remember that it was only this year that the Prince visited Mr Hardy on a motor bike. In fact the English spent a number of years condoning Mr Hardy; and they have never induced him to London. He was for years considered a terrible fellow, and a pessimist.

They can't expect foreign opinion to veer in an instant because of a prince and a motor bike.

Some shrewd Swede may even have investigated the nature of

[6] Robert Bridges was poet laureate from 1913 until his death in 1930. Austin Dobson (1840–1921) was a poet, man of letters, and student of the eighteenth century. Sir William Robertson Nicoll (1851–1923), Scottish Non-conformist divine and man of letters, founded *The Bookman,* anthologized contemporary writers, and wrote on the literary history of the nineteenth century.

their committee, and their Academic Committee, which used to call itself, or be loosely called, their "Academy".

This sub-division of the Royal Society of Literature (the latter a sort of palmes académiques institution with no licence to give palmes) was founded about twelve years ago when an American lady married to a Frenchman decided to give ONE HUNDRED POUNDS per annum as a reward to litterchure in them islands.[7]

Like the French Academy it was composed of forty members, mostly old dodos. It roped in a few estimable characters who thought England ought to have an intellectual life; they did not enjoy it.

We have record of one scene the late Maurice Hewlett [8] burying his head in his hands out of boredom, and the late Henry James touching him gently on the shoulder, and emitting the sepulchral irony "Come, come, we are not here to enjoy ourselves" (Anecdote told me by Monsieur Hewlett.) And as to the selection of members we have memory of a time when two candidates were proposed (B . . . . . and C . . . .) Mr X . . . . had written to S. M. suggesting "B. and not C.", and received the magistral letter:

WHY B . . . . . and not C . . . . , I thought they were two buttoks of one bum?

And I have a third memory of a Sussex cottage where the police descended upon us, namely Mr Yeats and myself, desiring me as an alien. And another morning we received news that Nobel award had gone to Tagore, and this filled us with merriment. It filled us with merriment because Mr Yeats had tried to get Tagore elected to the "Academic Committee" and the committee had voted against it. Yeats thought they wouldn't have Tagore because they thought him a nigger.

They refused Tagore and they chose in his place the Dean Inge.[9] And Mr Tagore is a very good poet in Bengali, and they none of them could understand that the award was made to Mr Tagore because of his poems in *bengali* and not for the translations of those poems into prose english.

It is quite possible that they have proposed Inge to the Swedish electors, if not this year, possibly last year.

---

[7] The Edmond de Polignac Prize for literature, established in 1911 by the Princesse de Polignac in memory of her husband. Awards were granted before the war to De La Mare, Masefield, James Stephens, and Ralph Hodgson.

[8] Maurice Henry Hewlett (1861–1923), novelist, essayist, and poet whom Pound knew.

[9] William Ralph Inge (1860–1954), influential British theologian and "gloomy dean" of St. Paul's, known for his admonitory sermons and essays about modern life.

And what Fleet St. (London journalism) overlooks in its present ferment, is the fact that William Yeats is a very great poet, and that every literate, english-reading man of my generation, or let us say of the decade of which I am the youngest member, has known Yeats' poems from adolescence, and loved them, and owned them and read them over and over, and that they rank with the work of the great minor poets (minor in the sense that they have sung one mood, or two moods, but not all moods); and that Yeats ripped away the rhetoric of english verse.

And in modesty he has commented, "I got rid of one sort of rhetoric, and seem to have invented another"; which is in a measure true, but does not cover the whole matter. For the first time in English there were lyrics that read from one end to the other, in a straight simple sentence, with no deflection of word-order.

And perhaps for the first time in the islands a great and known poet stood aside and made way for writers with a cleverer stage knack than himself; and even London had seasons of a theatre that was not wholly idiotic or pusillanimous, or merely a charlatan's rag bag, patched up with tatters of Nietzsche, Ibsen, or with top dressing of Oscar.[1]

So that the award has been an admirable award, and whatever one's mistrust of collective and incorporated intelligence one must admit that the Nobel awards have been in general well made; everyone disagrees with one award or another, but the list of recipients is neither pompous nor ridiculous. A wreath of this sort has its limitations; the award could not preserve M. Maeterlinck's writings, nor gain an audience for M. Spitteler. If one noted that the award to M. France was unproductive, and that the upkeep of active writers is more important than the laying of laurels on the doorsteps of their elders, that stricture bore rather on the conditions of the prize than on the action of the Swedish academy.

The decadence of Maeterlinck had showed them the danger of crowning young men. A danger that should not be a complete deterrent but which the hostile critic must allow for. And if, to recapitulate, the award had not gone to Yeats it might well have gone to another Irishman, and if it can not, for some national reason, go for two consecutive years to the same nation, one might nominate James Joyce as representative of the republic of letters, or of the Heimatlos; who are, at this moment, as respectable a collection of writers as is found in any one country.

If not for next year, for some year not too distant, for looking

[1] Oscar Wilde? or the head chef at the Ritz?

over the list of possibilities there seems no unlimited number. There is, admittedly, Mr Hardy; and the Italians would, since Fiume and his war service, offer D'Annunzio; and France has no writer of first magnitude; and I think none who could get a french quota of votes, unless by some desperate wrangle. And there is Mr. Conrad Korzeniowski? [2] Heimatlos or proposed by Poland, or by England? and who is not quite in Joyce's class as an author.

Idealism

In the discussions that have taken place here in Paris about Joyce's "eligibility" this word has been used as if in some way it would debar the author of "Ulysses". That is buncomb.

If Idealism means anything. If it implies anything more than a bandying of catch-words and shibboleths, and an attempt to force a personal panacea upon others; it should mean what?

Surely the highest idealism is that which tries to make others more aware of the relations between one thing, or one state of mind, and another; to make them more aware of the cosmos in which they exist.

And if "Ulysses" has any existence, it exists as a great work of Katharsis.

* * *

An insidious voice says "It has never gone to an American". Again buncomb. There has been only one American during the prize's time, of suitable magnitude; and one can hardly see Henry James in the act of receiving the medal. One can hardly see him in the act of realizing the existence of Sweden. One can still hear the slow suave voice: "Eh, I, eh belong to a body, eh, doubtless you also belong to it"

(mute interrogation on my part)

"and there is also another inner and more secret body, eh, doubtless you also belong to it. . . . ."

etc., ending magnificently: "and how my dear old friend . . . . eh . . . . Howells . . . . !" [3]

Mr James having with some difficulty complied with their request to send in some congratulations to be used at a dinner of honour to Howells, and the so called American Academy having suppressed 'em because they weren't sufficiently flattering to the national assininity.

[2] Joseph Conrad's Polish name was Teodor Jozef Konrad Korzeniowski.
[3] William Dean Howells.

Apart from all of which there is one reason *why no American or Englishman should be immediately eligible for any such international honour*. Namely 500 copies of a great work of literature have been seized and burnt in Washington D.C. and another 500 seized and destroyed in Southampton; and no writer of standing resident in either England or America has emitted one word of protest.

I refer to the seizure and destruction of copies of James Joyce's "Ulysses"; and if the Swedish Academy exists for the purpose of rendering some sort of international literary justice, there is this wrong to be balanced.

You would think we were in the time of Bayle; when the Dictionnaire was burnt in market place.

And at such a time it is fitting that a nation's authors should suffer for the ill deeds of the populace whom they have mis-educated or left in ignominious murkiness.

Joyce's sense of urbanity, expressed so genially in *Ulysses*, found satisfaction in Paris. He was becoming involved with a new and growing circle of friends and he gradually became a renowned figure and an acknowledged leader of the *avant-garde*. He told Wyndham Lewis that Paris was "the last of the human cities," [1] preserving its intimacy despite its size. Pound, on the other hand, had expressed dissatisfaction with Paris and indeed with all of the places he had been:

> The problem (O gawd, how one falls into *clichés*) facing (O gawd, O Montreal) . . . Is it possible to establish some spot of civilization, or some geographically scattered association of civilized creatures? One is up against this problem in a decadent wallow like London, in an enervated centre like Paris, in a reawakening Italy, in an inchoate America. [2]

Joyce was always interested in the actual city, Pound in the ideal city of the mind; Joyce never ceased being Leopold Bloom, while Pound, after his initial delight in Bloom, moved on to the more austere and aristocratic figure of Odysseus. Pound's "Cititatem Dei" was the idea he had fought for as a journalist and as an editor; he was trying to create such a "city of God" or of "the gods" in his poetry; "£," his sense of life, existed as a group of poems, or as a book, or as the heroic consciousness, wherever he himself might be. As he told H. L. Mencken in 1928, referring to his departure from America, "the State of Pound did very largely sever 20 years ago." While Joyce strove to make himself a native of whatever place he was in, Pound aspired to be an intellectual cosmopolite, a citizen of the world.

Pound departed for Rapallo in the fall of 1924 and in 1925 settled there permanently. He continued to work on *The Cantos* and Joyce on his history of the world. In 1925 they appeared together

[1] Ellmann, *James Joyce*, page 523.
[2] "Paris Letter," *The Dial*, LXXIII, 5 (November 1922), page 549.

in Robert McAlmon's *Contact Collection of Contemporary Writers*, represented by *Canto* XX, lines 1–60, and by what are now the first pages of the section of *Finnegans Wake* that reviews the origins of Humphrey Chimpden Earwicker's name and reputation.[3] Joyce suggested that McAlmon try to get a preface from Arthur Symons, since the writers gathered about Pound resembled the group of writers who had gathered about Symons and *The Yellow Book* in the 1890's.[4] Nothing came of Joyce's suggestion. Pound's only extant communication to Joyce in early 1925 is a letter about a French translation of *Dubliners*.

21 January 1925   *Siracusa*

Can't make out whether Jean de Gourmont wants to translate it or wants ME (porca santa) to trad. In any case as he is a gentleman, send him a line. His firm ought to do *Dubliners*. Also *you* might smoke 'em up to start the series of continental editions of contemporary English books—before Berlin does.

P.S. J.d.G.'s address is 71 rue des Sts. Pères, in case his handschrift is more illegible than mine.

A curious episode later in 1925 perhaps augurs a new coolness in their literary relations. Earlier in the year Ernest Walsh, who was starting a new magazine called *This Quarter*, had decided to dedicate an issue to Pound and had asked Joyce for an encomium. Joyce had responded warmly, expressing gratitude for Pound's friendly help of 1914–1920 and even for his advice and encouragement, which had come from "a mind of such brilliance and discernment" (perhaps an instance of Joycean hyperbole, for he said later that he had never taken Pound's advice on matters relating to his writing.)[5] Walsh had later got Joyce to let him print the Shem chapter of *Work in Progress*. Joyce had given Walsh the manuscript, but then had gone off on a holiday in eastern France. On his return to Paris in September for another operation on his eye he found himself baffled. He had tried to find Walsh, he wrote to Miss Weaver, but both Walsh and Shem had disappeared. Walsh had proposed earlier that Pound correct Joyce's proofs, but Joyce had written to Pound that he wanted nothing better than to check them himself and

---

[3] *Finnegans Wake,* New York: The Viking Press, 1939, pages 30–34.

[4] *Letters of James Joyce,* I, page 226.

[5] "Letter on Pound," *The Critical Writings of James Joyce,* edited by Ellsworth Mason and Richard Ellmann, New York: The Viking Press, 1959, pages 253–254.

asked if it would be possible to have his piece set first.[6] Pound's only reply was a letter to "Voices of Americans in Europe," *The Chicago Tribune* (Paris Edition), September 3, 1925:

From Mr. Pound

To the Editor of the *Tribune*.

Sir: May I avail myself of your sometimes hospitable letter column to state that I have no editorial connection with any current periodical; and that I am not a receiving station for manuscript, typescript, drawings, photographs or other paraphernalia, accompanied or unaccompanied by return postage (French, Guatemalian, or Etats Unisien).

EZRA POUND

Rapallo, via Marsala, 12 int. 5

Joyce sent the paper to Miss Weaver on October 10, remarking that there had been "other allusions since"; upon his return he had found "a very curious atmosphere" and he suspected (though he did not specify) the causes.[7] On October 22 he included Pound, Ford, and Walsh among those who had made no acknowledgment of "Anna Livia Plurabelle," which had appeared in the October issue of *Navire d'Argent*.[8] What Joyce was thinking of—it sounds as though he suspected some kind of conspiracy—is not certain, but it can be inferred that he expected less formality and more interest than he thought Pound was displaying. He apparently cared about Pound's opinion, though he might not agree with or even value it, and so was either miffed or disappointed.

In 1926 relations became further strained over Samuel Roth's piracies of Joyce's work. Roth, a New York publisher, had written to Joyce expressing his admiration and then in 1925 had begun to publish fragments of *Work in Progress* in his magazine *Two Worlds*. He paid Joyce $200 and promised more, but none came. Then, in July 1926, he began without authorization to print *Ulysses* in a second publication, *Two Worlds Monthly*. In an interview with the New York *Evening Post* on November 1, 1926, Roth claimed that he had "arrangements" with Joyce for the publication of *Ulysses*. Sylvia Beach issued a denial in a cable to the *Post* and in an open letter to the American press,[9] and Joyce tried to get Quinn to

---

[6] *Letters of James Joyce,* I, pages 233–234.
[7] *Letters of James Joyce,* I, page 234.
[8] *Letters of James Joyce,* I, page 235.
[9] Gorman, *James Joyce,* pages 307–308.

institute proceedings. When Quinn declined, Joyce wrote asking the advice and aid of Pound, who earlier in 1926 had forced Roth to remove his name as an editor of *Two Worlds*.

19 November 1926 *Rapallo*

Cher. J.: Sorry, I dunno no lawyer. I cabled my father to start proceedings against Roth last winter; but he didn't as he found it wd. be expensive. However I did succeed in getting my name off the cover. (In return for which recd. several obscene and abusive missives from the impeccable Roth.)

You are in worse shape than I was as you have taken money from him . . . and you have known for some time that he was a crook. All I can suggest is that you write to as many papers as possible, denouncing Roth, and stating that text is garbled and unauthorized. There is no known way of getting at R. as he has only "desk room," i.e. comes in now and again to get his mail in an office containing forty other desks (probably of various flavours and integrities).

I mean if you go to law you have nothing to get damages FROM.

Are you in communication with Collins? ?[1] If so, can you get any information from him about the art collector, Barnes.[2] Don't say it is for me.

Re your own affair: certainly write (typed letter? they won't read your script) and SIGN your letter to N. Y. *Post*. That is your best way of annoying R.

Also you better stir up JANE HEAP. It is to interest of *Little Review* as well as yours to stop Roth. I have no friends in America. I don't know whether McAlmon is in N. Y.; you can organize a gang of gunmen to scare Roth out of his pants. I don't imagine anything but physical terror works in a case of this sort (with a strong pull of avarice, bidding him to be BOLD).

He had nothing to make out of me, so consented to remove my name from his title page, after I had written to various offices protesting against his use of my name in his ad. That however was not fear of the law, he merely saw he had more to lose by having me on the war path than to gain by having my name on his sheet.

[1] Dr. Joseph Collins, author of several "The Doctor Looks at" books on literature, biography, love and life, marriage and medicine (cf. Dr. Gould's books on genius and eyestrain, etc.). Collins wrote "Ireland's latest literary antinomian: James Joyce," in *The Doctor Looks at Literature*, New York: George H. Doran Company, 1923, pages 35–60.

[2] Albert Coombs Barnes, American art collector who established the Barnes Foundation, Merion, Pa.

The man is quite clever. He has more interest in the matter than your lawyer wd. have.

Your only weapon is firmly abusive campaign in the press.

Also you can write to Roth, threatening action. You will get a good deal of impertinence in reply but still. . . .

You can also state in your letters to press that *Parts of* Ulysses *that were printed before suppression are copyright*, and that you are proceeding against Roth. (That may make his subscribers nervous about receiving future numbers.)

However, you have a skunk to deal with and the perfume will possibly fly.

Joyce started legal proceedings against Roth and organized an international protest. He asked Pound to sign. But Pound, along with his old adversary Shaw, was one of the few who drew attention to himself by refusing.

25 December 1926   *Rapallo*

Dear Jim: I answered S[ylvia] B[each]'s letter explaining why I do not care to sign your protest. I.e. I consider it a miss-fire, that omits the essential point and drags in an irrelevancy.

I am glad SOME use has at last been found for Claudel.

I enclose a note that you can use as p.s. to the general protest.

Merry Xmas and greetings to the family.

Enclosure

25 December 1926   *Rapallo*

My dear Joyce: My only reason for not signing your protest is that I consider it misdirected. To my mind the fault lies not with Mr. Roth, who is after all giving his public a number of interesting items that they would not otherwise get; but with the infamous state of the American law which not only tolerates robbery but encourages unscrupulous adventurers to rob authors living outside the American borders, and with the whole American people which sanction the state of the laws. The minor peccadillo of Mr. Roth is dwarfed by the major infamy of the law.

You are perfectly at liberty to publish this statement or to make

226

any use of it you think fit. Parts of *Ulysses are* protected, as they appeared in an American periodical, were copyright, and were not suppressed. I understand that Roth has reprinted these parts, in which case he is liable to due penalty.

Instead of using "a mountain battery to shoot a gnat," Pound wanted Joyce, as "the leader of European prose," to wage a full-scale war against the general evils of the copyright and pornography laws; if he did so Pound would testify by affidavit. But Hemingway told Joyce Pound's idea was "moonshine," and Joyce did not take up the proposal; he wrote "a courtly reply to say he assumed Pound felt his signature to be one of those which were supererogatory." [3] Later, in his defense, Roth claimed that Pound, acting as Joyce's literary agent, had authorized him to publish *Ulysses* in *Two Worlds*. At Joyce's request Pound made a formal denial at the American Consulate in Genoa; in the spring of 1928 he agreed to give evidence against Roth should it be needed. Joyce's legal proceedings had caused Roth to cease printing *Ulysses* in October 1927 (he had printed more than half the book). He was finally enjoined in December 1928 from using Joyce's name in any way.

When the Roth affair began Pound was preparing to resume the polemical activities of the war and the postwar years which he had laid aside to concentrate on *The Cantos*. A new magazine, *The Exile*, was to serve the same purpose as the earlier *Egoist* and *Little Review*—as an outlet for "personal utterance" or "propaganda" and as a refuge for writing which established literary journals would not print. At this moment too, Joyce found himself in much the same position he had been in when Pound wrote to him in 1913. Several fragments of *Work in Progress* had appeared in periodicals, but on his return from vacation in September 1926 he discovered that *The Dial*, which had accepted the Shaun book, declined to print it as it stood. Finding himself without a publisher, he recalled his manuscript and once again lapsed into discouragement. (Eugene Jolas, who would begin regular publication of sections of *Work in Progress* in *transition* in April, 1927, did not appear on the scene until late in December 1926, when Joyce met him and read selections to him.) His discouragement was accentuated when his friends began to turn against the book. To assuage his disappointment and to reassure himself he tried to get Miss Weaver involved in what he

[3] Ellmann, *James Joyce*, page 599.

was doing by asking her to "order" a section. She obliged, and he proceeded to write according to her specifications, remarking "I know it is no more than a game but it is a game that I have learned to play in my own way. Children may just as well play as not. The ogre will come in any case." [4] While this was going on Joyce sent the Shaun typescript to Rapallo, seeking Pound's opinion and hoping that he had found Shaun a place. With Pound's replies a friendly argument about literary judgments began.

15 November 1926 *Rapallo*

Dear Jim: MS. arrived this A.M. All I can do is to wish you every possible success.

I will have another go at it, but up to present I make nothing of it whatever. Nothing so far as I make out, nothing short of divine vision or a new cure for the clapp can possibly be worth all the circumambient peripherization.

Doubtless there are patient souls, who will wade through anything for the sake of the possible joke . . . but . . . having no inkling whether the purpose of the author is to amuse or to instruct . . . in somma. . . .

Up to the present I have found diversion in the Tristan and Iseult paragraphs that you read years ago . . . mais apart ça. . . . And in any case I don't see what which has to do with where. . . . Undsoweiter.

2 January 1927 *Rapallo*

Dear J.: First number of my new periodical designed to deal with various matters not adequately handled elsewhere has gone to press. I don't see that it can be much direct and immediate use to you. It comes out 3 times a year, so that serialization is out of the question.

I think, and always have thought, that the "sample of woik in prog" stunt was bad. *The transat.* did it because there simply wasn't enough copy to fill the so large review.

If I had an encyclopedicly large monthly, the kewestion wd. be different. Present view is that your daruk pool shd. be sold whole on *Ulysses* and that further distribution of bits wd. do final sales more harrum than good. However, I may be wrong. The law-court bit, livens up.

[4] *Letters of James Joyce*, III, page 144.

Wot I nevurtheles suggess re the oncoming review is that it will do no harm to have it circulate freely to such as will pay for it. There are plenty of seguidores after the act; but it can do no harm to establish a means of communication that in case of emergency will not have to stop, to hem, to haw, to whit, to whom, etc.

Notice of forthcoming novels, romans, etc., can be conveyed and at any rate, the air of ambiguity so . . . shall we say . . . widely ambient . . . etc. . . . . vb sap.

On the heels of Pound's refusal to sign Joyce's international protest against Roth and his rejection of Shaun came further doubts from his other old admirer. On January 29 Miss Weaver wrote of the protest: "I wish Mr. Pound had signed it, considering that the book in question is *Ulysses* and not the present one. And perhaps when the present book is finished you will see fit to lend ear to several of your older friends (E. P. to be included in the number) . . ." [5] In his reply on February 1, Joyce expressed his disappointment that she had not liked his work, asserted his own belief in it, and made his usual plea for encouragement, complaining that her reservations had given him "a nice little attack of brainache." He then delivered his candid judgment of Pound's critical acumen:

It is possible Pound is right but I cannot go back. I never listened to his objections to *Ulysses* as it was being sent him once I had made up my mind but dodged them as tactfully as I could. He understood certain aspects of that book very quickly and that was more than enough then. He makes brilliant discoveries and howling blunders . . . [6]

But Miss Weaver persisted in her coolness to what she called Joyce's "Wholesale Safety Pun Factory" and "the darknesses and unintelligibilities of your deliberately-entangled language system." [7] He had previously defended himself to Miss Weaver: "One great part of every human existence is passed in a state which cannot be rendered sensible by the use of wideawake language, cutanddry grammar and goahead plot." [8] He complained to William Bird that he could not understand Pound's and Miss Weaver's objections to the book's obscurity, for, while the action of *Ulysses* had taken place chiefly in

[5] *Letters of James Joyce,* III, page 154.
[6] *Letters of James Joyce,* I, page 249.
[7] Ellmann, *James Joyce,* page 603.
[8] *Letters of James Joyce,* III, page 146.

the daytime, the action of *Work in Progress* takes place at night. "It's natural things should not be so clear at night, isn't it now?" [9]

Joyce tried to counteract Pound's criticism and win back Miss Weaver's support by asking Pound's opinion about publishing the poems he had written since *Chamber Music*, many of which Pound had placed in *Poetry* during the London years. He explained to Miss Weaver on February 18 his strategy for having "the case of Pound's soundness of judgment at the present moment more gone into":

> Some time ago Mrs Symons asked me (from her husband) if I had not written any verse since *Chamber Music* and if it would collect. I said it would make a book half as big but I did not trust my opinion of it as I rarely thought of verse. There are about fifteen pieces in all, I think, and I suppose someone some-day will collect them. I mentioned this to Pound and asked could I show him, say, two. I left them at his hotel. A few days after I met him and he handed me back the envelope but said nothing. I asked him what he thought of them and he said: They belong in the bible or the family album with the portraits. I asked: You don't think they are worth reprinting at any time? He said: No, I don't.[1]

To Pound they were works of the past which not even the new and different title *Pomes Penyeach* could bring up to date; he responded by lauding a new discovery, Ralph Cheever Dunning. Taken aback, Joyce did not at first reply to Mrs. Symons. "It was only after having read Mr Dunning's drivel which Pound defends as if it were Verlaine that I thought the affair over from another angle." To his relief, Miss Weaver agreed with him about Dunning. Joyce wryly played on Pound's vehement denial and his erection of Dunning in a letter to Miss Weaver of May 12, when his pen accidentally made a blot: "The verses in [BLOT] Look at that! It must be Pound did it, I mean dun it." [2]

Despite his differing literary opinions, Pound continued trying to help Joyce, and even asked for help in return. Later in 1927 he wrote suggesting possible publishers. He also appealed to Joyce's Aquinian training by asking if he could explain "natural dimostra-mento," a phrase in Cavalcanti's canzone "Donna mi prega," which Pound was working on for his *Guido Cavalcanti Rime* (Pound mem-

[9] Ellmann, *James Joyce,* page 603.
[1] *Letters of James Joyce,* III, page 155.
[2] *Letters of James Joyce,* I, page 251.

tions his request in a letter to Olga Rudge, September 28, 1927: at Yale). Joyce replied in November:

I cannot find the phrase you ask about either in Father Rickeby's enormous edition of Aquinas or in the French one I have. The scholastic machinery of the process of thought is very intricate, *verbum mentale* and all the rest of it but I can find no such phrase as you quote. Perhaps it is used in logic or metaphysics. To my mind it does not convey as yet any very precise sense. These philosophical terms are such tricky bombs that I am shy of handling them, being afraid they may go off in my hands.[3]

He added a lighthearted jibe at Pound's rejection of *Work in Progress* and *Pomes Penyeach*. In *transition 8* (November 1927) a defence of *Work in Progress* had appeared by William Carlos Williams who, Joyce wrote Miss Weaver on November 4, was a schoolfriend of Pound's to whom Pound had denounced the book as "backwash," urging him to have nothing to say about it. Joyce remarked to Pound:

I have nicely exhausted myself a goodly share of kicks (some of them aimed at me from that well of English undefiled, Tasmania!) and a few halfpennies of encouragement for which I am deeply grateful. . . .
P.S. I forgot to send a little epigram I made after our last conversation, I think, about my new book. So here it is. I am writing it legibly.

E. P. exults in the extra inch
Wherever the ell it's found
But wasn't J. J. a son of a binch
To send him an extra pound?

The title I gave it (the epigram) was:
Troppa Grossa, San Giacomone![4]

Joyce was recalling his amusement at the retort to Pound with which Shaw had confirmed his refusal to subscribe to *Ulysses* ("I

[3] *Letters of James Joyce,* III, page 166.
[4] *Letters of James Joyce,* III, page 166.

take care of the pence because the pounds won't take care of themselves"). Also, his acknowledgement of Pound's donations of "clothes,
boots, time, quiet and money" in the limerick written at Sirmione in
1920.

True to their delight in puns and parodies, each parodied the
other's style. On June 13, 1925, Joyce had written to Miss Weaver
about the request of the painter Patrick Tuohy, who had painted
his father, that Joyce pose for a portrait. Between parodies of
Gertrude Stein and Robert McAlmon, after which he returns to his
own voice with "(Re-enter Hamlet)," he included a parody of *The
Cantos*:

> Is it dreadfully necessary
>   **AND**
> (I mean that I pose etc) is it useful, I ask
> this
>   HEAT!?
> We all know Mercury will know *when*
>   he Kan!
>   but as Dante saith:
>   1 Inferno is enough. *Basta*, he said, *un'inferno,
> perbacco!*
> And that bird—
>   Well!
> He   oughter know!
> ≡   (With apologies to Mr Ezra Pound) [5]

Pound returned the indirect compliment in a letter to Richard
Aldington on November 14, 1927, ridiculing "the revolution of the
word" as essentially a mosaic of nonsense syllabification.

My DeaHH Richard: [6]

       N O

> I do NOT take an idea which I expressed lucidly
> 13 years ago, and doll it up in the rags and bobs
> of Mssrs W. Lewis, and J. Jheezus Joyce.
> *Transition* has this a.m. arrived, and I "got" your
> insult re/Mr. Gillespie. [7]

[5] *Letters of James Joyce,* I, page 228.
[6] Transcription by D. D. Paige, at Yale.
[7] A. Lincoln Gillespie, Jr., "Music Starts a Geometry," *transition 8,* Paris,
November 1927.

The young follow poppa. In this case the young is
trying to follow three poppas at once. Me for the
root idea (as is nacherly and will probably be
more obviously prevalent in more and MORE young with
the flow of time), Jim and Wyndham for the
kombobo-whyliating of the arsebeforebehindside of word-y-
wobble hichthatch tho' why a kobbobibbleofanglomurkn
syllables shd. be forthe of meaning to before ness
less utile than the same with applyto greekand by none
more or by moremoreorless comprehended hellenicsyllables
is not.

In fact this new syllabation is defensible by logic,
but not practiced with moderation.

It is not clear what Aldington asked for, though he may have asked
Pound to write on how "the revolution of the word" (or perhaps
surrealism) might be related to Vorticism; he may even have asked
Pound to reply to Wyndham Lewis's attack on Joyce and Pound in
his just published *Time and Western Man*. Lewis had been much more
severe on Pound, pointing out the contrast between the archaism of
his poetry and his "fire-eating propagandistic utterances," especially during the periods of *Blast* and Vorticism, when he had
sensed a disparity between the pantechnicon and the Red Indian.
Pound was, paradoxically, "A Man in Love with the Past" and "a
sort of revolutionary simpleton." Lewis suggests that the outburst
of energy and new modernism which began with *The Exile* was a
recurrence of Pound's divided impulses of the *Blast* years.

The fit epilogue occurred a year later. Late in 1928 Joyce learned
that H. G. Wells was in Paris. Since Wells had admired and supported
his earlier work, Joyce hinted indirectly that he might do the same
for *Work in Progress*. On November 23 Wells declined with a thought-
ful letter. He contrasted their respective frames of mind and literary motives. Joyce's Catholic background placed him in "stark
opposition to reality," causing his mental existence to be "obsessed
by a monstrous system of contradictions" and his writing to emerge
as "quirks and fancies and flashes of rendering"; Wells, not unlike
Pound, turned his mind to "a big unifying and concentrating
process" and sought to promote "a *progress* not inevitable but interesting and possible." Wells admitted, however, that his training
had been scientific and that he was writing under the British "delusion of political responsibility," while Joyce's Catholic and revolu-

tionary training made him write under the Irish "delusion of political suppression." Wells closed his letter with the same generosity Pound had displayed during the 1910's (in his letter on "Sirens," for instance) :

> All this from my point of view. Perhaps you are right and I all wrong. Your work is an extraordinary experiment and I will go out of my way to save it from destruction or restrictive interruption. It has its believers and its following. Let them rejoice in it. To me it is a dead end.
>
> My warmest wishes to you Joyce. I can't follow your banner any more than you can follow mine. But the world is wide and there is room for both of us to be wrong.[8]

Pound, conversely, was losing patience; Joyce must have sensed the growing hostility to his work, for Wells's distinction between the expressive and the "constructive" (and to Joyce, propagandistic) led him to think of Pound. He commented to Miss Weaver on December 2: "the more I hear of the political, philosophical, ethical zeal and labours of the brilliant members of Pound's big brass band the more I wonder why I was ever let into it 'with my magic flute.' " [9] Joyce probably heard in *The Exile* the thump of drums and the sound of brass; Wells's distinctions foreshadow Joyce's and Pound's antipodal positions during the politically dominated 1930's. An isolated letter asking about Joyce's early translations of the German playwright Gerhart Hauptmann (he had translated *Michael Kramer* and *Vor Sonnenaufgang* in 1901) appropriately ignores Joyce's current work.

23 December 1928   *Rapallo*

Dear James: With respected greetings of the allegedly happy but in reality rather frigid season.

As a philological note: The Yeats alledges that in time past (80 or 90 years ago) thou madest some traductions of the plays of G. Hauptmann.

2ndly that these cd. not be used at the Abbey because it was then constitooted or red taped to do nowt but 100% green or Erse plays.

[8] *Letters of James Joyce,* I, pages 274–275.
[9] *Letters of James Joyce,* I, page 277.

If these juvenile indiscretions still exist the time may now have come to cash in on 'em.

The noble Gerhardt is struggling both with *Ulysses* (im Deutsch) and with the germanly traduced works Wm. He sez *Ulysses* in choimun is like looking at a coin through a microscope, can't see it cause it's aggrandized to such etc. . . .

Seems quite as likely that it was Grillparzer or Ibsen that you'd traduced, *but* you might lemme have the reel dope on the sichooat-shun. . . .

1930-1938

By 1930 Joyce was a world figure. Although *Ulysses* was banned in England and America, he was the most famous prose writer in his own language; all of his fiction had been translated into French and German, and translations had appeared or were about to appear in Russian, Swedish, Polish, and Japanese. In 1932 he signed a contract with Random House for the publication of *Ulysses* in the United States, though not until after Judge Woolsey's famous decision of December 1933 that it was not obscene did the book appear. *Work in Progress* was appearing regularly in *transition* and parts of it had been published in book form; in 1931 Joyce signed a contract with his old publisher Ben W. Huebsch for the complete book. From 1930 on he was forced to undergo a series of further eye operations. In 1931 he moved to London, intending to settle there, but he soon found that he was not attuned to Anglo-Saxon countries and returned to Paris. At the end of the year his father died, filling him with remorse and guilt for never having returned to Ireland. His father's death was somewhat assuaged by the birth of his first grandson on February 15, 1932, but in March his daughter Lucia suffered the mental breakdown which was to dominate Joyce's personal life until his death.

Pound meanwhile had set up his own cultural center in Rapallo. Yeats lived there periodically, Pound organized his famous chamber music programs, and the pilgrimages began that brought to Rapallo young poets, founders of little magazines, future editors, and old Ez's scholars, who undertook investigations of everything from the Italian Renaissance to modern banking. New sections of *The Cantos* appeared regularly, as well as evangelistic calls for reform like *How to Read* (1929) and challenges to established scholarship like *Guido Cavalcanti Rime* (1932). Pound also began to conduct his one-man campaign of reform-by-letter. Not only did he write to dozens of correspondents, old and new, known and unknown, but he became a prolific writer of letters-to-the-editor, addressing himself to periodicals all over the world. Seeking to spread the gospel of Social Credit economics he also became a regular contributor to *The New English Weekly*, the Social Credit paper founded by A. R. Orage on his return to journalism in 1932. He already admired Mussolini's economic system but had not yet begun to apply his economic theories openly and directly to the growing political conflict between democracy and fascism.

Joyce continued to see Pound when Pound came to Paris, retaining his whimsicality, his appreciation for past aid, and his amusement at Pound's brand of wit. Of one occasion he wrote to Miss Weaver:

> Pound says the most outrageously amusing things sometimes. Kicking his long legs around in the drawingroom he upset a little sacred image McGreevy (Lord knows why!) gave me at Xmas so that a thread got twisted round S. Joseph's neck, E.P. exclaiming 'Gee! I never knew that *that* blighter had been hanged too!'[1]

Despite his lack of sympathy with Joyce's linguistic mystifications, Pound remained genial and continued to hope that *Work in Progress*, like *Exiles*, was merely a necessary *jeu d'esprit* between works. In 1929 he had begun to correspond and cooperate with *Hound and Horn*, the Harvard miscellany edited by R. P. Blackmur, Lincoln Kirstein, Bernard Bandler, and Varian Fry, hoping that it might succeed *The Exile* and *The Dial* as a review in which his voice and ideas could be heard. He wrote to Kirstein on October 26 [?1930] (at Yale):

> (Privik and confidenshul. IF you can get a decent chunk of W[yndham]. L[ewis]. I will TRY to get a chunk of Monsieur Joyce written in plain and decent english or american and not choctaw. This is possibly Icarian, and nothing can be done till I see him in the spring but I hold out the offer . . . about which I request that you *speak to no one* whomsoever (save Bandler if he is supposed as co-edtr. to see all this correspondence.

In a piece published in the first number of Samuel Putnam's *New Review*, January–February 1931, of which Pound agreed to be a "subeditor," he assumes his old role as Joyce's Sancho Panza to jibe at the Homeric explicators and psychological analysts of *Ulysses*; he probably has in mind Stuart Gilbert's *James Joyce's Ulysses*,

[1] *Letters of James Joyce*, I, page 281. Thomas McGreevy, a friend of Joyce's, had written on Joyce's work.

1930, as well as the *Nouvelle Revue Française* ("n.r.f."), for which Larbaud had written his article on *Ulysses*, and the Bloomsbury group ("the Bloomsbuggars"), Virginia Woolf, John Middleton Murry, Aldous Huxley, Herbert Read, etc., who were interested in psychology, in the stream of consciousness, and in the unconscious as it was being exploited in surrealism. Pound was ready to become Joyce's bumptious squire as soon as Joyce gave up his quixotic "backwash" and returned to his real gifts and his true subject. The opening paragraphs explain the occasion of Pound's article. Wambly Bald was the literary columnist of *The Chicago Tribune*, Paris edition, one of Pound's forums for letters to the editor. William Carlos Williams's *White Mule* ran in most of the issues of *Pagany*, edited in Boston by Richard Johns from 1930–1933. Pound placed Wyndham Lewis's gigantesque satire on London, *The Apes of God* (1930), with *Ulysses* as one of the three great modern prose works in English (see below, pages 267–272).

from AFTER ELECTION [2]

On the 5th. of November of this year I learned, first from the Chicago Tribune and secondly by private advice from Mr Putnam, that I was an associate editor. The Tribune seemed to imply that I was concerned in some sort of manifesto which I had not at that date seen, although I had no great fault to find with the quoted fragments. Mr Bald further stated that I would remain on the sidelines and maintain an approbatory attitude for a decade. I am still groping for the basis of these assumptions.

When in all the course of my life which has itself been a series of joyous ejections, when have I ever displayed that mixture of indolence and self-restraint which keeps a man on the side lines? "What god, what hero or what man" [3] is assured of a solid ten years approbation, even from me who am now apparently introduced as an approver?

* * *

I APPROVE, all right, I approve of "WHITE MULE" by Bill Williams appearing on p. 4. of the summer issue of "Pagany", "a native quarterly"; the subtitle of White Mule is "a novel"; on p. 10, I find the italicised words *"to be continued"*. In the autumn issue of "Pagany" I find no "White Mule". I disapprove of not finding "White Mule".

[2] *The New Review*, Paris, I, 1 (January–February 1931), pages 53–54.
[3] Cf. *Hugh Selwyn Mauberley*, III.

I have not at the date of this writing seen the rest of the manifesto. Mr Putnam suggests that I will probably resign when I see it.

However there seems to be no bar to my expressing myself on the various points raised in Mr Bald's notice.

* * *

I thoroughly approve of Mr Joyce making experiments; he is at liberty to dine in restaurants I dislike; no man could write two "Ulysses", one after the other. I have the utmost respect for Mr Joyce his integrity as an author. Any popular entertainer would have woke Leopold Bloom the next morning and continued in a sequel. I should myself have been the first to enjoy such a sequel. I should give thanks to the various gods had he done it. I don't care a damn about the metaphysics and the correspondences and the allegorical and the anagogical and the scatological parallels of his opus. I don't care whether you spell it omosias or omoousias [4] or however thehellzbellz you do spell it or whether the father came out of the egg of the second emanation of the egg of the third emanation. Has not the author himself complained in my hearing that at least someone might have said they *enjoyed* the book and thought it "so goddammed funny"?

Give the goodman his relaxations. He wrote a dramedy when he had finished "The Portrait". Sign, if you like, my name "Sancho Panza".

Have we had enough of the n. r. f. and the pseuderasts; have we had enough of the pseuderasts and the Bloomsbuggars? Enough, enough, we have had quite enough and then had some and that some was goddamd too many.

I respect Mr Joyce's integrity as an author in that he has not taken the easy path. I never had any respect for his common sense or for his intelligence. I mean general intelligence, apart from his gifts as a writer.

* * *

In contrast with this most stubborn Irish we have ole Bill the most stubborn ox in America. Bill began with contortions and obscurities. Goin' East as J.J. went toward the sunset, Bill has

[4] Pound refers to *homoiousias* (of like substance) and *homoousias* (of the same substance). The Nicaean Council (A.D. 325) promulgated as orthodoxy that the Son was of the same substance as the Father, declaring heretical the Arian doctrine that the Son was of different substance (*heteroousias*) or merely of like substance. The Nicaean definition was the basis for the orthodox doctrine of the Trinity as one in *ousia* and three in *hypostasis* or *persona*.

arrived at the Joycian lucidity of "White Mule". Read it and then turn to The Portrait of the Artist as a Young Catholic.

Mr Joyce is perfectly right. I repeat and reJim that I respect him, but it would be jolly to see ole Poldy Bloom wakin up in the morning with his frowsy head beatin' the foot board. It would be jolly to see Cissy Caffrey gettin out a clean set of diapers for that dirthy young spalpeen young whatshisname. It would be jolly to hear the Croppy boy bein' orated over with the voice of all the sonzofbitches that ever made speeches in the lowsy louses of Parliament, and Poldy's new weepin meditations about the new measures in Ireland and the sacredness of the censorship and the rights of free fahrtin in public.

And when I saw three Irish honest plotters in London, and when I saw ten Irish ministers in Paris,—black is the day and helldamn the lot of them,—did I ever expect to see the hour that Pickwick would be publickly burned in the streets of Dublin beneath the statues of the three famous fornicatin' Irish heroes for corruptin the minds of the young.[5]

And now my dearly beloved brethrenletuspray and to HELL with the Free State.

This paragraph is an elegy.

* * *

Nevertheless I prefer THE APES OF GOD to anything Mr Joyce has written since Molly finished her Mollylogue with her ultimate affirmation.

THE APES is the only major manifestation we have had from north of the bleating channel for now nearly a decade. The yatter it has aroused appears to me mainly nonsense. One admits Mr Aldington's protest that Lewis might have been better employed depicting the retired airmen, labour members, pelman [6] students who constitute the only Britain that matters (inarticulate Britain) or rather one wishes that if a novel is to be the expression of ideas as well as, or instead of, the expression of a vitality, one would prefer ideas that have some relation to life as one oneself lives it.

Mr. Lewis had a theory that the scum on the top of the pond may in the long run poison the fishes.

Sometime we will have to resign ourselves to the fact that art is what the artists make it, and that the spectator has damn well to take what he gets.

[5] See Pound's letter to Joyce of December 21, 1931, below, pages 241–243.

[6] The Pelman Institute, London, and the Pelman System of teaching language and training the mind, the memory, and the personality.

In THE APES Mr Lewis has given us magnificent Rowlandson.[7] The chippchipp about identification of the "characters" with living unoriginals is of featherweight non-importance. In eighty years no one will care a kuss whether Mr X, Y or Z. of the book was "taken from" Mssrs Puffun, Guffin or Mungo. The colossal masks will remain with the fixed grins of colossi.

The tittering scholiasts will identify H. Z. his marriage with an event in European society that occurred eight weeks after the volume was printed, und so weiter. . . .

Pound consulted Joyce again late in 1931 about the Blarney Stone, probably wondering if the custom of kissing it grew out of primitive fecundity rituals in which the stone symbolized the god-king's masculine energy as the poem or the statue (according to Pound) symbolized the artist's. Pound's printed letterheads became a distinguishing mark during the Rapallo years and after; the following, given in its original form, was one of his first. He had begun dating his letters by the fascist calendar ("Anno X").

res publica, the public convenience
Rapallo, Via Marsala, 12 int. 5 [8]

EZRA POUND   21 Dec. 1931 Anno X

Dear Jhayzus Aloysius Chrysostum   Greetin's to you and to yr wives and descendents legitimate and illigitimate (se*lon*).

Blarney Castle, it come into me mind. Do you know anything, apart from the touchin' ballad; about it. I mean when did fat ladies from Schenekdety or Donegal first begin to be held by their tootsies with their hoopskirts falling over their privates to in public osculate: he [the] said stone

and for what reason? fecundity? or the obverse?
Whose stone, in short, was it?

I regret not havin the opporchunity to sing you my last ditty when in Paris or rather the last before I went thither, composed for yr/ special postprandial dilectation and then, domme, I forgot it. At least I think I forgot it, I can't remember having performed it.

When you get an address send it on; or come down and watch the icicles forming on the edge of the mare Thyrenno. benedictions

E.P.

[7] Thomas Rowlandson (1756–1827), British caricaturist.
[8] *Letters of James Joyce*, III, pages 237–238.

SONG FOR INFORMAL GATHERINGS

(to the familiar lyric measure)

O Paddy dear an' did you hear
The news that's going round,
The Censorship is on the land
And sailors can be found
ExPurgating the stories
That they used to tell wid ease
And yeh can not find a prostichoot
Will speak above her knees.

I met Esmond Fitzguggles [9]
And the old souse says to me:
'I fought and bled and died, by Xroist!
'That Oireland should be free,
'But you mustn't now say "buggar" nor
      "bitch" nor yet "bastard"
'Or the black maria will take you
'To our howly prison-yard.'

'They've had up the damn boible
'To examine its parts an' hole,
'And now we know that Adam
'Used to practice birt-controll,
'In accardance wid St. Thomas
'And dhe faders of the church,
'And when pore Eve would waant to fuck
'He'd lambaste her wid a birch.'

'We must prothect our virchoos',
Lowsy Esmong says to me,
'And be chaste, begob, and holy
'As our Lord was wont to be.
'And we must select our language
'So that it shall not offend

[9] Pound had known Desmond Fitzgerald at T. E. Hulme's Poets' Club dinners in 1909. Fitzgerald later became a minister in the Irish Free State. As Minister of Publicity he visited Joyce in 1922, told him that he was about to propose that Ireland nominate Joyce for the Nobel Prize, and urged him to return to his native country. In 1931 Fitzgerald was Minister for Defense.

'The fat ould buggerin' bishops
'Or their woives, worrld widout end!'

Sure I t'ought of Mr Griffeth [1]
And of Nelson and Parnell
And of all the howly rebels
Now roastin' down in hell
For havin't said 'Oh, deary me!'
Or 'blow' or even 'blawst'
An' I says to lowsy Esmond:
'Shure owld Oireland's free at last.'

O'Donal Hugh Red O'Donnel

Joyce's reply to Pound's letter seems more concerned with the relation between stone and speech than between stone and phallic power.

1 January 1932 [2]   [*Paris*]

Extracr [*sic*] from The Groves of blarney (Air: The Bells of Shandon) by Richard Milliken [3]

And there's a stone there that whoever kisses
IIE never misses
To grow eloquent.
'Tis he may clamber to a lady's chamber
Or become a member
Of sweet parliament.
A clever spouter
He'll soon turn out or
An out-and outer to be left alone.
Don't seek to hinder him
Or to bewilder him
Sure, he's a pilgrim from the Blarney stone.

[1] Arthur Griffith (1872–1922), Irish revolutionary leader, head of the Sinn Fein, and first president of the Irish Republic after the Anglo-Irish treaty of 1921. He edited the nationalist papers *The United Irishman, Sinn Fein,* and *Nationality.* Pound applied one of Griffith's principles of political action—"can't move 'em with a cold thing like economics"—to his poetry in *The Cantos.*
[2] *Letters of James Joyce,* III, pages 239–240.
[3] The stanza is actually by Francis Sylvester Mahony ("Father Prout") (1804–1866), and was written as an addendum to Richard Alfred Millikin's poem (Ellmann, *Letters of James Joyce,* III, page 239).

Extract from Work in Progress, Part I, section 6 (it is the second of the four masters, who here represents Munster, answering. He has been asked a riddle. What Irish capital city of six letters, beginning with D and endung with N etc etc' but he answers)

Dorhqk. and, sure, where you can have such good old chimes anywhere, and leave you, as on the Mash and how 'tis I would be engaging you with my plovery soft accents and descanting upover the scene beunder me of your loose vines in theirafall with them two loving loofs braceletting the slims of your ankles and your mouth's flower rose and sinking ofter the soapstone of silvry speech.[4]

Dear Pound: There is nothing phallic about the Blarney stone, so far as I know. The founder of the castle was a cunctator (or perhaps it was the defender of it). He kept on inventing excuses, parlays etc during its siege, I think in the time of Essex. The stone is flat and so far as I can remember let into the wall a few feet below a window. I never understood why it could not have been kissed from a ladder. I heard there were double bands of elastic to fasten the women's dresses. I did not kiss the stone myself.

I hope you had a pleasant *ceppo*.[5] Ours was saddened by the death of my father in Dublin. He loved me deeply, more and more as he grew older, but in spite of my own deep feeling for him I never dared to trust myself into the power of my enemies

It has been a great blow to me.

We send you and Mrs Pound our best wishes for the New Year. sincerely yours

James Joyce

While Joyce was in London in 1931 he had tried to arrange for publication by subscription of Pound's collected prose writings, and perhaps *The Cantos*, which had not yet found a commercial publisher. In 1929 Pound had conceived the idea of publishing his "Collected Prose Work (folio)," the record of his "folio mind," as "a single chunk," asserting "my one vol of prose is no more a series of ... vols than my cantos are a series of lyrics," and adding "the components need the other components in one piece with them." Pound

[4] *Finnegans Wake*, page 140.
[5] Ceppo di Natale, "Yule Log."

considered his prose and his poetry to be complementary versions of a synthetic digest, like *Ulysses*: "There is a difference between Ulysses and a series of Hen. James novels" (letter to *Hound and Horn*, August 30, 1930, at Yale). The project did not succeed in London or America. *Prolegomena*, containing *How to Read* and part of *The Spirit of Romance*, appeared as a first volume in France in 1932, but succeeding volumes were never issued; instead Pound compressed his prose into a more concise summary, *Make It New*, which Faber and Faber brought out in 1934. Joyce recalled his efforts in London when Ford asked him in 1932 for a testimonial to help advertise an American edition of *A Draft of XXX Cantos*. Joyce responded warmly, stating that although the scheme for Pound's prose had fallen through, publication of Pound's main work in his own country was far better. Joyce reiterated that but for Pound's efforts "I should probably be the unknown drudge that he discovered—if it was a discovery." [6] (He avoided, as usual, any comment on Pound's work.) Joyce continued to consult Pound about publication of his own work in Italy. In April 1932, in regretting that he could not accept an invitation to lecture in Florence, he suggested to the mayor "Se mi è lecito proporre un altro nome credo che il mio amico, il poeta americano Ezra Pound, il quale ha tradotto in inglese le opere di un grande scrittore fiorentino, Guido Cavalcanti, potrebbe benissimo rimpiazzarmi." [7] He was less sanguine about Pound's pictorial artistry: "And as for Pound's pen pictures—heaven preserve us! *Es tut mir leid aber es ist nichts zu malen*," he wrote Miss Weaver. [8] It is not clear whether Joyce meant drawings by Pound of Joyce or himself, or Pound's criticism or his letters, or perhaps even *The Cantos*.

In 1933 Pound summarized the history of his association with Joyce, and his early and late judgments about Joyce's work, in *The English Journal*.

PAST HISTORY [9]

For a man connected with education, the editor of this magazine is a marvel of open mindedness. He believes that men who make

[6] "From James Joyce," *The Cantos of Ezra Pound: Some Testimonials*, New York: Farrar and Rinehart, Inc., 1933, pages 12–13.

[7] *Letters of James Joyce*, III, page 244.

[8] *Letters of James Joyce*, III, page 250. Ellmann interprets: "'I'm sorry but there is nothing to paint.' A comic distortion of *'Nichts zu machen'* ('Nothing doing')."

[9] *The English Journal* (College Edition), Chicago, XXII, 5 (May 1933), pages 349–358.

literature know something that those who merely teach it do not. The longer and the more acrimonious the correspondence between us becomes, the more nearly impossible it seems to establish ANY communication between the two groups.

When Remy de Gourmont wrote me that a writer's sole pleasure was the untrammeled expression of what he was thinking ("*ce qu'il pense*") he used the present tense of the verb. He didn't refer to something the writer HAD THOUGHT.

Nobody thought it wd. be a nice thing for the aged Theodore Roosevelt to charge up San Juan Hill yet again in 1914 to wrest Cuba from the Spaniards. Frobenius [1] notes the same distinction between the tenses of the verb in the healthy stage of narrative production. His Africans talk about what the leopard and antelope *are doing* and *saying* NOW, not what they did or said in the time of Aesop. They call the Aesop, "school book exercise."

Everything I have to say about Joyce's *work as such*, has already been printed. Mr Hatfield [2] is eminently correct in saying that the gen. pbk. and "his readers" have not read it, and he might have added "it wd. be impossible for more than ½ a dozen of them to get at it." This fact may shed a little light on the difficulties one had in "putting him over," not as critic but as impresario—one who took on the job or "impressa."

Mr. Joyce from Birth till His Election to the Irish Academy [3]

I did not discover Mr Joyce. Mr Yeats discovered him, but discovered him as a writer of severe and conventional lyrics—the only Irish verse which had sufficient severity for me to consider it relative to "our own" imagiste and pre-Amygist ambitions in 1912 and '13 (vide my anthology *Des Imagistes* 1913–14).

A dirty, bigoted intrigue in Dublin caused the destructions of the first edition of *Dubliners*. As nearly as I can remember Mr. Mencken and the *Egoist* received some of these stories from me in typescript and printed them before the volume appeared.

The *Egoist* then serialized *The Portrait* and, at my suggestion, began publishing books, among which were *Tarr, Prufrock, The*

---

[1] Leo Frobenius, German anthropologist, an authority on the development of cultures. Pound admired his work and drew on his theories and discoveries for *The Cantos*.

[2] W. Wilbur Hatfield, editor of *The English Journal*.

[3] The Irish Academy was founded by Yeats and Shaw. In the fall of 1932 Yeats invited Joyce to join, but Joyce politely refused.

Portrait of the Artist, Quia Pauper Amavi (containing "Homage to Propertius"). *The Little Review* undertook the serialization of *Ulysses*, and from that date onward the story of Joyce's publication is fairly well known.

The significance of the story is: 1st, that there was then in Ireland the same brute bigotry that has since effaced that country from the map of mundane intelligence. It did so almost as soon as their party of intelligence had worked thru into an effective public manifest, i.e., hardly had they obtained more or less of "self-government" when they saddled themselves with a censorship almost, though not quite, as idiotic as our own.

2nd, that England as a "literary world" was dominated by three or four sets of detrimentals, among which:

A. publishers moved by no motive save avarice.

B. a few british gents. honest in financial matters, well dressed in daily life, and obtuse.

C. a generation of more hustling writers impervious to a number of values.

80% of such literature of my generation (from 1910 to 1930) as has any solid value, has been published only via specially founded "amateur" publishing houses. The whole of organized publishing, the solid wall of purveyors of literature, the Canbys, Gosses, weekly supplementers, etc., has been steadily against this 80%. Tho' the supplements and commercial house have come to heel *after the fact.*

These people have obfuscated your world (O general reader!) and you still waste time leaving them in control of the distribution of printed matter.

Not one of the writers who give vitality to present literature wd. have reached you had these people been left to their own devices or if a small hated group had not resisted their efforts (conscious or unconscious) to starve that group into submission.

The Portrait and *Ulysses* were serialized by small honest magazines, created to aid communication of living work; after a lapse of years, these vols. arrived at such a state of acceptance that parasitic publishers issued them. The Tauchnitz which cares only for money but pretends to other aims, issued *The Portrait* and the Albatross issued *Dubliners* and *Ulysses* in continental cheap editions, indicating that the books had passed out of the exclusive circle of people who think and want to know what is being thought, and into the general mass of people who read because an author has a "name," etc.

The facts about Joyce's writing are no different from what I have, at various times during the past 20 years, stated them to be. In many ways Joyce has not gone further than Henry James, at any rate H. J. was the first man to extend the art of the novel beyond the territory already occupied by the french. The serious student can find much of this matter analyzed and presented in H. James's prefaces, and in one novel, *The Sacred Fount*, which James refrained from discussing.

Joyce does not proceed from James, but directly from Flaubert and Ibsen.

In *Dubliners*, English prose catches up with Flaubert (as I indicated, I think, in *The Egoist*). This was a great and cheering event in those days.

The prevailingly active line-up in England in the 1900 to 1910s was the Wells-Bennett-Chesterton, that simply did *not perceive* more than two thirds of the human spectrum. As for Shaw, when Joyce later produced his magnum opus, Mr Shaw considered that no book was worth three guineas. That is the measure of Mr Shaw's values.

Prose did not begin in the 19th century. Flaubert wrote a certain kind of prose. Just as a great many inventions have followed Mr Edison's inventions or as Mr Edison may be said to have done a great deal of other people's work FOR them, so Flaubert did a great deal of the real or fundamental brain work for nearly all good narrative writers since his time. He told his stories by a series of precise statements as to what was visible, or what was done in the scene and by his characters. He often told more than the reader of average human laziness could take in effortlessly. He taught Maupassant to write. He wd. send his young friend out in the morning and tell him to come back describing some concierge in such a way that when Flaubert went past that concierge's loge or doorway he wd. know it was that particular concierge and not some other that young Maupassant had seen.

Maupassant wrote mostly short stories, never telling his reader more than the reader cd. lap up at a sitting. Kipling, O. Henry and all good and most successful short story writers since then have merely learned Maupassant's technique, either directly from him or indirectly from his imitators.

Naturally this process in the long run produced weaker, progressively weaker dilutations.

Joyce, we believe, went back to Papa Flaubert. English prose was mostly very sloppy. In *Dubliners* Joyce tells his stories by definite statement of things visible or things done. Ibsen has told about things felt, things dimly feared; Joyce began to present things felt and feared, but still used hard definite statement.

As Madox Ford had been preaching the virtues of the French prose, of what he called impressionist prose, for some years, and as the Imagist FIRST manifesto had demanded "Direct treatment of the THING whether subjective or objective, and the use of NO WORD that did not contribute to the presentation," a few people recognized the significance of Joyce's first prose book at once.

This question of the fundamental accuracy of statement is the ONE sole morality of writing, as distinct from the morality of ideas discussed *in* the writing.

Transpose this into science: an honest chemist tells you what is in his test tube whether it stinks or not. His honesty *as a chemist* consists in putting down the result of his analysis. An honest biologist isn't there to pronounce a favorable verdict on the patient regardless of what he finds by analysis.

A dishonest writer can do just as much harm as a physician who lies about an analysis and lets his patient behave as if that lie were the truth.

This perception of the writer's MORAL duty has been battle ground for nearly a century. Bigots do not like it, cowards do not like it.

The state of Ireland was so bad that they finally had a revolution to escape at least the diseases which they supposed to be due to English rule. Even that hasn't got it into some people's heads that Joyce was being RESPECTABLE and not merely smutty when he reported on Ireland as he did in *Dubliners*, *The Portrait*, and finally the great Gargantuan *Ulysses*.

My disgust with the American postal laws, which give utterly unqualified people right of decision about what books shd. pass through the mails, is in no way diminished by the accidental advertisement given *Ulysses*. *Ulysses* is probably the only new book of any great value that has had the benefit of such unintentional advertising.

The real circulation of a book shd. be counted by the number of UNDERSTANDING readers it attains, not by the number of half-wits who buy it for irrelevant reasons.

In *The Portrait*, Joyce is at the level of Flaubert's *Education* but does not go beyond the Flaubertian field.

Exiles is a bad play with a serious content; the effect of Ibsen is everywhere apparent; the play's many excellences are those of a novelist not of a dramatist. It was a necessary step. Joyce had to write something of that kind before he cd. write *Ulysses*.

Ulysses (as I have said, vide *The Dial* and *Le Mercure de France*) is a masterwork, in the line of great unwieldy books, *Gargantua*, and *Don Quixote*. It boils over the general form accepted as the form of the novel. Its immediate forerunner was *Bouvard et Pécuchet*.

Bloom is a better device than Flaubert's two heroes. This also I have indicated (in detail) in the two articles cited. Flaubert's two old buffers go down to the country and discuss and epitomize. Flaubert was digesting the social organism of his time. Bouvard and Pécuchet couldn't have tried canning cutlets in Gargantua's day.

The valid parallels for *Ulysses* are with Cervantes * chewing up the Spanish Romances, and with Rabelais † chewing up scholastic bunk, and the idolatry of written words in his own day. The parallels with the *Odyssey* are mere mechanics, any blockhead can go back and trace them. Joyce had to have a shape on which to order his chaos. This was a convenience, though the abrupt break after the *Telemachiad* (Stephen's chapters) is not particularly felicitous, I mean that to the reader who is really reading *Ulysses* as a book and not as a design or a demonstration or a bit of archaeological research, this chop-off gives no pleasure and has no particular intrinsic merit (tho' it has parallels with musical construction and can be justified by a vast mass of theory).

Parenthesis: Ben Hecht once said, "Anybody can write a short story. All you do is to take a man and a woman, AND bring 'em together." The meeting of father and son can be considered under a similar general equation of form.

Joyce has made, to date, 3 contributions to literature that seem likely to *be there* for as long as any of the rest of it. His last decade has been devoted to experiment, which probably concerns himself and such groups of writers as think they can learn something from

* A great many people at one time pretended to admire *Don Quixote,* and may indeed have admired it without any inkling of why it produced such an excitement in Spain. It contains long passages of parody, the fun of which is only appreciable by people who know what is being parodied, that is to say a mass of Spanish romances which no one in our time has read save possibly a few professors. University post-grad scholars sometimes learn of the existence of these forgotten books in the footnotes to scholarly editions of *Don Quixote* [E. P.].

† Rabelais' greatness consists largely in that vigour of mind which freed him from stupid respect for stupidity, whether it were the stupidity of mediaeval writers or that sometimes present in the latin "classics" which were upheld by all the snobbism of his time [E. P.].

it. It can hardly be claimed that the main design of his later work emerges above the detail. I pointed out, long ago, that the defect of Gongorism was something deeper than excessive ornament, or rather that *all* sorts of excess in detail can be considered under a general equation with Gongorism. Mozart wrote galimatias to amuse his young female cousin.

Mr Jefferson remarked that neologisms were justified when they helped to make clear one's meaning.

Mr Wyndham Lewis' specific criticism of *Ulysses* can now be published. It was made in 1922 or '23. "Ungh!" he grunted, "He [Joyce] don't seem to have any very new point of view about anything." Such things are a matter of degree. There is a time for a man to experiment with his medium. When he has a mastery of it; or when he has developed it, and extended it, he or a successor can apply it.

Ulysses is a summary of pre-war Europe, the blackness and mess and muddle of a "civilization" led by disguised forces and a bought press, the general sloppiness, the plight of the individual intelligence in that mess! Bloom very much *is* the mess.

I think anybody is a fool who does not read *Dubliners, The Portrait*, and *Ulysses* for his own pleasure, and—coming back to the present particular and specialized audience—anyone who has not read these three books is unfit to teach literature in any high school or college. I don't mean simply English or American literature but *any* literature, for literature is not split up by political frontiers.

I can not see that Mr Joyce's later work concerns more than a few specialists, and I can not see in it either a comprehension of, or a very great preoccupation with, the present, which may indicate an obtuseness on my part, or may indicate the Mr Joyce's present and my present are very different one from the other, and, further, that I can not believe in a passive acceptance.

In judging the modality of another intelligence one possibly errs in supposing that a man whose penetrations and abilities exceed one's own in a given direction shd. at least equal them in some other. In other words, the times we live in seem to me more interesting than the period of what seems to me reminiscence—which (to me) appears to dominate Anna Livia and the rest of the Joycean curley-cues.

I am, at 47, more interested in work built on foundations wherein I have laboured, than in that produced by Mr J's imitators, and feel that this is justified on human and critical grounds.

Awareness to the present is indisputably part of a great writer's equipment, it is a dimension to be measured, or a component in his specific gravity to be judged and computed, and if you ask me whether I believe that Joyce in 1933 is alive to the world as it is, a world in which technocracy has just knocked out all previous economic computations, and upset practically all calculations save those of C. H. Douglas; a world in which the network of french banks and international munition sellers is just beginning to be expressable on the printed page; in which class-war has been, or is as I write this, simply going out of date, along with the paddle-wheel steamer, and being replaced by a different lineup or conflict, I must answer that Mr Joyce seems to me ignorant of, and very little concerned with these matters. Anthony Trollope wd. have been more alert to their bearing.

Joyce's "Contribution and Influence"

It is impossible, in the course of a single article, to explain the contribution of a new or comparatively new writer to "people" unless one presupposes that they are to some degree familiar with the preceding history of literature.

Joyce's influence in so far as I consider it sanitary, is almost exclusively Flaubert's influence, extended.

That is to say Flaubert invented a sort of specific for literary diabetes. Injections of this specific into Maupassant and weaker injections into Kipling, Steve Crane, etc., prevented a good deal of diabetes (sugar in the wrong place) but the strength of this curative was weakened by time, or you may say, the "culture" was imperfectly continued.

Joyce got some of the real stuff, full strength, or in words already used: Wrote English as clean and hard as Flaubert's French.

This, plus Madox Ford's criticism and practice, plus the effect of a movement for the non-soppy writing of poetry, influenced let us say the early Hemingway and all of McAlmon, and via McAlmon has affected beneficently a whole group of younger writers.

Apart from his ambition for the perfect "form," Henry James set out to enrich the *content* of the novel. The Goncourts had complained that "realism" cd. deal with low life, and expressed a hope that it wd. in time be able to deal with more complicated and elaborate mentalities. This job James undertook, with various results which lie outside the scope of our present essay. Even when Joyce introduces theology and complicated *ideas* he is not preoccupied either with the amenities of certain highly specialized or etiolated

252

social groups of society, nor very much with manners as a fine art. Proust continued James' "line."

Criticism is not limited to saying that certain things are good or bad, but has also the function of sorting out and dissociating DIFFERENT kinds of endeavor. The criterion for a peach or a bull dog is not the criterion for an apple or a spaniel.

The later influence of Joyce has not been useful. This is no FAULT of Joyce's. It is perfectly permissible for a good physician to introduce a new and effective method into an hospital regardless of its being or not being his own invention. He may then retire to his laboratory and conduct research with whatever hope he can maintain in further progress. If some student runs off with the test tubes before the researcher has finished his work, and tries to use whatever is then in them as a specific against, say, consumption, you can not hold the researcher responsible.

As for further details of my ideas re/ the relation of *Ulysses* to Flaubert's unfinished Bouvard and Pécuchet, I explained my view in both the *Dial* and the *Mercure de France* over a decade ago. I can not see any way of abbreviating what I then said. Without reading both books, the teacher can not be expected to understand their relations. It wd. be impossible to explain the working of a taxi engine to a student who refused to learn the simple bases of physics (whether they were called that or not, and irrespective of whether he read 'em in a textbook or was told 'em in a garage).

I have simplified the concept of world literature to the best of my ability in *How To Read*.

The only way for an instructor adequately to know Joyce's "position" is to know more or less the state of human knowledge with regard to writing NOVELS before 1912; to know who were the great inventors and great performers and then to locate Joyce's work in relation to these known phenomena.

Unless the words Flaubert, Ibsen, Henry James have specific meanings for the reader no essayist however patient can explain Joyce's relation to them, or anyone's relation to them, without at least writing three other essays, one on each of these writers, and probably another ten on their forebears, in fact, without doing a complete history of the novel. Once and for all the reader can dismiss the idea that he can solidly KNOW anything about ANY literary form or performance if his knowledge is limited to one language. This is more obviously impossible in a case where a writer's greatest admirations are books written in alien tongues, or when his modes of thought have been fostered by say French and Latin of various epochs and not (in Joyce's case emphatically NOT) by the sort of sloppy writing that was accepted in England in the latter XIXth century and early XXth.

On the other hand, a reader who has from whatever source attained sound criteria of excellence can approximately judge the excellence of a book in so far as that book does not exceed the varieties of excellence that he has been taught to look for.

In "Past History" Pound prepared a new kind of attack against Joyce's work and confirmed the lines of his own development. Literature should pay attention to economics and politics and to what is going on at the present moment; preserving public morality is more important than exploring psychological hinterlands. In 1934 Pound felt a new resurgence of energy and a crystallization of the "totalitarian synthesis": "With the dawn of the year XII of the present era, the chronicler's old sap moves again; for the first time since we were that way ourselves, I am ready to take rash chances, to put my money on this year's colts." [4] He had met Mussolini on January 30, 1933; on the impetus of that contact with contemporary history he wrote during February both *ABC of Economics* and *Jefferson and/or Mussolini*, the books that reflect his "coming up to date" in *Cantos* XXXI–XLI. This new surge of energy made him answer in 1934 when asked to do another piece on Joyce: "I will not LOT'S WIFE. There is too much future, and nobody but me and Muss/ and half a dozen others to attend to it" (December 8: at Yale). Between 1934 and 1940 Pound published forty-one cantos— it had taken him fifteen years to complete the first thirty—and several prose books dealing with literary criticism, political thought, and intellectual autobiography. He continued to write voluminously for Social Credit journals. To *The New English Weekly* he contributed his economics poems under the pseudonym "Alfred Venison," and, between 1934 and 1936, the column "American Notes." For "American Notes" he read *The Congressional Record* and American papers in Rapallo, then commented for London on such complex American phenomena as Roosevelt, the New Deal, Huey Long, Father Coughlin, and the various activities and schemes germinating in the Congress. He even became a crackerbarrel philosopher, as in his 1935 rubric "EZ Sez: Being Some Pithy Promulgations," for the Santa Fe *New Mexican*.

[4] "Date Line," *Make It New,* page 15; *Literary Essays,* page 83.

Joyce became a focus for Pound's impatience with passéism and the stream of consciousness. In March 1930 Pound had written to E. E. Cummings of a piece Cummings had sent him: "Ever a pleasure to have something to decipher that *ain't* dear Jim or oedipus Gertie." He laid out his position fully in a letter to Robert McAlmon, February 2, 1934:

Here we are again. My usual rôle of butting into something that is not strictly my business. But I think you *and* Hem have limited yr. work by not recognizing the economic factor.

Lot of damn rot and "psychology," people fussing with in'nards which are merely the result of economic pressure. Sort out the cussedness and the god damn idiocy which people *keep* after the pressure is removed and the meanness etc. due to Λ) immediate need; B) habit begotten of need and worry (plus reaction, booze etc. when the blighters can't stand staying conscious a minute longer).

I think the whole of egoistic psychological nuvveling is gone plop because the people who go on imitating Dostoiev. and the whole damn lot of 'em *won't* look at the reality. I.e. what was economics, or inevitable 30 years ago, is now just plain god damn stupidity, and people not having the guts to think *what* the monetary system is. Hell knows the neo-communists won't. They think the revolution is GOING TO BE in 1918 in Moscow.

Lot of psychic bellyache *not* a problem any longer, any more than man being melancholy for lack of a pill. Just as damn silly as dying of thirst in an attic because some kid has turned off the water from the basement.

People too lazy to examine the facts are not intelligent enough to write interesting books (reduced to bulls and memoirs depending on personalities).

And thass *that*. J. J. drunk no more dam interest than anyone else drunk . . . or rather that is an exaggeration. Still I do think any character in a Simenon "tec" w[ould] probably make a better fardel to be carried upstair[s]. An so forth . . .

Later in 1934 Pound became excited about E. E. Cummings's book about Russia; because Cummings had seen something new and had therefore "presented a subject," *Eimi* was a live book. *Eimi* elicited a comparison with Joyce's work. Pound had "gone to bat for Joyce sufficiently often"; now, impatient with "the snobbism that has steamed up around Joyce's writings in regress," he doubted that Joyce or Gertrude Stein "have said anything that will be of any interest in itself, apart from their varieties of galimatias."

> . . . Joyce's mind has been deprived of Joyce's eyesight for too long. You cannot say it is closed altogether, but Joyce knows very little of life as it has been in the large since he finished "Ulysses."
>
> He has sat within the grove of his thought, he has mumbled things to himself, he has heard his voice on the phonograph and thought of sound, sound, mumble, murmur.
>
> Three decades of life have been lived since he began writing, of the last two he has learned almost nothing. Of the dominant and cleaving ideas of the last decade he is nearly unconscious.[5]

Crises existed in the conscious world of public policy. Or, if one were to explore body and soul, one should explore the "sane." Pound wrote to Olga Rudge on December 1: "Chap named Miller has writ a bawdy [*Tropic of Cancer*] which will be very useful to put Wyndham and J. J. into their proper cubby-holes; cause Miller is sane and without kinks" (at Yale). Still, however, Pound acknowledged the cathartic power of *Ulysses;* on March 28, 1935, he wrote to Eliot that although Miller's book is presently "the only book a man cd. read for pleasure," still it does not "out Ulysses" Joyce.

But in his customary blunt way, Pound began to use the terms of drunkenness and excretion to characterize the possessor of the un-wavering eye who had administered the laxative bolus. The great Katharcizer, drunk with the stream of consciousness and with the curly-cues of language, had himself to be purged from the ranks of those who would define the present and prepare the future. In 1935 and 1936 Pound began to agitate Wyndham Lewis and William Carlos Williams to form with him a new cenacle, with manifesto, for preserving civilization. In letters to Lewis in late 1936 he first somewhat reluctantly included Joyce "if not too soused." But then he excluded Joyce by implication, for one motive for his manifesto was that "this flow of conSquishousness Girtie/Jimmee stuff has about FLOWED long enuff" (at Cornell). And, in a list of "Living Writers?" which includes Cocteau, Lewis, Eliot, Williams, "Ez," Frobenius, and McAlmon, Joyce is conspicuously absent (to Williams, at

[5] "E. E. Cummings Alive," *The New English Weekly,* London, VI, 10 (December 20, 1934), pages 210–211.

Buffalo). In a letter to Hilaire Hiler, March 10, 1937, while describing a "real mag" for present purposes, he hit on a characteristic *mot juste:* "No need of *transition* crap or Jheezus in progress. I am about thru with that diarrhoea of consciousness. Why ain't I called it that before and not in a private epistle? All I thought of when I saw J. J. last was: 'in regress'."

For Pound, the "living" Joyce was dead. The author of *A Portrait* and *Ulysses* would continue to live in his memory until and even after Joyce's death, but the "allegorizing" Joyce would remain no more alive than Pound thought him in the 1930's. Much later, from St. Elizabeth's, came scorn for the "Joyce inflation" (Pound's term for the budding "Joyce industry"); describing to Wyndham Lewis the "Square $ Series," his postwar organ for writing that he considered had been ignored or suppressed by the publishing powers, he said "no cigarette butts of the late J. J. or other spent rockets" (undated: at Cornell).

As Pound's advocacy of the future grew more shrill and his expressions of support for extreme political forces in a disintegrating Europe began to harden into slogans, Joyce became uncomfortable about Pound's increasing hostility to his work and about their disagreement over the importance of economics and politics. Hemingway has recorded that the last time he saw Pound, in Paris in 1934, it was at Joyce's request. Joyce asked Hemingway to come along to dinner with Pound because Joyce was convinced that Pound was "mad" and was "genuinely frightened of him." Hemingway recalled that throughout the dinner Pound spoke "very erratically." [6] Away from Pound, however, Joyce retained his combination of acerbity and wit. At the time of the *Anchluss* in 1934 (perhaps with the dinner in mind), when newsboys were shouting in the streets about "l'Autriche," he wrote to Miss Weaver, "I am afraid poor Mr Hitler-Missler will soon have few admirers in Europe apart from your nieces and my nephews, Masters W. Lewis and E. Pound." [7] When Mussolini invaded Ethiopia a year later he joked to his daughter-in-law Helen Joyce about Pound's political zeal:

May the 17 devils take Muscoloni and the Alibiscindians! Why don't they make Pound commander-in-chief for Bagonghi and elect me Negus of Amblyopia? [8]

[6] Charles Norman, *Ezra Pound,* New York: The Macmillan Company, 1960, page 322.

[7] *Letters of James Joyce,* III, page 311.

[8] *Letters of James Joyce,* I, page 381.

Joyce's barb, in the lingo of *Finnegans Wake*, catches with amusing exactness an essential difference between the two men: Pound struts as the generalissimo of "big-muscles" Mussolini, attacker of the Abyssinian cutups (who would rather be someplace else). Joyce, the peaceful bystander and victim, is the sultan of dim-sightedness, or perhaps the vision-blurring vinous libation itself, both eyes ambling in a land of shades.

Joyce was determined to finish his book and was burdened with family troubles. He expressed his long-standing indifference to political and social events conclusively in 1937 when Nancy Cunard sent him a questionnaire seeking his views on the Spanish War. When she asked if he was going to answer it, he replied:

> No! I won't answer it because it is politics. Now politics are getting into everything. The other night I agreed to let myself be taken to one of the dinners of the P.E.N. Club. The charter of the P.E.N. states that politics shall never be discussed there. But what happened? One person made a speech, referring to one angle of politics, someone else brought up a conflicting argument, a third paper was read on more politics. I wanted the P.E.N. to take an interest in the pirating of *Ulysses* in the United States, but this was brushed aside. It was politics all the way.[9]

Pound, also approached by Nancy Cunard, refused to get involved in an argument about communism or any other sort of "ism." "Personally," he said, "I am against taking sides in a sham conflict."[1] As usual, he considered the cause of the war to be not the beliefs of the participants, but the manipulations of international finance and the armaments industry. Both writers were equally stubborn or equally quixotic.

The world drifted toward a second war; the first war had brought Pound and Joyce together, but this one, even as it approached, divided them. The only relic of the late 1930's is an exchange of letters in the fall of 1937. Pound wrote to Joyce (the letter has been lost) to inquire about publication or performance of some Purcell sonatas. Joyce relayed Pound's inquiry to a publisher who, he discovered, had already brought out several. On November 12 he conveyed the information to Pound and at the same time asked

[9] Ellmann, *James Joyce*, page 717.
[1] Noel Stock, *Poet in Exile: Ezra Pound*, New York: Barnes & Noble, Inc., 1964, page 173.

for an introduction to Gerhart Hauptmann, who was then living in Rapallo. Joyce wanted to send Pound a copy of *Michael Kramer*, which he had translated in 1901, for Hauptmann to autograph.

8 December 1937   *Rapallo*

J-J-J-Jayzus me daRRRlint: The ribbon iz pale and the carbon brighter and dis is deh feast of the angel or whatever, so you better have the carbon as the angel stops the sale of typink ribbuns . . . .

NOW: about Haupy. I *will* NOT. And fer various reysons . . . .NO sane man *likes* wrappin up parcels. It wd. do you no bloody good. Miss Yunkmans is married and Mr. Yauwner is no longer wid him (meanin wid Haupy). His Missus likes paper and string and standin in pust offices as little as I do.

Send the bloody book *here,* and when his nibs gets here I will lay it on the café table before him and say the grreat Jayzus James the Joyce in excelsis, rejoice in excelsis, wants the Xmas angels to sign it.

Like what Gabriel said to Mary (or vice versa) in Fra Angelico's pixchoor. He sez: "I waaaant that." Or rather *she* sez. "I WANT that in WRITIN'."

In *Guide to Kulchur,* written in 1937 and published in 1938, Pound placed Joyce in "the new paideuma," his experiment in defining culture as what remains fixed in the mind and has become almost part of one's nature. Joyce appears at the turning point between "the sorting out" of the 1910's and the *"rappel à l'ordre"* of the 1920's. The turning point is reflected in Pound's preference for the aesthetic method of the sculptor Constantin Brancusi, whose work he had reviewed in 1921. Brancusi was then trying to get all forms into a single form, to "approach the infinite *by form";* he was revolting against art which, like *Ulysses,* tries to "excite transient . . . interests by more monumental and melodramatic combinations"; such art is a monument to the past rather than aspiration toward an unknown perfection.[2] Pound mentions in connection with Brancusi Charles Humbert René, Marquis de La Tour du Pin Chambly de la Charce (1834–1924), French Catholic sociologist and syndicalist, in whose work he became interested in the 1930's. La Tour du Pin was the principal theorist of the Catholic social movement of the end of the nineteenth century and author of *Les*

---

[2] "Brancusi," *The Little Review,* Autumn 1921; *Literary Essays,* pages 441–445.

Phases du mouvement social chrétien (1897) and of *Vers un ordre social chrétien* (1907). Brancusi represents the aesthetic *"rappel à l'ordre,"* while La Tour du Pin represents Pound's shift from the artistic mode to the cultural "totalitarian synthesis."

MONUMENTAL [3]

I AM not dealing with Mr Joyce in this volume. I have small doubt that no reader will have taken this book, up to this moment, for anything save an universal receptacle, yet it has limits, and its edge is a demarcation. In 1912 or eleven I invoked whatever gods may exist, in the quatrain:

> Sweet Christ from hell spew up some Rabelais,
> To belch and . . . . . and to define today
> In fitting fashion, and her monument
> Heap up to her in fadeless excrement.

"Ulysses" I take as my answer. Yet ten years later when Brancusi inveighed against the "monumental", I did not at once grasp his meaning. "Ulysses" is the end, the summary, of a period, that period is branded by La Tour du Pin in his phrase "age of usury".

The reader, who bothers to think, may now notice that in the new paideuma I am not including the monumental, the retrospect, but only the pro-spect.

The katharsis of "Ulysses", the joyous satisfaction as the first chapters rolled into Holland Place, was to feel that here was the JOB DONE and finished, the diagnosis and cure was here. The sticky, molasses-covered filth of current print, all the fuggs, all the foetors, the whole boil of the European mind, had been lanced.

[3] *Guide to Kulchur,* Chapter 13, page 96.

1939-1945

In 1939 Pound visited America. One of his professed purposes was to try to prevent the war that was threatening. He visited Washington, but since President Roosevelt was too busy to see him he had to be satisfied by discussions with Secretary of Agriculture Henry A. Wallace and various congressmen, including Senator William Borah of Idaho, the state in which he was born and had lived during the first eighteen months of his life. He returned to Italy in the summer. When the war broke out in September, Pound had "got to the end of a job or a part of a job (money in history)" with the completion of the John Adams cantos and was trying "to tackle philosophy or my 'paradise' "; he found, however, that philosophy was as difficult for him as it had been for Joyce (had Joyce sought it) and was requesting help from George Santayana.[1] But the fact of war and questions of political economy were drowning out poetry. Pound found himself writing for Japanese and Italian papers, then undertaking economic pamphlets (in Italian) which supported fascist economics and laid the blame for the war on the capitalist democracies. It was becoming, as he recalled later, "Arguments, arguments and arguments"—"economic stuff in Italian" with some Confucius translation thrown in.[2] Joyce, meanwhile, had finished his book and *Finnegans Wake* was published in England and America in May 1939. But when the war broke out he became discouraged and displaced. After France fell in the summer of 1940 he tried to return to Zurich, where he had sat out the first war, but had difficulty in obtaining permission from the Swiss and an exit visa for Lucia. Finally the required permissions were obtained, however, and in December he settled in Zurich with his family. But he was near the end. On January 10 he was overcome by stomach cramps. X-rays revealed that he had a perforated duodenal ulcer. An operation was performed, but on January 13, 1941, Joyce died. Appropriately, in his last written communication, he

[1] Pound, *Letters*, December 8, 1939, and January 16, 1940.
[2] *Paris Review*, 28 (1962), pages 46–47.

thought of Pound as one whom his brother Stanislaus might call on for help in Italy.[3]

Joyce had never quite known what to make of Pound. Was Pound the Red Indian and pantechnicon of Wyndham Lewis, the American breed of "revolutionary simpleton" whose art is "Mongol, inhuman, optimistic, and very much on the precious side, as opposed to European pathos and solidity"? Or was he more complicated, a new world prophet and technologist who nevertheless felt that "The curse of me and my nation is that we always think things can be bettered by immediate action of some sort, any sort rather than no sort"? Was he the "wonder worker" of the 1910's, the conductor of the big brass band of the 1920's, or the lonely commander-in-chief-elect of Mussolini's Bagonghi? One may doubt whether Joyce could really understand the peculiarly native brand of American Pound represents. It is probable, therefore, that Joyce's view is best expressed in the medium that was most his own, his art. Joyce memorialized their association fulsomely in *Finnegans Wake*, the experiment over which they diverged.

Joyce may have perpetrated a preliminary spoof in 1929, after Pound had rejected Shaun for *The Exile.* The two "Letters of Protest" in *Our Exagmination Round His Factification For Incamination of Work in Progress* are reputed to have been written by Joyce himself.[4] Vladimir Dixon's "Litter" to "Mister Germ's Choice" sounds like Joyce's parody, of a Poundian Uncle Remus parody, of Joyce's style. "I opened the window and in flew Enza," "the prewailent distemper," might remind us not only of the disagreements over *Finnegans Wake* but also of the fortuitous events that brought the two writers together; it might also suggest how despite differences they seemed unfailingly attached to each other, perhaps in ways not yet fully explored.

In *Finnegans Wake*, Pound appears in various guises.[5] Naturally his name lends itself to associations with food and money, as befits

[3] *Letters of James Joyce,* III, page 507.

[4] *Our Exagmination* . . . , Samuel Beckett et al., Paris: Shakespeare and Company, 1929; 2d ed., New York: New Directions, 1962, pages 189–194; *Letters of James Joyce,* III, pages 187–188.

[5] As a neophyte reader of *Finnegans Wake* I have had to rely for a start on *A Second Census of* Finnegans Wake: *An Index of the Characters and Their Roles,* Adaline Glasheen, Evanston, Ill.: Northwestern University Press, 1963; *A Skeleton Key to* Finnegans Wake, Joseph Campbell and Henry Morton Robinson, New York: Harcourt, Brace and Company, 1944; *A Concordance to* Finnegans Wake, Clive Hart, Minneapolis: University of Minnesota Press, 1963; *The Books at the Wake: A Study of Literary Allusions in James Joyce's* Finnegans Wake, James S. Atherton, New York: The Viking Press, 1960; and *The Art of James Joyce: Method and Design in* Ulysses *and* Finnegans Wake, A. Walton Litz, London: Oxford University Press, 1961. I do not claim to have included all possible allu-

his grubstaking and his later emphasis on economics and social questions. But he also appears through, or is associated with, the loud,
public, authoritarian figures of Humphrey Chimpden Earwicker
and Shaun the Post. In one sense HCE and Shaun are John Joyce
Sr. and Joyce's brother Stanislaus; in another Earwicker is the
complete artist, a divine figure, while Shaun and Shem the Penman
(Joyce's figure for himself) are earthly aspirants who seek to
encompass the antipodal roles of the common man and the perfect
creator. In accord with his early promotion of Joyce's work, Pound
is heard through the loud drum, the radio, and the signifying
thunder. When HCE's voice comes through a babel of radio voices it
is as though "the cockshyshooter's evensong evocation of the
doomed but always ventriloquent Agitator, (nonot more plangor-
pound the billows o'er Thounawahallya Reef!" (page 56), were
Pound's advertising of Joyce: the man in the street hears the popu-
larizing barker as Joyce-Bloom dreamed of Pound in 1922. Shem
hears the voice of Pound's letters in Anna Livia Plurabelle's, "as
unbluffingly blurtubruskblunt as an Esra, the cat" (page 116—a
pun on "arsE"-backwards Esra, the phallic poet who objected to
the "cloacal obsession"). "A maundarin tongue in a pounderin
jowl" (page 89), also like ALP's, expresses amusingly Pound's
Chinese refinement but his thumping garrulousness; the play on
"maundarin" (begging) may suggest how Joyce and Pound are
complements of the artist.

As in *The Cantos*, the Confucian element in *Finnegans Wake* is
strong. HCE is in one of his faces a confusionist-Pound, a dead
ringer for the sage who reverences Mt. Taishan, his chin playing
footsie with an oriental cloudcuckooland: "has the most conical
hodpiece of confusianist heronim and that chuchuffuous chinchin of
his is like a footsey kungoloo around Taishantyland" (page 131).
Only such an encyclopedic gasser, American variety, would at thirty
(in 1915) have had the audacity to begin a long, gigantically
radiating, raging rag-bag, full of circuses and circlings, aimed at
holding up the world:

he's as globeful as a gasometer of lithium and luridity and he
was thrice ten anular years before he wallowed round Raggiant
Circos; the cabalstone at the coping of his cavin is a canine

sions to Pound or to have exhausted possible references or possible overtones. The
passages quoted are only those which, without a full study of *Finnegans Wake*,
seem to me plausible and revealing allusions to Pound; they are explained only in
reference to the relations between Pound and Joyce. Page numbers refer to The
Viking Press edition, 1939.

constant but only an amirican could apparoxemete the apeu-
presiosity of his atlast's alongement: . . . (pages 131–132)

Such a figure is mocked in "And his pounds that he pawned from the
burning" (page 322), the chorus sung by the drinkers in the tavern
when a figure of HCE Jr. comes in from a voyage to the accompaniment of a burst of Chinese; Pound is not only John Peel (or John
Bull or the fabulous voyager), would-be raiser of the dead, but
probably also one of the fragments shored (or shelved, *Canto* VIII)
from burning (or falling) London.

One of the fully developed Shaun-figures, the proponent of universal culture, Professor Jones, seems to owe a good deal to a
Poundian original. The Professor expatiates on the "dime-cash
problem," seeking support from Lévy-Bruhl's anthropology (cf.
Frobenius) and opposing Spinoza's and Spengler's romantic pessi-
mism; his citation of "a recent postvortex piece infustigation of a
determined case of chronic spinosis" (page 150) recalls Vorticist
muscle-flexing and Wyndham Lewis's attacks in *Time and Western
Man*. The Professor's use of a translation from the Javanese, "The
Mookse and the Gripes" (cf. the Noh plays), and of the classical
tale of Burrus and Caseous, spoofs Pound's didactic use of mythic
recurrence and metamorphosis as his theory of history in *The
Cantos*. The Professor's peroration includes a Poundian challenge
and claim:

I'll beat you so lon. (Bigtempered. Why not take direct action.
See previous reply). My unchanging Word is sacred. The word
is my Wife, to expivise and expound, to vend and to velnerate,
and may the curlews crown our nuptias! Till Breath us depart!
(page 167)

Should a beggar artist be given a dime? Without pondering, the
Professor has expounded the answer "No" and denied "impulsiv-
ism." His refusal, probably Ireland's, seems to belie Pound's earlier
generosities; but insofar as Joyce has Pound in mind in this respect
it is a reminder that Pound refused to sign the protest against Roth
and that in late 1926 and 1927 he rejected the Shaun chapter and
Finnegans Wake itself. (Joyce's letter of November 1927 had regretted that Pound had not given even a pennysworth of encouragement to *Pomes Penyeach* or to Shaun; the Confucius-*Cantos* and
Professor Jones passages, written during the summer of 1927, may
have been the "extra pound" of Joyce's postscript.)

Not only were Shaun and Shem competitors, but Joyce and Pound as well; indeed the aggressive Shaun-fessor's interminable demonstration and his "I'll beat you so lon" is followed by a surprise reversal in which his audience, Shem-the-beggar and everyman, trumps him. Similarly, Joyce joins the crowd to beg relief from Pound the whited-sepulchre imagist, turned onlocker of an endless wordhoard, who dubbed him the "non-conformist parson from Aberdeen," and who considered words too sacred for Joyce's shenanigans: "Or ledn us alones of your lungorge, parsonifier propounde of our edelweissed idol worts!" (page 378). When Shaun accuses Shem of cooking up a thundering Irish stew the accusation redounds by pun on the accuser ("the more potherbs you pound," etc., page 190). Again:

> . . . it's snugger to burrow abed than ballet on broadway. Tuck in your blank. For it's race pound race the hosties rear all roads to ruin and layers by lifetimes laid down riches from poormen—

—better explore the dreams of HCE than lash yourself in a rearward race toward the future, for the usurers have always fleeced Tovarisch (pages 565–566). Since the competition is on his home ground, Joyce of course wins: if Pound is like HCE, HCE becomes finally a more capacious symbol than Pound's daylit, worldly imagination can summon from history, or than he can ventriloquize. Pound is more like Shaun, who aspires to be his father but fails. During the trial of Yawn, Shaun disintegrates to ALP, then to a more mysterious figure, nearer to Finn himself, who appears sitting on a knoll. When the inquisitors challenge him he dares all "ollaves," i.e., all singers, perhaps especially multivoiced bards living in Italy:

> —I mean to sit here on this altknoll where you are now, Surly guy, replete in myself, as long as I live, in my homespins, like a sleepingtop, with all that's buried ofsins insince insensed insidesofme. If I can't upset this pound of pressed ollaves I can sit up zounds of sounds upon him. (page 499)

By reaching inward instead of outward, Joyce claims, he has plumbed to a principle or pattern of human history that is beyond Pound's grasp. Yet despite his "triumph" Joyce has conceived Pound as a fully developed opposite, of all the modern writers perhaps his most worthy and significant antagonist. We would see them as complements.

Joyce defined Pound in relation to himself; if he did not understand Pound in Pound's own terms, he seems to have known and reacted both to him and to his work more fully than has been thought. In one respect he understood the "ventriloquent Agitator" well enough to have predicted his direction much as his own had been predicted in 1912. As the great feast in HCE's tavern opens we hear the sound of a radio, gift of the innkeeper's customers, emerging above the continuous brawl to tell of HCE's and Ireland's shame, "bawling and whowle hamshack and wobble down in an eliminium sounds pound so as to serve him up a melegoturny marygoraumd, eclectrically filtered for allirish earths and ohmes" (pages 309–310). In the month of Joyce's death Pound began to use over Rome Radio his "maundarin tongue in a pounderin jowl," in all the tones and timbres Joyce had heard, to explain to America its folly and its betrayal of its heritage.

Pound's talks, which finally earned him a charge of treason against the United States, continued from January 1941 until July 1943 (Pound also wrote scripts for others). It is difficult to know what the broadcasts were like before December 7, 1941, for the United States government did not begin transcribing them regularly until January 29, 1942, when Pound returned to the air after having gone back to Rapallo "to seek wisdom from the ancients," "to figure things out." [6] But scripts of the previous talks are doubtless in Pound's possession and will eventually fill in the picture, for in 1948 Olga Rudge published six of his talks, several of which must have been given before America entered the war.[7]

[6] Pound spoke over Rome Radio twice a week. Between December 7, 1941, and July 23, 1943, United States authorities transcribed 122 shortwave broadcasts, some of them repeats of the same talk; they are available at The Library of Congress.

Whether Pound chose to remain in Italy or was refused a visa on the last American diplomatic train is unclear (Norman, *Ezra Pound,* pages 383–384). I leave aside here the questions of Pound's alleged treason against the United States and of his legally determined insanity. These must be faced, and I shall consider them elsewhere, where they may be viewed with the necessary combination of dispassion, compassion, and full understanding of the personal, literary, and historical evidence. In what follows I present merely Pound's memories of Joyce.

[7] *"If This Be Treason . . . . . . ,"* Siena, Italy, 1948; printed for Olga Rudge by Tip. Nuova, 1948. Miss Rudge appends a note: "These 'talks' are printed from the original rough drafts. No cuts, corrections or changes have been made. I have not been able to consult the author about this or other matters. I trust he will not feel that I have taken him too 'au pied de la lettre,'" page 2. The following excerpts should be read accordingly; it should be noted, however, that the talks transcribed by the United States government are similarly informal.

Three of these talks dealt fulsomely with Joyce. In the first two, "E. E. Cummings" and "E. E. Cummings/examined," [8] Pound elaborated his view that *Ulysses*, Wyndham Lewis's *Apes of God*, and Cummings's *Eimi* form "a trio or triad," which encompass "Hist. morale contemporaine. History of contemporary morals; manner and customs, the REAL history of the ERA." His main argument was that *Eimi* was "the liveliest . . . the best bet, the greatest," partly because Cummings continued the American tradition of Thoreau, Whitman, and Henry James (Pound was feeling his America strongly, with both love and hate). He said of *Ulysses*, on the other hand, with its occasional "heaviness" and its London-fog-like "glooms":

Mr J's book was the END, it was the completion (literarily speakin) of an era. It cooked up and served the unmitigated god damn stink of the decaying usury era.

It showed a Dublin, so de Bosschère said, that might have been Brussels.

It was whole, entire, gentile and jew'first great book in contemporary english, insistin on Mr Blum (jew) as existin, and as the father, in some senses, of the man who declined to be a jesuit- all that damn allegory symbol etc. insisted on.

Me saying "affair de cuisine", at least in so far as the structure modeled on Homer's Odyssey, etc. Joyce hittin like hell for his allegories, symbologies, bubkologies[9] and the whatnots.

BUT the main point hit by de Bosschere—THAT might have been Brussels, as well as Dublin.

As technique, the end of the Flaubert process, grown out of Bouvard and Pécuchet.

And I went out with the big bass drum, cause a masterwork is a masterwork, and damn all and damn whom wont back it, without hedgin.

As for Joyce and the author of *Apes of God*, who had survived the end of the period Joyce had monumentalized, and even, unlike Pound, remained in London:

[8] *Op cit.*, pages 3–15.
[9] It is hard to tell whether Pound's coined "-ology" is derived from English (Molly Bloom's mammary powers?), or Greek (βουβών, groin: Stephen? Bloom? Molly?), or Yiddish (*bubkus*, beans; idiomatic, nothing—does Joyce know beans? or what?).

Well Mr Lewis made the BOUNDARY line, DEFINED the limit of Mr. J's Ulysses. (I said HUSH, at the time) I said wait till they *see* it.

After the tree has *grown* you can begin prunin the branches.

Well old Wyndham grumped: as follows, he said about J's Ulysses "Don't seem (meaning Mr Joyce doesn't seem) to have a very NEW pt. of view about anything". In the old style of painting, say Rembrandt or Durer or Carpaccio, or Mantegna when a painter starts painting a picture he damn well better NOT git a new point of view till he has finished it.

Same way for a masterpiece of lit. new pt. of view shd BE either before a man starts his paintin: his recordin contemporary Anschauung, contemporary disposition to life, or AFTER he is thru his portrayin.

That was Ulysses LIMIT, it painted a dying world, whereof some parts are eternal.

Joyce's limitation had been that he "had no philosophy, not so you would notice it. Nothing much alive and bustin the old partitions." He had "some ruck end of theology and a VERY conventional outlook," whereas Lewis had "philosophic views," however "wrong headed."

Pound concluded his comparisons:

My point is that you got to read ALL three vols. to see that the novel did not die with Ulysses. I know brother Estlin sez Eimi isn't a novel. So's your old grandpop. IS Mr Rabelais' big book a novel: or more than. . . . Three books by three painters. NO; Joyce was not a painter not a bohemian, a small bourgeois, to the UTMOST.

Consequently *Ulysses* was not, like *Eimi* or *Apes of God*, "physic and warning," but "a certificate of demise." But the idea that the three books are "the REAL history of the ERA" remained with Pound. He wrote to Wyndham Lewis from St. Elizabeth's "PROportion between Uly/bloosy/liaases/Eimi/Apes cd/ be COMpared if the only critic of the age warnt in bug house" (at Cornell).

As for *Finnegans Wake*, Pound called it in the fourth talk "an aimless search for exaggeration":

Joyce hit his high in Ulysses/ There was still exuberance/
In Finnegan he is hunting/ he is experimenting with a tech-
nique/ bourgeois diversion/

I havnt patience to wade through it/ thank god I am not
employed to estimate the amount of real metal in low grade
ores/ (no pun intended) [1]

The third talk in Miss Rudge's little book, "James Joyce: to his
memory," must have been given in 1941, shortly after Joyce's death
(it is not clear whether it was given before or after the talks on
Cummings). It is much more orderly and finished than the other
talks, perhaps having been prepared for publication. It reflects the
fact that Pound's indifference to and open scorn of "retrospect" did
not exclude those parts of the past which, when he wanted to, or felt
moved to, or had to, he could bring to life. As in many of his
broadcasts, the division between the passéist Pound and the
modernist Pound, between private and public, between elegy and
evangelism, between poetry and polemics, is reflected in the division
in the speech between Joyce on the one hand, and Mussolini and
Hitler on the other. But in recalling the new Rabelais whom he had
invoked, Pound expresses in his best spontaneous voice, unmarred by
the masks of ideology or resentment or strident irrelevancy, his deep
respect and affection. He has seldom if ever written prose in this
vein that can match it. Here the "ventriloquent Agitator," the poet
of many voices, used the radio as the apt medium for expressing the
kind of modern language he had created. This mode foreshadows the
language and tone of *The Pisan Cantos*.

JAMES JOYCE: TO HIS MEMORY.[2]

One winter day in 1912 or thereabouts in Stone Cottage, in
Sussex I asked Yeats (Wm Butler Yeats) whether there were any
poets in Ireland fit to contribute to an anthology of poetry unlike
his own. Joyce being then the only Irish writer not absorbed in the
"twilight," I asked his permission to use his poem "I hear an army",
for despite the differences of surface, despite the old lavender of his
Chamber Music this poem because of the definiteness of the visual
image it presents had an affinity with the aims of the then nascent
Imagist group.

From then on the latin elegance of his writing in Dubliners and le

[1] *Op. cit.,* "A French Accent," page 24.
[2] *Op. cit.,* pages 16–20.

Portrait lifted him into the first rank and there was no longer any question of his being even remotely part of a small movement. He was in the great line of Flaubert and the arc of his work rose to the "romanzone", the pot-wolloper "Ulysses" with a necessary parenthesis in "The Exiles" wherein he was digesting what he had learned from Ibsen.

In what I wrote of each of his books as it appeared from 1913 to 1922 there is nothing I have wished to withdraw. I prefer obstetrics to funerals. It is more exhilarating to fight for a new fine writer against prejudice than to bury him when his reputation is made.

The world has lost a great dining companion or an after dinner companion and in private a humourist. A humourist endowed with a rich contempt but almost no bitterness in fact if Joyce ever really loathed any human being save R......[3] I can not recall it. This complete snot of a British consul, later ambassador, riled Jim at a difficult moment, and the fury of his portrait of the demon barber is his lasting reply.

As to the Wake of Wakes which is Finnegans, a pity, a thousand pities that Joyce cd. not attend his own funeral. The oirish miniSter was absent; faith he may not have known a wake was in progress, or the unlikeliness of a wake in Geneva or whatever god forsaken Swiss valley dear Jim was buried in, may have deterred him. But the humour of the situation was of Joyce's predilected variety.

Sure, said the, of all things BRITISH minister, or ambassador or whatever the sassenach send out to Switzerland: A great oirishman, AND, sez the ambassador a GREAT ENGLISHMAN has gone from us.

Shades of St Pathrick. It seems says the deeplomat that a part of our own youth has gone with him.

Well that's true enough. But as for mr Joyce a great englishman, its like the mandated territories, its like.

We want the earth, yr. hats and shoes and anything that is still yours.

Or as John Adams said, I think to General Howe it was that he said it: receive me in ANY role save that of a British subject.

However, what they can't take when living, they lay claim to when it is coffined.

Tact was ever a British virchoo. At any rate Jim had his revanche for the persecutions of snotty R......

He was buried with honours and buried a damn sight too soon. Humanly speaking.

[3] Sir Horace Rumbold, British Minister to Switzerland, 1918.

I don't think this last work a safe model for infant writers, nor did he himself so consider it. In fact that technique, for someone lacking Joyce's own particular contents is not greatly to be recommended. A man who has made three masterworks has a right to experiment. There is no reason for obstructing the traffic. With Dubliners, the Portrait and Ulysses, Joyce's position is sure. And Ulysses stands in the light of "big books" of fiction. From the Golden Ass on through Gargantua, Don Quixote, Bouvard and Pécuchet. But that line did not *end* with ULYSSES; e. e. cummings wrote EIMI; where the technique is necessary to the subject, and the critics of fiction, of the "over-size" novel, can compute the weight and size of Ulysses, better by comparing it not only with its precursors, but with cummings' work and with Wyndham Lewis' "Apes of God" (bis). Criticism gains nothing, understanding of literature as such gains nothing by supposing that only one book has been written, or that *one* author exhausts the whole range and scope of an era. Ulysses stands properly in relation both to forerunners and to successors. It was in its author's own mind a mine of rich COMEDY, not a crucifix set in a chapel or a bag of saint's bones to be worshipped. If we were diverted by Mr Wells' suggestion that Joyce had cloacal obsession, and that such books should be kept in locked cupboards it may as well go on record that in the storm of abuse in the 1920's Joyce emitted only one mild complaint, thus verbatim: If only someone had said among all those critics, that the book is really damn *funny!*

In short it was not writ to take any man's joy out of living. Nor was that Joyce's practice in private, when free from chapel attendants. May his spirit meet with Rabelais' ghost at Chinon and may the glasses never be empty. If he was a great writer, he also had a fine tenor voice, for Blarney Castle me darlint, or the Frau in Amsterdam, and to a considerable age he could kick to the chandelier as well as any young girl.

A recent American pall bearer, obviously preferring funerals to birth tried to bury a whole generation along with our eminent Irish colleague. This wont do, even for an American lachrymose weekly book review. Mr Lewis is still quite as alive as Joyce ever was. Mr WYNDHAM LEWIS, not the pseudo or D. B. Wyndham but the real Wyndham Lewis. And as to possum Eliot, here I see by the pypers he has been convertin the Archbishop of YORK to Christianity, though they seem between 'em to have got a bit of bolschevism mixed into the recipe. But at any rate the ole possum is still goin' strong under tribulation and stuka bombardment. And I repeat for the health of letters and criticism. Even Ulysses can be considered the first trilogy of live books, that is the series Ulysses, cummings' EIMI and Lewis' Apes of God. This is a healthier way of reading Ulysses than that of considering it the END of double decked stories, however much it be truly the tomb and muniment of a rotten era portrayed with the pen of a master.

The pall bearer tried to bury me also with the lament that I had ceased etc/ and had "*given* myself to fascism".

Now I have no more "GIVEN myself" to fascism in the sense used by the N. Y. reviewer than I had GIVEN myself to Mr Joyce. I suggest he meditate on a line in the Malatesta Cantos.

"Books, arms, and of men of unusual genius
both in ancient times and our own."

As a writer I am given to no one and to all men. As a critic for 30 years I have observed MEN of unusual genius, and this not limiting my observation to writers only. Genius can exist in all kinds of activity. As to the Genius of Mussolini and Hitler I am not alone in observing it. In fact if the American reader wishes to measure the effect of one of these men of genius he can not do better than take up W. Lewis' volume, written in 1931.[4] The Germans weren't pleased with it at the time. It is not a flattering portrait, it is beyond all possible doubt a true portrait, painted with no touch of favour. It depicts Germany at the time when Hitler took over.

It now serves as no pro-German record could serve to measure what Hitler has made of what no other man in 1930 wd have dared to imagine was OPPORTUNITY.

It is a more remarkable record than I managed to make in my comparison of Mussolini and Jefferson, because after all I was here in Italy, I had been coming to Italy since 1898, and had been in residence here eight years. I was, moreover, stressing certain items of interest, not as Lewis was in his "Hitler" making a general portrait of the whole situation but merely insisting on the constructive elements in fascism and particular facts of the corporate state which deserved comparison with the best efforts of the Founders of the North American system.

America wd have led a calmer life in the interim had I been able to arouse a little more interest in the matter THEN rather than now.

---

[4] *Hitler,* London, Chatto & Windus, 1931. But Lewis later considered Hitler a "Jingo god" and a threat to European culture: *The Hilter Cult,* London: Dent, 1939.

Just as the Republican Party wd/ be a happier institution if they had had the sense to nominate Uncle Geo. TINKHAM [5] instead of the tin horn double twister Rip van Wilkie. Rip van winkle wobble the Wendle.[6]

Pound delivered his last word on Joyce in the only appropriate manner, in his poetry, while he was trying to put back together a world which for him had fallen apart. The broadcasts of 1942 and 1943, in which he quixotically defended the Constitution by attacking the American government, are the confused mixture of fascist apologetics, economic theory, anti-Semitism, literary judgment, and memory. He admitted on one broadcast, "I lose my thread at times, so much that I can't count on anyone's mind." [7] He included his own. In another he revealed his desperation:

> There is so much that the United States does not know. This war is proof of such vast incomprehensions, such tangled ignorance, so many strains of unknowing, I am held up, enraged by the delay needed to change the typing ribbons, so much is there that ought to be put into young America's head.
>
> I don't know what to put down, can't write two scripts at once. The necessary facts, ideas come in pell-mell, I try to get too much into ten minutes. Condensed form is all right in a book; saves eyesight. The reader can turn back and look at a summary.
>
> Maybe if I had more sense of form, legal training, God knows what, I could get the matter across the Atlantic, or the bally-old Channel. . . .
>
> Got to choose between two or four subjects or I will get nothing over in any one talk. . . .[8]

He was anticipating not merely the collapse of the fascist state of Italy, but the disintegration of an entire structure of ideas which had made up the "city" of his mind as "the last American living the tragedy of Europe." [9] After his surrender to American forces in 1944 and his imprisonment at Pisa, he found that his world had to be recaptured and restored, slowly and meticulously. He discovered

[5] Congressman George Holden Tinkham (R–Massachusetts, 1915–1943), a friend of Pound's whose fight against the League of Nations won for him the title "founder of isolationism"; he opposed the New Deal, arguing that Roosevelt's recovery program could succeed only if the President took the United States into war (Eustace Mullins, *This Difficult Individual, Ezra Pound,* New York: Fleet Publishing Corporation, 1961, pages 198–200).

[6] Wendell Willkie.

[7] From Pound's broadcast of March 8, 1942.

[8] Broadcast, July 6 and July 7, 1942.

[9] *Paris Review,* 28 (1962), page 51.

a new reality as the solidity and color of the past, remembered in
affection, flowed in upon him and were caught elegiacally in voice and
word:

> nothing matters but the quality
> of the affection—
> in the end—that has carved the trace in the mind
> dove sta memoria [1]

Only by reconnecting himself to past history—to both the history
of western culture, as represented in the particular historical knowledge that he could call up without source books, and to his own
"life and contacts"—could he discover his self. Or perhaps he rediscovered, at a greater distance and in a new way, the self of his
London years, when, as at Pisa, he had been locked in close encounter with everybody's world. At any rate, we can read *The Pisan
Cantos* in one of its dimensions as a monument to the generations
that lived through the period between the wars. As Joyce's *Ulysses*,
and Pound's *Hugh Selwyn Mauberley* and *A Draft of XVI Cantos*
had been monuments to the civilization that produced and endured
World War I, *The Pisan Cantos* is a tragic and elegiac monument to
Europe in 1945.

Pound's work with Joyce and his analyses of Joyce's books had
been "timely" expressions of his own absorption in an immediate
present. In *The Pisan Cantos*, however, Joyce comes alive in permanence, remembered from the meeting at Sirmione:

> Tout dit que pas ne dure la fortune
>
> In fact a small rain storm . . .
> > as it were a mouse, out of cloud's mountain
> recalling the arrival of Joyce et fils
> > at the haunt of Catullus
> with Jim's veneration of thunder and the
> > Gardasee in magnificence
> But Miss Norton's memory for the conversation
> > (or "go on") of idiots
> was such as even the eminent Irish writer
> > has, if equalled at moments (?sintheticly)
> > certainly never surpassed
>
> Tout dit que pas ne dure la fortune [2]

[1] *The Cantos of Ezra Pound*, New York: New Directions, 1948, sixth printing
(with author's errata), *The Pisan Cantos*, 1948, page 35.
[2] *Ibid.*, page 34.

The passage is more than a reminiscence. It reconstitutes an aspect of Pound's personality by relating him to the past, to the present, and to persons. Within the elegiac frame of a general truth which includes his own loss of fortune, at the Disciplinary Training Camp at Pisa, which is contained in the landscape, the weather changes. It is a rainstorm. It may be *ridiculus mus*, but to Pound it is more, for it brings as a flash of memory the arrival of Joyce and his son at Sirmione. But Sirmione is Sirmio—as Joyce himself had commemorated in his limerick, a place of poets: particularly, of Catullus. Rain, memory, and veneration expand through the evoked emotion to a panorama of nature, which for an instant casts the meeting against an enlarged background of both local and universal magnificence. Yet Pound is still Pound. He will not be dispersed into a sentimentalized version of himself. Therefore he fills in the Joycean picture by veering back to their literary disagreement about *Finnegans Wake;* Joyce's fictional "go on" may have been no more convincing than somebody's memory of real "go on," indeed might have been a mad experiment after all. Finally, the elegiac impersonal refrain clouds over the vignette. Yet it has been carved; it perseveres with the repose of art as a trace in Pound's mind, in the natural scene, on the page, and in time.

Joyce takes his place when Pound reassembles his companions of the 1910's. The place is a city of the dead, an Elysian version of Pound's London; it is almost as though Joyce had been there, with Pound and the others, and he appears as he might best like to have been remembered:

nor is it for nothing that the chrysalids mate in the air
                              color di luce
green splendour and as the sun thru pale fingers
Lordly men are to earth o'ergiven
              these the companions :
Fordie that wrote of giants
        and William who dreamed of nobility
              and Jim the comedian singing:
                  "Blarrney castle me darlin'
                  you're nothing now but a StOWne"
and Plarr talking of mathematics
        or Jepson lover of jade
Maurie who wrote historical novels

and Newbolt who looked twice bathed
are to earth o'ergiven.
And this day the sun was clouded
—"You sit stiller" said Kokka
"if whenever you move something jangles." [3]

The rigid sheath of tradition, memory, and good manners makes movements painful and precarious, but Pound sits upright and still, trying not to rock the boat, seeking the dignity of a temple image. The perception at the beginning affirms nature's generation of diaphans and winged light, which in turn affirm the unconquered flame of the human shades, shipmates in the same boat. The tone of their passage is elegiac. But their track is still fresh.

Finally, we can be reminded of their common exploration:

orient reaching to Tangier, the cliffs of the villa Perdicaris
Rais Uli, periplum
Mr Joyce also preoccupied with Gibraltar
                                    and the Pillars of Hercules
not with my *patio* and the wistaria and the tennis courts
or the bugs in Mrs Jevons' hotel
    or the quality of the beer served to sailors [4]

Both Bloom and Pound can be imagined still standing at the Pillars, where two old worlds meet, less concerned with tourist accommodations or with Circe than dreaming of the *nostos* that will bring them to a new world. That new world is also home, and they never lose their determination to be off and moving.

[3] *Ibid.*, pages 10–11; the final two lines are illuminated by *Guide to Kulchur*, page 83.
[4] *Ibid.*, pages 25–26.

Appendix A

In the poems of *Lustra* Pound was seeking a poetic representation
of modernity, analogous to Joyce's representations in the short
story and the novel, by adopting such roles as Whitmanesque bard,
public censor, exile, traditionalist, and realist. Elkin Mathews's
exasperated reader produced a delicious series of expostulations
that reflects London's reaction to Pound's new style: "An impudent
piece," "Poor Walt Whitman! Let's hope he will survive it," "Better
keep his *baser passions* to himself. No one else wants them," "We
shall get ourselves rather disliked (this is quite true)," "*Beastly,*"
"Smelly like its subject," "Papyrus. How truly beautiful," "Delicious lasciviousness," "Profane and flippant," etc. He concluded his
comments:

> The only poems worth reading are the translations. . . . The
> splendid self conceit (see page 39 [probably "Salvationists"])
> of the author—Poet! (save the mark!) is the only redeeming
> feature of most of the others, which with a few exceptions are
> more fitted for the Waste Paper Basket than for the literary
> public.

Lustra had already been set up in type, but Mathews had misgivings
and the printer also balked; Mathews marked sixteen poems for
deletion or alteration.

A flurry of correspondence ensued. Mathews sent the proofs to
Yeats, asking him to mediate. Yeats, Pound said, "quoted Donne at
him for his soul's good" and reminded him that one of his favorite
books was *Tom Jones*. In a space of five days Pound wrote Mathews
at least five letters, two postcards, and a public note, consulted
Pinker and the Home Office, and got an opinion from Augustine
Birrell, who then exchanged notes with Mathews. The upshot was a
private edition of two hundred copies and a trade edition, called by
Pound "castrato," which excluded nine poems. Pound followed his
outraged refusal to delete or change poems with a more temperate

argument appealing to Mathews's good sense; his note, based upon "Meditatio Anent the Difficulties of Getting 'A Portrait of the Artist as a Young Man' Printed in England," was to be added to the edition if poems were deleted. These documents complete the perspective on the "book war" of 1916–1917.

All of the papers cited and printed are from Mathews's papers concerning the affair, which are at the University of California, Berkeley.

[c. 29] May 1916   *5, Holland Place Chambers, Kensington.*

Dear Mathews: I have written to Mr Yeats with very considerable moderation.

I do not recognize anyone's right to interfere with the freedom of letters, nor can a serious writer be expected to abandon the tongue of Shakespeare for the meouing of Wordsworth and Al. Tennyson and Mr Gosse.

It is nonsense to imagine that there can be trouble over poems which have already appeared not only in England but in America which latter country is supposedly much more silly and prudish and uninformed. A man's book is infinitely more private than a magazine.

I do not write [*crossout:* for the public which] as that pandar to public imbecilities Mr Chesterton, nor yet for the Meynell's [1] nursemaid. I write for a few hundred people who are familiar with the classics and who are bored to death with modern inanities because the latter have no directness.

Re/   The poems I have mentioned in the note to Yeats, it is obvious that the proofs sent him had been marked by someone in a state of unreflecting excitement. The poems in that list can not cause any disturbance.[2]

As for the printer holding you up, on such a poem as the one about Cabaret Dancers, that also is nonsense, it was one of the two poems which he printed from on his specimen page, so it is nonsense

[1] Wilfred Meynell, journalist, biographer, and poet, and his wife Alice Meynell, poet, essayist, suffragette, and journalist. They had five children and were noted for their devout Catholic household.
[2] "Salutation The Second," "Commission," "Further Instructions," "The Seeing Eye," "Faun," Coitus," and "Ιμέρρω."

for him to pretend now that he "didn't know it was there". If he was going to fuss he should have done it then.

You will remember that you got into the same sort of funk over the "Goodly Fere", and even insisted on putting a note at the end of it, excusing yourself. No one has ever been able to [crossout: learn] guess why the note was put there, and there never was any scandal over that poem.
You can of course put a note in "Lustra" saying the poems are reprinted at my wish exactly as they have appeared in "Poetry," "Poetry and Drama" etc. (the ones marked in Yeats' proofs seem to be mostly from those magazines.)

In fact there must be a note of acknowledgement to the magazines, anyway, as per enclosure [arrow to note between rules, below].

I must have six [longhand: complete] sets of proof [crossout: as soon as possible] [longhand: at once, to get opinions on them.], also a list of the printers minimum demands, before I can send any terms. The proofs Yeats had were obviously blue-penciled in excitement. Marking poems like the "Faun" and "Pagani's", is simply hysteria, there is no possible thought in either which could have disturbed Mrs Barbauld[3] or Miss Jane Austen.

This much you can be certain of, whatever you take out of this book posterity will put back into it, and they will do so ridiculing an age and a bad taste that removed it.

Note: Most of the poems in this volume have already appeared in the following magazines: "Poetry", "Poetry and Drama", "Smart Set", "BLAST", and "Others"; and in the provisional edition of Cathay. To the editors of the magazines the author wishes to make due acknowledgement.

Then you can add anything you like.

As for your request to Mr Yeats, I am willing to sacrifice a few of the shorter poems on the altar of bigotry, and also to make a few verbal deletions, but if any deletions are made I must have leave to print the final note, which I enclose.

Yours sincerely
Ezra Pound

[3] Anna Laetitia Barbauld (1743–1825), poet, miscellaneous writer, and editor.

The deletions in this book are none of mine and I do not give them my approval. It is thirty nine years since Edmond de Goncourt wrote of an earlier preface by himself and his brother

Thirteen years ago my brother and I wrote in an introduction to "Germinie Lacerteux":

"Now that the novel is wider and deeper, now that it begins to be the serious, passionate, living great form of literary study and of social research, now that it has become, by analysis and psychological inquiry, the history of contemporary ethics-in-action (how shall one render accurately the phrase 'l'histoire morale contemporaine'?), now that the novel has imposed upon itself the studies and duties of science, one may again make a stand for its liberties and its privileges." [4]

There ended his quotation of the preface written in the sixties; he continued:

In 1877 I come alone and perhaps for the last time to demand these privileges for this new book, written with the same feeling of intellectual curiosity and of commiseration for human sufferings.

It has been impossible, at times, not to speak *as a physician, as a savant, as a historian.* It would be insulting (*injurieux*) to us, the young and serious school of modern novelists, to forbid us to think, to analyze, to describe all that is permitted to others to put into a volume which has on its cover "Study," or any other grave title. You cannot ask us at this time of day to amuse the young lady in the rail-road carriage. I think we have acquired, since the beginning of the century, the right to write for formed men, without the depressing necessity of fleeing to foreign presses, or to have, under a full republican regime, our publishers in Holland, as we did in the time of Louis XIV and Louis XV.

Poetry is as serious and as grave a form of expression as is the prose of a novel, or if poetry be not so respectable a form of expression then the serious writer must give up verse altogether, for if he

[4] Pound clipped this passage and the following from "Meditatio" and pasted them in.

may not at times express himself "as a physician, as a savant, as an historian" he had better give up writing altogether, or seek out some country [*longhand, crossout:* language] [*longhand:* or form] wherein such expression is permitted him.

If the writers of the past had been dependent upon the present regulations or habits of book-printing [*longhand:* in England] the following authors and books could not have come down to us as they stand, they would have been either suppressed or interfered with in some way.
Sappho, Anacreon, Theocritus, Zenephon, Herodotus, great stretches of the Greek Anthology, Aristophanes, Catullus, Horace, Juvenal, [*longhand:* Martial] (need one name over the classic writers [*crossout:* two thirds] [*longhand:* so few] of them would have [*crossout:* been put aside] [*longhand:* escaped)] Villon, Rabelais, Voltaire. [*crossouts illegible*] The Divina Commedia itself could not stand as we have it, Shakespeare and the greater part of the Elizabethans, Burton, Pope [*insert:* Fielding, Sterne, Smollett, *longhand:* Heine,] Flaubert, De Maupassant, Tolstoi, wherever one looks for the lasting element in literature, one finds books that could not appear, [*longhand:* under present English conditions.] and the greater part of these books are in no way indecent or salacious.

I write for a few hundred people who are already aware of the classics, and who will be for the most part greatly surprised that any such difficulty in printing exists in this twentieth century. I would point out among contemporary english work of great value Mr James Joyce's "The Portrait of the Artist as a Young Man", which has gone to America to be published, and Mr Wyndham Lewis' novel "Tarr" which may have to follow it. I leave the verdict of these things to the future. There is no doubt as to where it will rest.

This age can not expect its poets to compete with its prose writers unless it allow them an equal directness
                              [*crossout:* Ezra Pound]
of expression, and it can not expect us the contemporary writers, to hold our own against the writers of the past if it deny us the traditional media of our art.

When you have denied a man the language of Catullus, Villon, Heine, Shakespeare and Dante, you have denied him a very great deal.

Ezra Pound.

30 May 1916   5, *Holland Place Chambers, Kensington. W.*

Dear E. M. This is to put your mind at rest on the subject of prosecutions. I have gone into the matter with Mr Pinker, as I said on my post card. No prosecution is of any effect unless the Home Office takes it up. And I am not the sort of person whom the Home Office attacks, and the Home Office will not make a fool of itself over my book, nor would any informed man stand against the defence I have made in my note.

The present panic among printers has been caused by the suppression of Lawrence's "Rainbow". I am not for one instant going to compare my book with the Rainbow. There is no immoral tendency in my work. I don't know that there was in the Rainbow, but it was nearer the order of W. L. George [5] and "Three Weeks" [6] than to the order of Catullus and Heine. It was a novel sexually overloaded, a sort of post-Wellsian barrocco and it depended for its sale precisely on its sexual overloading.

Now "Lustra" does not depend on any such thing. It is [*long-hand:* where it is harsh] clean cut satire, written in the speech of the best English classics and with the vocabulary of all the classics that ever were.

However let us look at the legal status of even such a work as the "Rainbow", and observe what protection we have against cranks.

/ / / / /

I happened to be seeing Mr Pinker about Joyce. He was much annoyed that Joyce's novel had to go to America to be published and said "It's a pity you can't get a printer who is something better than a scared ass."

Then I said the suppression of the Rainbow had sent all the printers off their chump. and that I was even having trouble over my poems.

[5] Walter Lionel George, English social critic. In 1909 he began to use fiction to spread his social and philosophic ideas.
[6] By Elinor Glyn, 1907.

He then told me what had happened in Lawrence case. He put the whole blame on Methuen. Some crank went to a magistrate and said the book was immoral. Methuen admitted it. Then the magistrate gave various orders, *in excess of his powers*. If Methuen had declined to obey, or if they had denied that the book was immoral, *NOTHING* could have been done until the Home Office moved. The Home Office had inspected the book (Mr Birrell being asked for an opinion said the book was too dull to bother about) and decided that they would do nothing.

Now there is no immoral tone in Lustra. There is open speech, that is all, that is the whole of any possible complaint. Moreover on personal grounds I know that the Home Office is well disposed toward me. Those very words were written to me only a few weeks ago and I had very definite proof of the fact, to back up the statement. The printers do not figure in the matter.

As for what you said to Yeats about "not only men come into this shop, *but ladies*". Mrs Shakespear [7] merely gasped and said: "Well, I suppose we are ladies of *some* sort. Or if we aren't, who IS? ! ! !".

The book, the whole of the mss. was submitted to the inspection of four perfectly well bred women before I brought in the mss. to you. I asked their advice about what I was to include.

The more closely you examine the poems the less will you be able to find any trace of depravity.

I find certain expressions that I can alter with no loss to the meaning. I have particularly left out the more violent poems, [*longhand:* & have included] very few of those used in **BLAST**.

The copy sent to Yeats, shows obvious marks of excitement. I am not going to be unreasonable, but I certainly am not going to omit such poems as "Further Instructions" or the "Cabaret" poem, nor yet the prefatory poems, though I do not consider them as good poetry as some containing more concrete expression. Still they act as a preface and are necessary to the form of the book. Beauty unrelieved goes soft and sticky.

My wife was very much surprised that you should have pitched on the "Cabaret" as unfitting, and said to Yeats "If he can't print *that* he had better leave England at once."

[7] Mrs. Olivia Shakespear, Pound's mother-in-law, a friend of Yeats and a cousin of Lionel Johnson.

I think you, with your recluse life, have perhaps got a little out of touch with the tone of contemporary London. You are one man when you are reading the English Classics in Chorley Wood, and another when you come into the day's round of occupation.".

Now do be calm a moment and think what I have said in the Cabaret poem. It is probably the best I have done since the Goodly Fere (excepting a few of the Chinese poems). It is not so good as the Ballad because it is slightly argumentative and didactic.

It says simply: "There is a sort of life which has a surface glitter, it is fundamentally sordid, or possibly innocent. Here is your cabaret, there is no particular romance or wonder about it, a few hard worked people with no particular lure of tragedy (à la Arthur Symons) but with a dull lower middle class life ahead of them, My dear Hagedorn, don't get excited. . On the contrary there need be no particular vice connected with these manifestations. In Venice the danseuse and her husband used to come in early, quite domestically. They left the baby upstairs and then came out onto the platform and sang "Donna è mobile". They are human beings like anyone else."

There is the gist of that poem, and I defy anyone, who will examine it calmly, to find anything to object to.

Again YOU CAN'T POSSIBLY BE PROSECUTED FOR POEMS THAT HAVE ALREADY APPEARED and created no scandal. And practically all the poems in this book have already appeared, [*insert:* the few exceptions] probably will have appeared before the volume comes out.

You can of course show all these letters of mine to the printer, and do try to persuade him to THINK about the matter. [*longhand:* not to go off his head at a first impression.]
It is said that the first impression of any work of genius is disagreeable. Certainly any new move in art or any ressurrection of old modes is always met with a protest, *a purely ephemeral* protest.

This book is, I hope, not a dull book. I believe it shows life fairly, and without slush and sentimentality. (Remember I forgot to put Ovid and Chaucer into my list of classics where they belong.).

If the book is not dull, neither is it trivial, nor undertaken in a trivial spirit. It expresses, I believe, a "philosophy of life", or what I would rather call a "sense of life" [*crossout:* philosophy being] which is common to all the classics, and which never went out of literature until the stultifying period of the counter-reformation, or in English in Wordsworth and Tennyson.

Do remember the troubles over the printing of Landor's "Imaginary Conversations" and how foolish the opposers of them now seem, and how we ridicule the people who called Shelley an atheist etc. etc. and etc.

Do try to think of the book as a whole, not of individual words in it. Even certain smaller poems, unimportant in themselves have a function in the book-as-a-whole. This shaping up a book is very important. It is almost as important as the construction of a play or a novel. I neglected it in "Canzoni" and the book has never had the same measure of success as the others. It is *not* so good as the others. I was affected by hyper-aesthesia or over-squeamishness and cut out the rougher poems. I don't know that I regret it in that case for the poems weren't good enough, but even so the book would have been better if they had been left in, or if something like them had been put in their place.

I am thinking of a few short satirical lines, when I ask you to consider this question of the "Book as a whole."

Don't think I am in a rage. I simply want you to use the best part of your mind in a question of literature. I am not going to quibble over a few words. I find I can change "whore" in place to "volaille" and in another to "girl". [*longhand:* if the good Elizabethan word is taboo.]. I am not sure that one of the lines, at least, will not gain by the restraint. I can of course change a title like "Coitus" if it scares you. But it is really better than "Pervigilium", and that poem has already appeared in "Poetry and Drama".

The poems have come out in bunches of about ten pages long in America during the past four years and I have never heard one word about their being indecent. There has been every sort of attack but positively not one attacker has thought of bringing that charge. ((Dell in Chicago was the first man to see that I was writing [*crossout:* like a Latin of] in latin tradition as distinct from greek. . All

285

the fuss has been on a question of form and now the whole country has gone quite cracked and is doing apparently nothing but bad imitations of the free verse which they so recently condemned.))
But no word about anything being immoral, not even in the land of Anthony Comstock.

Yours ever
Ezra Pound

[c. 31] May 1916   *5, Holland Place Chambers, Kensington. W.*

Dear E. M: I am nearly crevé de rire. The printer has so enjoyed himself ere he permitted himself to be shocked. On page 38. in his fury for precision he has emended my fine Elizabethan "cuckold" to "cuckolded".

The man has a sense of english and a desire to preserve its purity.

Of course there is no reason why I should not use the noun instead of the past participle in this particular line. But having had the pleasure of the emendation, of the dispute or initiation of dispute on a fine linguistic point of this sort, he really should not relapse from the air of the "spacious days" into the intellectual degradation of the counter-reformation period.

I judge he is not a hellenist, he seems to confuse the greek PHALOS, plu. PHALOI (meaning the point of the helmet spike) with the latin Phallus, meaning John Thomas.

yours
E. P.

2 June 1916   *5, Holland Place Chambers, Kensington. W.*

Friday evening

Do for god's sake send me a set of proofs *unmarked*. This thing [*insert:* you have sent] is like the Greek statues in the Vatican with tin fig leaves wired onto them.

Yrs.
E. P.

Appendix B

The letter John Quinn sent to Pound on March 27, 1917, includes copies of Quinn's correspondence with E. Byrne Hackett and B. W. Huebsch dealing with his effort to purchase some proofsheets of *A Portrait* corrected in Joyce's hand. Pound enclosed this "evidence" in his letter to Joyce of April 19, 1917. The Quinn-Hackett-Huebsch exchanges follow Quinn's "brief," numbered as he arranged and designated them (omitted sections deal with Hackett's offer to sell Quinn some autograph letters of Joseph Conrad). The packet of letters is at Cornell.

27 March 1917   *31 Nassau Street, New York*

My dear Pound: This letter is about two things: one for you personally, and the other about Joyce and his book.

(1) *As to yourself:* Your father a short time ago in a letter inquired whether I had or had seen your first book. I thought I had all your books. He gave me the name of one that I did not have, and it is a very interesting one. It is the one printed in Venice "A Luma Spento". Your father sent me a copy of it. I wrote to him that I should like very much to have it. He replied that it was yours, but that he didn't know whether you would sell it. For a first book it is a corker and I am very anxious to have it, if you have got a copy for yourself. As your father said it was yours and as he said he had a copy, I told him I was going to make you an offer for it. I think that eight pounds for a first edition of that kind is fair. So I enclose London draft to your order for eight pounds, which I hope you will think is fair for it.

So much for that.

(2) Re Joyce: As Joyce took the matter up with you, I will have to bother you by taking it up from my end with you also. I have got to show up a * * * * * of an Irish-* * * * * named Byrne Hackett, who claims that he knew Joyce in Clongowes. Here is the story:

287

Young Padraic Colum, a friend of Joyce, who was at my house a month or so ago, said that he had heard that Joyce's book "The Portrait" had some changes from the text, and had been toned or softened down. I told Colum that I was sure he had been misinformed. The next day I telephoned to young Huebsch. He told me that it was not true. He offered to send me down the pages of "The Egoist" from which the book had been set up to prove it. He added that in fact the book had one episode which was not in "The Egoist." He accordingly sent the thing down. I acknowledged it by telephone. I said to him that as a matter of curiosity I should like to have those pages. He said that he was sorry but that he had already "given them to Byrne Hackett" adding that if he had not given them to Hackett "nothing would give him greater pleasure than to give them to me".

You don't know this young Hackett. He is one of a tribe of three, pointed nosed, priggish, conceited, ungrateful, ex-Irish. It took me a long time to wake up to the Hacketts.

This young Hackett used to be connected with the Yale University Press. A year or two ago I suggested that he publish your things. I believe he wrote to you. That was at my suggestion. He has now left the Yale University Press and is running a second-hand and old and new and middle-aged alleged-rare-book store in New Haven. So I wrote to him about the manuscript. I made him a sporting offer of ten or twelve pounds for it. I enclose you with this a copy of my letter to Hackett of March 3d offering him ten or twelve pounds but adding "you (Hackett) can be the judge of that". This is the letter marked "1".

I got back a letter from Hackett which was priggish as well as hoggish as well as dishonest. It is the letter of March 5th, marked "2". I don't like to have people start their letters by saying "You may not be aware" or "Should you not wish" and so forth. The implication in his letter of March 5th that he had arranged for the publication of it with Huebsch was of course false. He said: "The manuscript came directly to me from Miss Harriet of the 'Egoist' and was sent to me at the instigation of Ezra Pound, with whom I had some correspondence at the University Press. I put the manuscript in Huebsch's hands." That was a dishonest attempt, as I regarded it, to develop some ownership in the alleged MS. He delightfully failed to say that it was at my suggestion that he wrote to you in the first place. This is the letter marked "2".

I replied on March 8th by a letter to young Hackett, which by the way I dictated in the Surrogates' Court. If ever a man showed his * * * * * and meanness, Hackett did in his letter of the 5th. It was a typically dishonest and grasping letter. My letter of March 8th ought to have made a dead * * * * * ashamed of himself. This is the letter marked "3".

He replied on March 12th sending me $75 on the theory that I had already cabled $50 to Joyce and asking me to return the manuscript to Joyce. This is letter marked "4".

I replied on March 13th returning his check for $75 and repeating that I would not take orders from him in regard to the matter and asking him to return my check for $75 [*sic: $50*], adding that: "I have had $50 worth of amusement out of the episode".

That day I cabled to Joyce as follows:

"New York, March 13, 1917.

James Joyce,
Seefeld Strasse 54,
Parterre Rechts,
Zurich, Switzerland

Portrait meeting with good success. Reviews very favorable. I will be glad cable you twenty pounds for sheets Egoist and page manuscript addition with interlineations and corrections by you, used by Huebsch for printing book. Cable whether acceptable.

John Quinn"

On March 20th I wrote Huebsch a letter returning the manuscript temporarily to him pending the receipt of a cablegram from Joyce. This is letter marked "5".

On March 20th I received a short note from Hackett of a more or less de-natured sort of impertinence, as though he still felt that he had some rights to it. This is letter marked "6".

This was acknowledged by Mr. Curtin, my secretary, on March 20th by a note marked "7".

On March 22d your cable was received as follows:
"Marconi London
Quinn,
31 Nassau St. New York

Joyce accepts. Money to be sent via me.

Pound"

289

Mr. Curtin handed me that cable just as I was leaving the office and I directed him to send a note to Huebsch, which is letter marked "8".

Finally comes my letter of March 23d to Huebsch [marked "9"], written the next day, telling him that I would send you and Joyce a copy of the correspondence so that Joyce might see the quality of Mr. Hackett's disinterestedness "or meanness in money matters".

This closes the matter.

I send you these letters in duplicate so that you can send a set to Joyce as well as to keep one yourself, if you want to. I send you this letter in duplicate. So that you can send the copy of this my letter to you to Joyce.

I enclose you with this London draft to your order for twenty pounds.

From beginning to end I have tried to do a good turn to Joyce. I admit that I wanted to show Hackett up too, and if ever a man was shown up, I think he has been shown up by me. Joyce is getting twenty pounds for one page of MS. in his handwriting. For one can get The Egoist with the numbers containing his book for ten or twelve shillings.

It has puzzled me why Joyce didn't reply to my cable direct to me. It is possible that he thinks that I am an American thief or an American crook, or that there was something crooked about my cable, or that I was trying to get some rights from him that I was not entitled to. When he knows the whole facts he may feel like sending me a word of thanks for the thought that I had in mind when I made my "sporting proposition" to Hackett of sending ten or twelve pounds to Joyce. Suspicion is a damned good thing, but I get so much of it from rich bastards that I don't like to see it in a man that I want to think well of.

I daresay you have seen James Huneker's two columns on Joyce in The New York Sun. I told Huebsch to send you copies of that.

I am glad to send this twenty pounds to you for Joyce. It is actually twenty pounds for one page of MS., which is about what a page of MS. by Meredith or Swinburne would bring, or more.

As I have said, I am sending you a carbon copy of this my letter, together with a copy of the Hackett correspondence, so that you can send it all to Joyce if you care to.

As to *The Portrait*, it is going well here. In Huneker's article he asked the question 'Who is James Joyce' and so on. I dictated an answer to it, used one or two phrases in your letter, told about "Dubliners" and "Chamber Music", and gave my opinion of Joyce. Mitchell, the editor of The Sun, said that two columns in The Sun on Joyce was all that they felt like printing now, and that my letter was a little too long. I then revised it and sent it to Vanity Fair. It is going to appear, with a portrait of Joyce which Crowninshield, the editor of V.F., got from Huebsch, in the May number. I corrected proofs last week. I used some facts out of your letters to me, without of course quoting you. But I did quote from your article in The Drama what you said about The Portrait.

I will send you a copy of Vanity Fair, and also mail a copy to Joyce.

Young Hackett, with the dainty name of Francis before the Hackett, had a review in The New Republic of a week or two ago. He could not help saying some good things about the book. But all through his review, which I assume Huebsch has sent or will send to Joyce, were mean digs. For example, he entitled his review "Green Sickness". He then alluded to the book as an "unpleasant book", which I think was dirty, for there was nothing unpleasant about it. He complained that it was "lacking in incident", as though it were a detective story. He then referred to "the mortal sin of masturbation which obsessed the character of the book" and so on, giving one the impression that the book was all about masturbation or birth control or some other damned Washington Square sexism. Then he said that it was hard reading in parts and that it would have been clearer if it had been paragraphed in sections, *a la* H. G. Wells. What I think was back of the spitefulness in his review was pure jealousy. Hackett is a conventional book reviewer. He isn't so grasping in money matters as the other Hackett whom I skinned as per the enclosed letters. Dainty Francis Hackett has got the same pointed nose and has insinuated himself into The New Republic. The chief man in The New Republic is a ***** named Walter Lippmann. Henri Bergson, with whom I have had two or three long talks lately, told me that a thing like The New Republic would not live in Paris for two weeks. He agreed with me that its strength came from a cocksure habit of uttering banalities, *a la* Wilson, with the air of omnipotence and inspiration. I told him that that sort of stuff went here chiefly because of the cock-sureness with which the banalities were given out. Young Hackett left a weekly paper in Chicago, where he had been doing book reviews, some five years ago with the announced intention of writing a novel. He went to Ireland for a year "to complete his novel". He returned from Ireland three or four years ago with the novel still unwritten or uncompleted. He has no more capacity for writing a novel than I have for painting a portrait—or less, for if I started painting a portrait I'd finish the damned thing even if I botched it or bitched it. Along comes Joyce therefore and does the trick; does *the* Irish novel, and the little soul of little Francis Hackett can't permit itself to give him unstinted praise. Hence "green sickness" and "unpleasant and difficult reading" and "obsession for the mortal sin of masturbation" and "lacking in incident" and "not paragraphed according to Wells".

Perhaps Joyce may get from this a little closer idea of the Hackett appreciation and the Hackett disinterestedness.

But to hell with them! [*Pound's insert:* i.e. The 2 Hacketts.] I'm through with both of them, and I don't want ever to hear from them or of them again.

As Joyce didn't reply direct to my cable, I shall not reply direct to him. So when you write to him please tell him that I congratulate him on the success of his book. My dictation of the Vanity Fair article was designed to help the book along. I am not a critic. I am not even a practiced writer. But I thought that what I did say would stimulate interest in the book. At any rate James Huneker liked it very much, for I sent it to him when I had it in the form of a letter to The Sun apropos of his article. And J. B. Yeats Senior liked it very much. I hope Joyce won't think it was too personal.

Sincerely yours,
John Quinn

P. S. Friday March 30, 1917.

Since dictating the above, I have received three sets of the revised proof of my article on Joyce. I enclose two of the proofs to you with this. I have made some corrections on one of the copies. One you can send to Joyce, and one you can keep yourself. I hope that Joyce won't object to my talking about him personally. It is the way to get people interested in a writer. I wrote my article to aid the sale of the book. Dozens of people will buy the book because I write about it, who would not notice a puff by a professional critic or who would never read book reviews.

Sincerely yours,
J. Q.

1.

3 March 1917   *31 Nassau Street, New York*

My dear Hackett: I very much wanted the MS. of Joyce's book. Joyce had told me that what Huebsch had was not a MS. but was what appeared in the "Egoist". A question came up regarding whether there had been any changes from the story as it appeared in the "Egoist" and the book, and I called up Huebsch about it, and then he told me that he had promised the thing to you. I don't want to have you lose the benefit of your forethought, but I make this sporting suggestion. Huebsch sent me the "Egoist" from which the book was set up. I daresay you have seen it. The book follows what appeared in the "Egoist" very closely, except for minor typographical changes, and has punctuation, paragraphing, capitalizations, and so forth, and one page of MS. in Joyce's handwriting inserted, and two insertions in the text, in place of two canceled pages of what appeared in the "Egoist".

This is the sporting proposition that I have to make: that I send to Joyce, not to you, what you think is fair, on the theory that Joyce needs the money more than you need the print as it appears in the "Egoist". My proposition is that you hold the scales of justice; that you let me know what you think the thing is worth, and that I will cable or send that to Joyce. This may sound a devilish cheeky thing to do. It is prompted as much by my wanting to help Joyce out (for £100 goes a very little distance in these days) as it is to have the story in the "Egoist". I should say ten or twelve pounds would be quite a fair price for it, but you can be the judge of that.

If this thing strikes you, let me know and I will send you the print in sheets as I got them, for you to look at and pass upon as to what you think a fair price would be. . . .

With kind regards, I am
Yours very truly,
John Quinn

E. Byrne Hackett, Esq.,
c/o The Brick Row Print & Book Shop, Inc.,
104 High Street, New Haven, Conn.

293

5 March 1917 *The Brick Row Print and Book Shop, Inc.*
104 High Street, New Haven, Conn.

My dear Quinn: I am quite willing to have one-half of the fine piece of philanthropy you have in mind for James Joyce. I set a present value of $100. on this Manuscript, made up of the printed pages of the 'Egoist' with certain additions and changes in Joyce's handwriting and will agree to have you retain it on your sending $50 to Joyce and $50 to me.

You may not be aware that I knew James Joyce at Clongowes. We were in the same class there, though I have not kept track of him, nor he of me. The manuscript came directly to me from Miss Harriet of the 'Egoist' and was sent to me at the instigation of Ezra Pound, with whom I had some correspondence while at the University Press. I put the manuscript in Huebsch's hand.

Should you not wish to pay this price, I will agree to sell the manuscript and give Joyce $50 from the proceeds. I can dispose of it readily but would much prefer that you should have it above any one else. . . .

With kindest regards, believe me,
Sincerely,
Byrne Hackett

EBH:HEP
John Quinn, Esquire
31 Nassau St., New York City.

3

8 March 1917 *31 Nassau Street, New York*

E. Byrne Hackett, Esq.,
Brick Row Print and Book Shop,
104 High Street,
New Haven, Connecticut.

My dear Hackett: I received yours of the 5th yesterday.

In my letter of the 3rd I made what I called a "sporting proposition," that I send to Joyce "what you think is fair. * * * My proposition is that you hold the scales of justice; that you let me know what you think the thing is worth. * * * I should say ten or twelve pounds would be quite a fair price for it, *but you can be the judge of that.*"

I stand by my offer, even though I do not think that it is worth $100. It has only one page of his actual MS. and four lines of interlineation in his handwriting. But as I made the proposition that you should be the judge, I stand by it. I accordingly enclose with this my check to your order for $50. I will send to Joyce the equivalent of the other $50 in a draft payable to him in Switzerland. That closes the matter.

I understand that the MS. "came to you" *physically* from the Egoist. Technically I do not think that either Huebsch had the right to present it to you, or that the Egoist had the right to present it to you. The MS. with the corrections by Joyce was and of course is *Joyce's property.* After Huebsch was through with it he, of course, held it *as Joyce's property.* I understood that in the mix-up it came to you from the Egoist as a thing *to be published* and *not as a gift from the Egoist.* Unless the Egoist intended to make a gift of the printed matter with those MS. corrections to you, quite apart from the question of *sending it for publication merely,* the legal ownership belonged and now belongs *in Joyce* and is neither in Huebsch nor in you nor in the Egoist. But as Joyce is getting what I think he will consider a good price for one page of MS. and four MS. lines, and as I said in my letter of the 3d to you I was prompted "as much by my wanting to help Joyce out", as by wanting to have the story as it appeared in the Egoist, which by the way one can get for a couple of dollars, for the Egoist is not out of print and back numbers are easily obtainable, I have closed the matter on the terms that you suggested. I understand that you *physically* received the copy from the Egoist and that you *physically* put the copy in Huebsch's hands *for publication.* But of course neither one of those *physical* acts had anything to do with the ownership of the MS. *after* Huebsch was through with it *for the purpose of setting up the book.*

Your letter interested and amused me. It made me realize the value of being classmates in School. Personally I should be ashamed to make a profit out of anything that had ever been given to me by anyone, whether the gift was authorized or not. I have heard of people selling wedding presents. Of course you know that Watts-

Dunton was very bitterly attacked in his lifetime because he sold, shortly after Swinburne's death, the Swinburne MSS. that Swinburne had given to him. I imagine that if you had kept up your acquaintance with Joyce after your Clongowes days, for say a year or two, you might be willing to give him $75 and you keep only the $25, and that if the acquaintance had continued even longer you might perhaps be willing to allow him up to even $90. I can imagine your thrifty business sense not under any circumstances wanting to let him have the whole $100. Just where the alleged "warm-hearted Irish sentiment" that might be expected, has been diffused or evaporated, it would perhaps be useless to inquire. Possibly it is the cold Connecticut-Yankee-New Haven denatured atmosphere. I am certain that if you had located at Cambridge, the golden light of Harvard would have kept alive that alleged Irish warm-hearted spirit that is supposed to inhabit the natives of the island and would have made you responsive to my suggestion all for Joyce's benefit. I would have thrown my hat up if you had said in reply to me, "make it $100 and give it all to Joyce". I should have said "There is the real warm-hearted Irishman, in spite of the Connecticut-Yankee-New Haven environment." But I am afraid that you have been infected with Yankee-itis. . . .

Coming back to the Joyce thing, I have several sets of the Egoist, three or four complete ones at least. It would be simplicity itself for me to have had the printed book read with one of my bound volumes of the Egoist containing it and indicate the changes, or rather make one of my duplicates of the Egoist conform to the printed book which would be the same as the so-called MS., with the exception that it would not have the *one page* of MS. in Joyce's handwriting and the four lines of interlineation in his handwriting. But, as I said in my letter of the 3d, I made a sporting proposition and was prompted by wanting to help Joyce out. And there you are! I have no doubt that Joyce will be surprised at getting $50 and will be glad of it. It might be better for me to cable it to him rather than run the risk of the delay and uncertainty of sending a draft.

Yours very truly,
JOHN QUINN

P.S. The foregoing was dictated by Mr. Quinn at the Surrogates' Court this morning, where he went direct from his apartment for the trial of a case, in the Judge's chambers during an interval in the examination of witnesses. As Mr. Quinn has been tied up all day,

when I talked to him on the telephone this afternoon he asked me to
sign the letter in his name and send it.

T. J. Curtin

4.

12 March 1917   *The Brick Row Print and Book Shop, Inc.*
104 High Street, New Haven, Conn.

John Quinn, Esquire
31 Nassau Street,
New York City.

My dear Quinn: I returned from Boston on Saturday evening to
find your note, enclosing check. Under the circumstances, I could
not think of retaining your check.

If the manuscript in question is not my property, I have no desire
to sell it to you or anyone else. You impugn my good faith in the
transaction ungenerously, I think.

If you have already cabled Joyce $50 on the basis of your pro-
posed purchase, I would like to bear half of it and I enclose, therefore, my check for $75.

You will please return the manuscript in question to B. W.
Huebsch and oblige,

Faithfully yours,
E. Byrne Hackett
per H. E. Plechner

EBH:HEP
Mr. Hackett left the office, being called out of town, before the
signing the above.

H. E. Plechner

5.

20 March 1917   *31 Nassau Street, New York*

Dear Mr. Huebsch: Referring to my talk with you on the telephone
this afternoon, in the course of which I read to you the cable which I
sent to Mr. James Joyce the early part of last week, and referring
to your statement that pending the receipt of an answer from Joyce

297

you thought you should be the custodian of the sheets, and referring also to your statement that you acknowledged unreservedly that the property in the sheets with the corrections was in Joyce, and that you had secured only the right to publish the literary work as a book—a very frank and, I may add, a very just acknowledgment on your part—I return you herewith the sheets which you sent to me. Mr. E. Byrne Hackett has no more right to them or in them than your office cat has. If you will glance at his letter to me, a copy of which I sent you, you will see that he rather peremptorily ordered that I return the thing to you. I am not accustomed to obeying the orders of people whose right to give orders I never have recognized. We all carry out orders and we all receive as well as give orders. But right-minded people do not attempt to give orders until they have a right to give them, and self-respecting people do not receive orders unless the giver has a right to give them.

I am sorry that there was only one carbon copy of my note on Joyce made. Crowninshield has the original. As soon as the single carbon copy is returned from Mr. Yeats, Mr. Curtin of my office will send it to you.

Sincerely yours,
John Quinn

P.S. Please send me 5 more copies. In the old days I used to buy and give away Synge's and Yeats' things by the dozen. But lately I have stopped, partly from lack of time and partly because people as a rule don't appreciate what is *given*. But Joyce is so big I can't deny myself the fun of seeing how others of my friends take him.

J.Q.

6.

19 March 1917   *The Brick Row Print and Book Shop, Inc.*
104 High Street, New Haven, Conn.

My dear John Quinn: Enclosed please find your cheque for $50.00 payable to my order.

B. W. Huebsch must decide whether you are to retain the Joyce Manuscript. As far as I am concerned you have absolutely no right to do so.

Faithfully
E. Byrne Hackett.

John Quinn Esquire

7

20 March 1917 *31 Nassau Street, New York*

Mr. E. Byrne Hackett,
Care of The Brick Row Print & Book Shop,
104 High Street,
New Haven, Connecticut.

Dear Sir: I am requested by Mr. Quinn to acknowledge the return to him of his check to your order No. 5359 dated March 8, 1917, for $50, undeposited.

Yours very truly,
T. J. Curtin

22 March 1917 *31 Nassau Street, New York*

Dear Sir [Huebsch]: Just as Mr. Quinn was leaving the office this afternoon I handed him a cable which had just arrived reading as follows:

"London, March 22, 1917; 3:28 P.M.

Quinn,
31 Nassau St.
New York.

Joyce accepts; money to be sent via me.

(Signed) Pound"

He directed me to say that he would send the twenty pounds to Joyce and to ask you to kindly return to him the two parcels of manuscript which he sent to you yesterday.

Yours very truly,
T. J. Curtin

9

23 March 1917 *31 Nassau Street, New York*

Dear Mr. Huebsch: Just as I was leaving last night Mr. Curtin handed me a cable from Pound which I told him to send to you in a note. I am sending Pound the money in a letter which will go tomorrow. I propose to send Pound the correspondence between Mr. Hackett and myself; so I should be glad if you would return to me the copies of it that I sent to you. After Pound has read the correspondence he will send it to Joyce. Pound and Joyce will then each have a rather clear idea of the quality of Mr. Hackett's disinterestedness or meanness in money matters, whichever way one looks at it.

The thing is now mine, mine without any obligation to Mr. Hackett, legally mine, rightfully mine, and Joyce is twenty pounds better off, and no thanks to Hackett. Most men would be ashamed of the transaction clearly disclosed in the correspondence. I am sorry to find out that Hackett was so grasping about a person whose friend he pretended to have been. I should hate to think that all Irish were that way. I know they are not.

In dictating my letter to Pound I am taking pains to put quite clearly before him that you unreservedly acknowledged Joyce's right in the thing absolutely and that in sending it to Hackett you acted in perfect good faith.

As the draft for twenty pounds will go forward tomorrow, I should be glad if you would let me have the thing back by tomorrow so that your responsibility regarding the custody of it may be at an end.

If you have had a chance to read the carbon copy of what I wrote on Joyce, which will appear in Vanity Fair in May and for which Vanity Fair is paying me $65 which I am going to turn over to the French Tuberculosis fund, I shall be glad if you will send that back also with the Joyce bundle. It is the only copy I have and I promised to let a friend have it by Sunday.

Yours very truly,
John Quinn

Appendix C

Although numerous phrases and passages were added to Bloom's morning visit to the garden jakes in "Calypso" for the 1922 edition, Pound's deletion of "about twenty lines" can be identified with fair certainty. The following passages did not appear in *The Little Review*, V, 2 (June 1918), pages 50–52; they are cited from *Ulysses*, New York: Random House, The Modern Library, New Edition, Corrected and Reset, 1961, pages 67–70 (bracketed italics indicate contiguous passages that Pound did not delete).

Page 67, lines 21–23
[*He felt heavy, full: then a gentle loosening*] of his bowels [*.He stood up*], undoing the waistband of his trousers [*. The cat mewed to him.*]

Page 67, lines 27–28
A paper. He liked to read at stool. Hope no ape comes knocking just as I'm.

Page 68, lines 30–38
He kicked open the crazy door of the jakes. Better be careful not to get these trousers dirty for the funeral. He went in, bowing his head under the low lintel. Leaving the door ajar, amid the stench of mouldy limewash and stale cobwebs he undid his braces. Before sitting down he peered through a chink up at the nextdoor window. The king was in his counting house. Nobody.

Asquat on the cuckstool he folded out his paper turning its pages over on his bared knees. [*Something new and easy.*] No great hurry. Keep it a bit. [*Our prize titbit. . . .*]

Page 69, lines 3–16
Quietly he read, restraining himself, the first column and, yielding but resisting, began the second. Midway, his last resistance yielding, he allowed his bowels to ease themselves quietly as he read, reading

still patiently, that slight constipation of yesterday quite gone. Hope it's not too big bring on piles again. No, just right. So. Ah! Costive one tabloid of cascara sagrada. [*Life might be so. It did not move or touch him but it was something quick and neat.*] Print anything now. Silly season. [*He read on*], seated calm above his own rising smell[. *Neat certainly. . . . He glanced back through what he had read and*], while feeling his water flow quietly, he [*envied kindly Mr Beaufoy . . .*]

Page 70, lines 1–6

He tore away half the prize story sharply and wiped himself with it. Then he girded up his trousers, braced and buttoned himself. He pulled back the jerky shaky door of the jakes and came forth from the gloom into the air.

[*In the bright light*], lightened and cooled in limb, [*he eyed . . .*]

Index

304

309

Sartoris, C., 19
Savitsky, *see* Bloch-Savitsky, Ludmilla
Schelling, Professor Felix, 8
Scheurer-Kestner, 204
Secker, Martin, 59, 79
Serruys, Jennie, 180
Seven Arts, 83, 92
Shakespear, Olivia, 283
Shakespeare and Company, 130, 188
Shakespeare, William, 51, 55, 194, 207, 278, 282
Shannon, Dr. John R., 99
Shaw, George Bernard, 47, 51, 55, 65, 129, 136, 189, 192, 198, 209, 226, 231, 246, 248
Shelly, Percy Bysshe, 285
Shenandoah, 200
Shorter, Clement King, 72
Simenon, Georges, 255
Sinn Fcin, 243
Sinn Fein, 21, 243
Slack, Monro, Saw & Co., 95
Slatin, Myles, 193
Small, Maynard & Co., 116
Smart Set, 17, 18, 19, 25, 32, 279
Smollett, Tobias, 281
Social Credit, 151, 236, 237, 254
Society for the Prevention of Vice, New York, 129
Society of Authors, Playwrights & Composers, 5, 6, 16, 75, 77
Sorcière, La, 53
Spectator, 18
Spengler, Oswald, 264
Sphere, 120
Spinoza, Baruch, 211, 264
Spire, André, 181
Spitteler, Carl, 216, 219
Stage Society, 47, 67, 74, 92, 105, 124, 125, 141
Stein, Gertrude, 8, 157, 211, 232, 255, 256
Stendhal, 27, 39, 44, 49, 52, 57
Stephen, *see* Joyce, *A Portrait, Ulysses*
Stephens, James, 120, 218
Sterlina, Signore, 147, 148
Sterne, Lawrence, 55, 134, 201, 281; *Tristram Shandy,* 196, 201
Stock, Noel: *Poet in Exile: Ezra Pound,* 258
Strindberg, August, 26, 29, 203; *Adolphe,* 203
Sullivan, Sir Arthur, 153, 181; *Box and Cox,* 181
Sun (New York), 105, 290, 291, 292
Surrealism, 233
Svevo, Italo, 31
Swift & Co., 117, 118
Swift, Jonathan, 134, 208, 213

Swinburne, Algernon (A.C.S.), 123, 290, 296
Symons, Arthur, 23, 126, 223, 284
Symons, Mrs. Arthur, 230
Synge, John Millington, 32, 52, 209, 298

Taft, William Howard, 200
Tagore, Rabindranath, 20, 216, 218
Tailhade, Laurent, 60
Tauchnitz, 60, 247
Tennyson, Alfred Lord, 278, 285
Tertullian, 70
Thackeray, William, 119
Théâtre de l'Oeuvre, 180
Theocritus, 281
This Quarter, 223
Thoreau, H. D., 267
Three Mountains Press, 212
Thring, G. Herbert, 78
Times (London), 86, 87, 92, 94, 106
Tinkham, George Holden, 273
Tolstoi, Leo, 281
Transatlantic Review, 214, 228
transition, 227, 231, 232, 236
Tree, Sir Herbert Beerbohm, 55
Tribune (Chicago, Paris edition), 224, 238
Tribune (New York), 25
Tribune (New York, Paris edition), 199
Trollope, Anthony, 251
Tuohy, Patrick, 232
Turgenev, Ivan, 52
Two Worlds, 224, 225, 227
Two Worlds Monthly, 224

Unanimism, 27
Uncle Remus, 262
United Irishman, 243
U.S. Penal Code, subsection 211, 130, 209–210
U.S. Post Office, 185
Untermeyer, Louis, 83

Vanderbilt, William K., 111, 181
Vanderpyl, Fritz, 181
Vanity Fair, 107, 116, 213, 214, 291, 292, 300
Venus, 122
Venus de Milo, 67, 68, 140
Verlaine, Paul, 230
Versailles Peace Conference, 12, 156
Victoria, Queen, 42, 145
Vildrac, Charles, 26, 29, 118
Villon, François, 281, 282; *see also* Pound, *Villon*
"Voices of Americans in Europe," 224
Voltaire, 52, 90, 208, 281; *Dictionnaire Philosophique,* 208
Vorticism, 5, 17, 30, 31, 32, 34, 35, 36, 41, 48, 102, 233

313

314